Palgrave Studies in Screenwriting

Series Editors

Steven Maras
Media and Communication
The University of Western Australia
Perth, Australia

Kathryn Millard
Department of Media, Music Communication
and Cultural Studies
Macquarie University
Sydney, Australia

J.J. Murphy
Department of Communication Arts
University of Wisconsin-Madison
Wisconsin, USA

Palgrave Studies in Screenwriting is the first book series committed to the academic study of screenwriting. It seeks to promote an informed and critical account of screenwriting and of the screenplay with a view to understanding more about the diversity of screenwriting practice and the texts produced. The scope of the series encompasses a range of approaches and topics from the creation and recording of the screen idea, to the processes of production, to the structures that form and inform those processes, to the agents and their discourses that create those texts.

Advisory Board:
Adam Ganz, Royal Holloway, University of London, UK
Ian W. Macdonald, University of Leeds, UK
Jill Nelmes, University of East London, UK
Steven Price, Bangor University, UK
Eva Novrup Redvall, University of Copenhagen, Denmark
Kristin Thompson, University of Wisconsin-Madison, USA
Jeff Rush, Temple University, USA
Paul Wells, Loughborough University, UK

More information about this series at
http://www.springer.com/series/14590

Steven Maras
Editor

Ethics in Screenwriting

New Perspectives

Editor
Steven Maras
Media and Communication
The University of Western Australia
Perth, WA, Australia

Palgrave Studies in Screenwriting
ISBN 978-1-349-71359-2   ISBN 978-1-137-54493-3   (eBook)
DOI 10.1057/978-1-137-54493-3

Library of Congress Control Number: 2016946988

Cover image © YAY Media AS / Alamy Stock Photo

Printed on acid-free paper

This Palgrave Macmillan imprint is published by Springer Nature
The registered company is Macmillan Publishers Ltd.
The registered company address is: The Campus, 4 Crinan Street, London, N1 9XW,
United Kingdom

PREFACE

This collection of essays and interviews on ethics in screenwriting seeks to open up new perspectives on a topic that is of interest to academics, writers, as well as readers/viewers of film, television and their scripts. Rather than cast final judgement on what is good or bad screenwriting, or declare the secret to *virtuous* screenwriting, the essays presented here do something different. They investigate ethics in screenwriting as an area or problem-domain that can be approached in different ways. Issues of good and bad screenwriting are certainly considered, but in a way that recognizes that competing ideas of right and wrong can emerge out of ethics, and that reflective ethical judgement is required to work through a range of poten-tially conflicting loyalties and responsibilities. While many of the essays broach philosophical ideas and perspectives, these are grounded in par-ticular practical problems to do with screenwriting or narrative technique.

All of the essays in this volume seek to go beyond a more general discussion of ethics and media, literature or film to engage with specific aspects of screenwriting and story practice. At the same time, each chapter seeks to consider the question of ethics specifically; that is, to go beyond a mention of ethics to consider what kind of ethics is in play, or can be put into play, in certain contexts. The essays range widely across differ-ent aspects of screenwriting practice, from questions of actuality and dis-closure to character creation and narrative form. They also move from discussion of particular scripts to a more general discussion of storytelling and narrative technique, in the belief that a critical perspective on 'story' and 'storytelling' can help guide our understanding of what ethical or responsible narrative practice might look like.

Resisting a sharp distinction between theorists and practitioners, the audience for this collection ranges from screenwriters to scholars with an interest in screenwriting research and media ethics more widely. Increasingly, the distinction between these two groups has become permeable, with many practitioners taking an interest in theoretical perspectives, and many scholars establishing themselves in academia as working screenwriters and image-makers. Ethics is a vital area of interest to a range of researchers working at different points along this continuum of theory and practice, and the collection caters for readers with different interests. Philosophically minded readers may be drawn to the discussion of the ethical philosophy of figures such as C. S. Peirce or Emmanuel Levinas, while other readers may be drawn to case studies such as that of double storytelling in Danish television, or the work of screenwriter Jean-Claude Carrière, to mention just a few examples (see the more detailed chapter summary below). The inclusion of two interviews—with Indigenous Australian screenwriter and cinematographer Warwick Thornton, and UK screenwriter Jimmy McGovern—actively soliciting the views of preeminent screenwriters on questions of ethics enhances a practitioner focus.

This collection emerges out of a particular research context, which explains its shape and character, and of which I offer this brief sketch. First, in relation to my own work, after presenting an overview of research trajectories in screenwriting research at the Screenwriting Research Network (SRN) conference in Copenhagen in 2010 (see Maras 2011), I became aware that ethics was an under-researched approach. At that time I was teaching and researching more widely in media ethics. Preparing for the SRN conference at Macquarie University in Sydney in 2012, I noticed how wider debates about media ethics had yet to establish themselves in the growing area of screenwriting research. In terms of my own work I sought to address this mainly through work on UK screenwriter Jimmy McGovern (see Maras 2015)—a research interest that is evident in this volume. Second, in February 2014 an energetic discussion of screenwriting ethics took place on the SRN mailing list (SCREENWRITING-RESEARCH-NETWORK@JISCMAIL.AC.UK). It was acknowledged that ethics was a wider discussion across society, incorporating issues of correct representation, government regulation, the work situation of screenwriters and its impact on ethics, the choices made by screenwriters, the role of audiences and how ethics is elaborated in classrooms. This discussion crystallized the decision to proceed with a book proposal. Responding to a call for papers, each of the contributors offered chapter abstracts, and once accepted so began a period of developing each essay. The story of the meeting of these two trajectories hopefully explains how this collection emerged but also why, as well as editing or perhaps more accurately 'curating' this collection, I offer several contributions as author/interviewer.

While it is important to acknowledge specific contexts, wider trends and questions should not be ignored. Over the past 20 to 30 years a 'turn' to ethics is evident in cultural theory across a range of disciplines (see Booth 1988; Carey 1999, 39; Garber et al. 2000; Couldry et al. 2013, 3). This work has prompted the question, 'What is the benefit of talking about ethics?' Shouldn't ethics and morals be done and not talked about? Shouldn't ethics consist of more than talk? A striving to be in the right; a struggle to comply with a personal conception of moral or professional behaviour, perhaps? As Lawrence Buell notes, there is a great deal that happens when we talk about ethics: it can be an expression of earnest debate over values and the limits of what we can do in a situation; a (re-) negotiation of relationships; an imperative in which we must confront what we must or 'ought' to do; and a place where we imagine ethical conduct as professionals (Buell 2000). Ideally, discussion of ethics spans the abstract and the embodied. In other words, it happens across discussion of different concepts and ideas drawing on the insights and limitations of particular material situations. In line with this, all of the essays that follow explore, or indeed cultivate, an ethical perspective within a particular practical context or problem.

Ethics *in* Screenwriting

This collection is titled *Ethics in Screenwriting*. It is worth explaining why this phrase was chosen over alternatives such as 'Ethics of Screenwriting', 'Screenplay Ethics', or 'Screenwriting Ethics'. In line with a proliferation of areas such as film ethics (Bergen-Aurand 2009), literary ethics (Garber et al. 2000; Egan 2004), documentary ethics (Sanders 2010), image ethics (Gross, Katz and Ruby 1988), entertainment ethics, archive ethics, story ethics, narrative ethics (Adams 2008), ethics of media (Couldry et al. 2013) or communication ethics and rights (Hamelink and Hoffmann 2008), it would seem straightforward to propose and project screenwriting ethics as a separate, discrete realm of its own. There are, however, two complicating factors to this proposal, both examined in Chapter 1. The first has to do with the normative assumptions we make about screenwriting. What idea of screenwriting do we use to mark out this realm? Which concept of screenplay would guide 'screenplay ethics'? The danger is that any single model will marginalize alternative forms of scripting. 'Writing' is, as I have argued, not limited to the writing of paper-based screenplays (Maras 2009, 1–2). Once we begin to consider a plurality of forms of scripting practices (see Millard 2014, 28–41), another issue opens up, which is that 'screenwriting' blurs or melds with cinematography, short-film making, documentary filmmaking; not to mention rehearsal, acting, sound recording and editing. This makes any clear demarcation between screenwriting ethics and other forms of ethics very difficult to construct. In other words there is no absolute demarcation between screenwriting ethics and, say, film ethics, unless one draws on a normative model of screenwriting, which would itself have ethical effects.

A second complicating factor is that it is not clear the screenwriter has their own unique or discrete zone of responsibility. This is due to the historically low autonomy of many forms of screenwriting—although the exact degree of 'relative autonomy' is always important to note (Newcomb and Lotz 2002, 62), as there can be differences in status even between staff and freelance or 'work for hire' writers. The low autonomy of screenwriting has in part to do with the structure of control and division of labour of many modes of film practice, whereby the screenwriter is but one of several key personnel involved in the creation or conception of a moving image work, and may even share the space of writing with other writers. However, autonomy arises as an issue in another way. Namely, due to the fact that the object most commonly linked to the screenwriter—the written script—is in itself part of a wider process of actualization and crystallization whereby the 'screen idea' is crafted and melds into the final screen work (see Macdonald 2013). In this situation the role/s and responsibility of the screenwriter is conditional on the role/s and responsibility of other image-workers. Because of this limited, diffuse or even inter-dependent zone of responsibility the screenwriter may have little control over what aspect of their script finally appears on the screen, or the way it is performed, recorded and edited for audiences.

Given these two complicating factors, even if we desire to name such a thing as 'screenwriting ethics' it does not have a discrete or simple domain of practice. If we turn to an alternative notion like the 'ethics of the screenwriter' and define screenwriting ethics as 'any ethical or moral dilemma faced by the screenwriter', we would be left with a very expansive and complex area with amorphous boundaries. In terms of analytical neatness, then, there is much in favour of the argument that rather than set up a specific area of screenwriting ethics we should categorize most ethical issues faced by screenwriters under broader, relevant headings such as story ethics, professional ethics, performance ethics, documentary ethics. This would allow screenwriters to benefit from discussion of ethics across a diverse space, and also share insights and ethical camaraderie with other media professionals.

This option, however reasonable, may concern some readers given the historical neglect of the script and screenwriting in academic approaches, which is only recently being addressed by a range of screenwriting researchers (see, as a sampler of early monographs, Sternberg 1997; Stempel 2000; Murphy 2007; Price 2010; as well as the international *Journal of Screenwriting* established in 2010). As Jill Nelmes writes, 'Even though the screenplay has been in existence since the first scenarios of the early twentieth century the form has received little academic attention' (2011, 1). There is a risk, then, that scripting will remain something of an invisible practice in accounts of ethics dominated by texts and professions, and in academic contexts in which screen literacies and practices have a precarious place (see Harper 2016). This would defeat the impulse behind this collection, which is to open up ethics in screenwriting as a vibrant area and topic of debate.

One of the advantages of the phrase 'ethics in screenwriting' is that it allows us to critically reflect on normative questions, focus on the '*in*', look at the specific links between screenwriting practice and ethical considerations, and ask what forms of responsibility arises from those links. At times, there may be little to differentiate the responsibility of the screenwriter from that of the director or producer or the storyteller or media professional in general. In other words, we may not need to name something 'screenwriting ethics' to talk about ethics in screenwriting, or even to be an ethical screenwriter. This is not to suggest that claims for the ethical autonomy of the screenwriter and responsible screenwriting should be ignored. Indeed, to the contrary, they should be examined carefully, sympathetically, as well as critically. The absence of an entirely separate or 'stable' space of 'screenwriting ethics' in which to ground the project of thinking about ethics in screenwriting indeed presents a conceptual challenge; but at the same time, it offers a new frontier for thinking about media ethics in a dynamic area of practice that has always sat at the crossroads of multiple academic and industrial disciplines.

CHAPTER SUMMARY

While developed separately, each of the essays in this volume contributes to a wider project of providing new perspectives on ethics in screenwriting. The essays do not attempt to promote a single foundational theory of ethics, but consider ethics across a wide range of media and screen cultures. Although broad, the organization of the collection follows three headings: 'Writers and Production Environments'; 'Actuality and History'; and 'Character and Narrative'. These flesh out the 'new perspectives' referred to in the title of the collection and help organize the three parts of the book.

In 'Ethics Beyond the Code', I introduce the collection by working through a particular problem facing any screenwriting researcher interested in ethics and morals; namely, the problem that, historically speaking, issues of ethics and screenwriting have been handled primarily through a discussion of the morality of film under the Hays Office production code in the USA during the 1930s and 1940s. At the same time, this approach limits discussion of ethics to a coded form of morality. Not discounting the fact that ethical debates may take on a different character in different parts of the world, I would contend that 'code' based thinking, even beyond the USA, represents a significant disciplinary paradigm or discourse that inhibits wider exploration of ethical questions in screenwriting. Thus, developing ethical analysis as an approach in screenwriting research involves thinking beyond an emphasis on codes. Through careful analysis of the production code and its moral discourse, I make a case for the need for new perspectives exploring ethics in screenwriting. Contemplating new perspectives, I argue, means reevaluating the way representation has been cast in moral debates. What I hope to show in this first chapter is how debates about screen morality have been constructed within a narrow representational arena that allows for a very limited construction of the relationship between ethics and screenwriting, cast within a climate of concern over the powers of influence of the moving image and extreme suspicion over entertainment.

The first part of the book examines a set of perspectives which have been gathered together under the umbrella of 'Writers and Production Environments'. This heading teases out the unique situational issues that confront any discussion of ethics in screenwriting. Production environments, and the writer's situation within them, represent an important site for contextualizing and expanding out the space of representation of ethics.

In 'The Concept of "Double Storytelling" in Danish Public Service TV Drama Production', Eva Novrup Redvall continues her analysis of screenwriting principles and practices fostered at the Danish broadcaster DR that she began in her book, *Writing and Producing Television Drama in Denmark: From* The Kingdom *to* The Killing (2013). Focusing specifically on Danish public service TV drama, Redvall examines the unique case of a public broadcaster explicitly commissioning projects with ethical and social connotations. She traces the emergence of the dogma of 'double storytelling' in DR and its operation in the context of DR Fiction. Her analysis explores the institutional commitment to ethics embodied in double storytelling, its emergence as a policy, and operation as a commissioning and storytelling principle.

In 'Ethics, Style and Story in Indigenous Screenwriting: Warwick Thornton in Interview', I examine the work of filmmaker Warwick Thornton, who has deep roots to Indigenous communities in Central Australia. His 2009 feature film, *Samson and Delilah*, winner of the prestigious *Caméra d'Or* at the Cannes Film Festival, among numerous other awards, is noteworthy for its innovative use of style and approach to story, using non-professional actors. In the interview that forms the second part of the chapter, Thornton elaborates on his stylistic choices, his relationship to writing, Indigenous communities, and reflects on his working methods, as well as his earlier short films.

In 'On Morals, Ethics and Screenwriting: An Interview with Jimmy McGovern', acclaimed Liverpool-based screenwriter Jimmy McGovern teases out questions of morality and ethics in his scripts, and gives special focus to the representation of working class morality on the screen. Refusing the role of screenwriter-philosopher, McGovern nevertheless outlines the central place of moral and ethics in his conception of a good story. In addition, while refusing the role of crusader, he teases out the importance of truth-telling and the need to be mindful of justice, especially when writing about historical events such as the Hillsborough Stadium tragedy, the Liverpool Docks dispute, Bloody Sunday and joint enterprise laws in the UK.

The three chapters in this part explore issues to do with public service broadcasting, Indigenous screenwriting in Australia and working class morality. They are complemented by the case studies examined in other parts of the book, and also contribute to the investigation of actuality and character in the other parts. Further work in this area could usefully elaborate on ethical questions arising from different methods of working and different production cultures (Caldwell 2008; Banks, Conor and Mayer 2015).

The second part of the book 'Actuality and History', examines issues around the writing of historical narratives, but also the deployment of actuality in screenwriting—themes already touched on by McGovern and Redvall in earlier chapters. These topics have long been debated in the context of documentary film (Gross, Katz and Ruby 1988) and represent an obvious and important direction in which to extend the representational space of ethics in screenwriting. While there exists a great deal of literature exploring the specific relationship between history and film and television, very little focuses on the situation of the screenwriter. Felicity Packard and Ben Stubbs work to address this gap in '*ANZAC Girls*: An Ethical Auto-analysis', where they reflect on the writing of the Australian TV series *ANZAC Girls*, a six-part drama series made for the Australian Broadcasting Corporation which explores the important, but under-represented role of nurses in World War I. Drawing on Packard's experience working on the project, the chapter explores the way the screenwriter can write a historically oriented screenplay that is mindful of truthful representation whilst remaining dramatically and commercially appropriate. Using *ANZAC Girls* as a case study, Packard and Stubbs develop a framework for thinking through the responsibilities of the screenwriter in relation to history, including questions of truthful representation; subjectivism; the double story; and ethical dramatic construction. They highlight the special role of titles and disclaimers in the presentation of history.

In 'The Ethics of Actuality in the Scripting of Enrique Rosas's *The Gray Automobile*', María Teresa DePaoli continues the discussion inaugurated by Packard and Stubbs in a different way. DePaoli explores how difficult it can be to make ethical judgements regarding actuality in nonfiction film, in cases where the conditions of actuality are fluid and the lines between fact and fiction, objectivity and fabrication are blurred. Drawing on historical and archival research DePaoli examines the myriad issues raised by the most famous film of Mexico's silent period, Enrique Rosas's *The Gray Automobile* (1919); a film especially noteworthy for its use of actual footage of the death of members of the gang at the heart of events depicted in the narrative.

In 'Blurring Boundaries, Transmedia Storytelling and the Ethics of C. S. Peirce', Renira Rampazzo Gambarato and Alessandro Nanì offer a different perspective on actuality, by focusing on the ethics of transmedia storytelling where game designers and writers purposely blur fiction and reality in order to craft complex forms of scenarios activated across a number of platforms. Drawing on the semiotic and ethical theory of

American philosopher C. S. Peirce, Gambarato and Nanì explore the ways in which transmedia stories lay down forms of interpretation which create complex borders for the game or narrative (sometimes associated with the slogan 'This is not a game' in the context of Alternative Reality Games (or ARGs)). Drawing on case studies from Sweden and Brazil they open up a new way of thinking about transmedia narrative through Peirce, and also survey the ethical debates emerging in this area. Like Packard and Stubbs they consider the ethics of disclaimers in guiding the viewer through ethically complex situations.

The third part of the book focuses on issues of 'Character and Narrative', a strand of inquiry already touched on in chapters contributed by Thornton and McGovern, and the chapter by Packard and Stubbs. Characters often play a key role in scripts in focalizing particular ethical situations and dilemmas. Different narrative techniques can create irony, comedy and satire, and contribute to what is called the 'treatment' of ethical issues. While traditional debates surrounding screen morality may focus on decency or indecency, this approach narrows down the discussion of character behaviour to a significant degree. In this part of the collection the authors consider the way characters are used in scripts to explore particular ethical tensions and problems.

In 'Doubled Ethics and Narrative Progression in *The Wire*', Jeff Rush looks at the handling of ethics in screenwriting through ideas of character and personal conflict. He suggests that the privileging of character conflict through concepts such as narrative 'spine' is limiting, and works at the expense of treatment of public conflict and wider social issues. Suggesting that some long-form television represents an alternative approach, Rush develops an analysis of the celebrated serial *The Wire* focused on what he terms a 'doubled' ethics, one that combines a focus on character growth alongside the larger, social world of the story. Drawing on narrative theory, especially the work of James Phelan, Rush develops an approach to character and narrative focused on concepts of narrative judgement and alignment. In making this argument, Rush teases out the relationship between personal and public conflict, and borrows from moral philosophy to show how personal conflict can be examined through an ethics of care, and public conflict in terms of an ethics of justice. Rush also revisits theories of television as a 'cultural forum', showing how doubled ethics contributes to ethical debate.

In 'Writing from the Mouth of Shadows: Creativity as Ethics in the Screenwriting of Jean-Claude Carrière', Felipe Pruneda Sentíes explores

Jean-Claude Carrière's view that the screenwriter works in the 'mouth of shadows' as a creative ethics in its own right. While Carrière's work has become a key reference point for screenwriting researchers, Pruneda Sentíes explores new perspectives on his approach. Drawing on Levinasian philosophy, and the work of Chloé Taylor and Nancy Yousef, Pruneda Sentíes suggests that Carrière's comments on creativity express a broader ethical commitment to knowledge, perception and experience. Pruneda Sentíes shows how principles of estrangement and 'positive othering' guide Carrière's approach to characters and collaborators. Through this discussion, 'ethical blindness' is reclaimed as an enabling approach to knowledge, and the Other, in our forming of relations with the world.

In 'Screenwriting as Dialogic Ethics After *Animal Kingdom*', I continue this focus on relational ethics. Drawing on the work of philosopher Martin Buber I explore how dialogic ethics provides a framework to consider the construction of ethical relations in screenwriting. David Michôd's 2010 Australian feature *Animal Kingdom* drew acclaim for its performances and won the World Cinema Dramatic Competition at the Sundance Film Festival in 2010. The film focuses on how its main protagonist, following the death of his mother, reunites with his estranged extended family, who also happen to be career criminals. I argue that the film and script use characters and situations to perform and explore different ethical or moral positionings in a world in which categories of Good and Evil are open to a range of powers and forces.

Linked to the theme of 'new perspectives', each part of the collection expands the space of representation of ethics in screenwriting in different directions, leading to a more complex view of screenwriting as a narrative practice than often assumed in debates over screen morality and decency. The final chapter in the collection, 'Ethics, Representations and Judgement', forms a contribution to thinking about character and narrative, but works as a conclusion revisiting some key themes posed earlier. In this chapter, I return to the problem of thinking about ethics in screenwriting 'beyond the code' and attempt to develop a more positive account of the interactions between ethics, representations and judgements. This involves developing the link between thinking about representation and relations, and the problem of how to navigate, mediate and represent the latter. The chapter reflects on the implications of making ethical judgements, the role of narrative in developing moral awareness, as well as the relationship between screenwriting practice and ethical practice. Drawing on the theory of 'world projection' put forward by American philosopher

Nicholas Wolterstorff, and applying it to Jimmy McGovern's 2014 script for a 90-minute television feature *Common*, I develop an alternative perspective on representation through a concept of 'ethical work'. I suggest that considering this ethical work could play an integral part in forming judgements about screen works and scripts.

This collection does not exhaust all of the topics that can be discussed under the rubric of ethics in screenwriting. In terms of ethical theory, there is room to broaden our engagement with ethical philosophy. A range of thinkers, such as (but not limited to) Paul Ricoeur, Nick Couldry, Onora O'Neill, Nancy Fraser, Martha Nussbaum, bell hooks (see Valdivia 2002) and Judith Butler, offer ideas rich in possibilities for researchers interested in ethics in screenwriting: from the ethics of recognition, to violence, to translation, to truth-telling, to the ethics of care, and through to the ethics of voice and dialogue. In terms of more applied screenwriting practice, much remains to be discussed on topics as wide-ranging as narrative ethics, authorship, documentary scripting, to working with communities, to consent, through to questions of cultural identity and ethics posed by queer, 'black' and feminist screenwriting. There is room for thorough examination of Indigenous and national ethical cultures to accompany a well-rounded examination of diverse storytelling cultures across the world (Khatib 2013). Finally, the research aspects of screenwriting promises to be a fertile area for deeper investigation of matters of consent and honesty (Weerakkody 2015, 52, 85). It is hoped that this collection, and the new perspectives it presents, forms a useful focal point for further discussion of ethics in screenwriting and robust foundation for future work.

EDITOR ACKNOWLEDGEMENTS

My acknowledgements begin with the Screenwriting Research Network, an eclectic coalition of researchers who have been considering new forms of screenwriting and scripting since its first meeting in 2007. It is my interaction with this community that has not only led me to this subject matter, but also linked me to many of the contributors in this volume, and others who expressed interest in it, or sustained it. My thanks as editor go to all the contributors for their persistence, patience and understanding through many drafts. I am grateful to Chris Cheshire, Alison Ray, Cathie Payne, Jule Selbo, Ian David and Margot Nash for their advice and feedback on different chapters, and especially Teresa Rizzo for her serving as a sounding board and reader for many chapters. My thanks to the

Palgrave editorial and design staff who worked on the book, including Felicity Plester, Chris Penfold, Harry Fanshawe and Lina Aboujieb, and especially the anonymous reviewers on the project for their constructive engagement. Gail Harper provided valuable assistance with the index. I wish to express a special thanks to my fellow Palgrave Series Editors Ian Macdonald, J. J. Murphy, and Kathryn Millard for their support of the project, and especially to Kathryn for her supportive editorial work and astute guidance over a very long development period. Throughout the gestation of this work I thank my family and all of my friends for their support and encouragement, for which I am very blessed.

The script for Jimmy McGovern's *Common* is accessible in the public domain in the BBC Writer's Room at http://www.bbc.co.uk/writersroom/scripts/common

The script of David Michôd's *Animal Kingdom* is accessible in the public domain at http://www.sonyclassics.com/awards-information/animal-kingdom_screenplay.pdf

Excerpts from *ANZAC Girls* screenplays used by the author and reprinted are courtesy of Screentime Pty. Ltd. © 2013.

REFERENCES

Adams, Tony E. 2008. 'A Review of Narrative Ethics.' *Qualitative Inquiry* 14 (2): 175–94.

Banks, Miranda, Bridget Conor, and Vicki Mayer, eds. 2015. *Production Studies, The Sequel! Cultural Studies of Global Media Industries.* London: Taylor and Francis.

Bergen-Aurand, Brian. 2009. 'Film/Ethics.' *New Review of Film and Television Studies* 7 (4): 459–70.

Booth, Wayne C. 1988. *The Company We Keep: An Ethics of Fiction.* Berkeley: University of California Press.

Buell, Lawrence. 2000. 'What We Talk About When We Talk About Ethics.' In *The Turn to Ethics,* edited by Marjorie B. Garber, Beatrice Hanssen and Rebecca L. Walkowitz, 1–14. New York: Routledge.

Caldwell, John Thornton. 2008. *Production Culture: Industrial Reflexivity and Critical Practice in Film and Television.* Durham, N.C.: Duke University Press.

Carey, James. 1999. 'Journalists Just Leave: The Ethics of an Anomolous Profession.' In *The Media and Morality,* edited by Robert M Baird, William E. Loges and Stuart E. Rosenbaum, 39–54. Amherst, NY: Prometheus Books.

Couldry, Nick, Amit Pinchevski, and Mirca Madianou, eds. 2013. *Ethics of Media.* Houndmills, Basingstoke, Hampshire: Palgrave Macmillan.

Egan, Kathryn Smoot. 2004. 'The Ethics of Entertainment Television.' *Journal of Popular Film and Television* 31 (4): 158–66.

Garber, Marjorie B., Beatrice Hanssen, and Rebecca L. Walkowitz, eds. 2000. *The Turn to Ethics*. New York: Routledge.

Gross, Larry P., John Stuart Katz, and Jay Ruby, eds. 1988. *Image Ethics: The Moral Rights of Subjects in Photographs, Film, and Television*. New York: Oxford University Press.

Hamelink, Cees J., and Julia Hoffmann. 2008. 'The State of the Right to Communicate.' *Global Media Journal (American Edition)* 7 (13). http://www.globalmediajournal.com/open-access/the-state-of-the-right-to-communicate.pdf

Harper, Graeme. 2016. 'An Ethics of the Academy's Embrace: The Writer, the Screen and the New Literacies.' *New Writing* 13 (1): 145–52.

Khatib, Lina, ed. 2013. *Storytelling in World Cinemas, Volume Two: Contexts*. New York: Columbia University Press.

Macdonald, Ian W. 2013. *Screenwriting Poetics and the Screen Idea*. Basingstoke: Palgrave Macmillan.

Maras, Steven. 2009. *Screenwriting: History, Theory and Practice*. London: Wallflower Press.

Maras, Steven. 2011. 'Some Attitudes and Trajectories in Screenwriting Research.' *Journal of Screenwriting* 2 (2): 275–86.

Maras, Steven. 2015. 'Jimmy McGovern through an Ethical Lens.' *Journal of Screenwriting* 6 (2): 203–20.

Millard, Kathryn. 2014. *Screenwriting in a Digital Era*. Basingstoke: Palgrave Macmillan.

Murphy, J. J. 2007. *Me and You and Memento and Fargo: How Independent Screenplays Work*. New York: Continuum.

Nelmes, Jill, ed. 2011. *Analysing the Screenplay*. New York: Routledge.

Newcomb, Horace, and Amanda D. Lotz. 2002. 'The Production of Media Fiction.' In *A Handbook of Media and Communication Research*, edited by Klaus Bruhn Jensen, 62–77. London: Routledge.

Price, Steven. 2010. *The Screenplay: Authorship, Theory and Criticism*. Basingstoke: Palgrave Macmillan.

Redvall, Eva Novrup. 2013. *Writing and Producing Television Drama in Denmark: From* The Kingdom *to* The Killing. Basingstoke: Palgrave Macmillan.

Sanders, Willemien. 2010. 'Documentary Filmmaking and Ethics: Concepts, Responsibilities, and the Need for Empirical Research.' *Mass Communication and Society* 13 (5): 528–53.

Stempel, Tom. 2000. *Framework: A History of Screenwriting in the American Film*. 3rd ed. Syracuse, NY: Syracuse University Press.

Sternberg, Claudia. 1997. *Written for the Screen: The American Motion-Picture Screenplay as Text*. Tübingen: Stauffenburg.

Valdivia, Angharad N. 2002. 'bell hooks: Ethics from the margins.' *Qualitative Inquiry* 8 (4), 429–47.

Weerakkody, Niranjala. 2015. *Research Methods for Media and Communication*. 2nd ed. South Melbourne: Oxford University Press.

CONTENTS

1   Ethics Beyond the Code   1
    Steven Maras

Part I   Writers and Production Environments   31

2   The Concept of 'Double Storytelling' in Danish
    Public Service TV Drama Production   33
    Eva Novrup Redvall

3   Ethics, Style and Story in Indigenous Screenwriting:
    Warwick Thornton in Interview   55
    Steven Maras

4   On Morals, Ethics and Screenwriting: An Interview
    with Jimmy McGovern   77
    Steven Maras

Part II   Actuality and History   97

5   *ANZAC Girls*: An Ethical Auto-analysis   99
    Felicity Packard and Ben Stubbs

6   The Ethics of Actuality in the Scripting of Enrique
    Rosas's *The Gray Automobile*   125
    María Teresa DePaoli

7   Blurring Boundaries, Transmedia Storytelling
    and the Ethics of C. S. Peirce   147
    Renira Rampazzo Gambarato and Alessandro Nanì

Part III   Character and Narrative   177

8   Doubled Ethics and Narrative Progression in *The Wire*   179
    Jeff Rush

9   Writing from the Mouth of Shadows: Creativity
    as Ethics in the Screenwriting of Jean-Claude Carrière   197
    Felipe Pruneda Sentíes

10   Screenwriting as Dialogic Ethics After
     Animal Kingdom   217
     Steven Maras

11   Ethics, Representations and Judgement   231
     Steven Maras

Index   259

LIST OF TABLE

Table 1.1   Summary of ethical perspectives in media ethics   17

NOTES ON CONTRIBUTORS

María Teresa DePaoli is Associate Professor of Spanish at Kansas State University. She received her doctorate degree from Purdue University in 2001. Her research centres on Latin American literature, film, media, as well as cultural studies, and she has published numerous peer-reviewed articles. DePaoli is the author of *The Story of the Mexican Screenplay: A Study of the Invisible Art Form and Interviews with Women Screenwriters.* (2014). She is also the co-author (with Laura Kanost) of *Las Guionistas: A Bilingual Anthology of Mexican Women Screenwriters* (forthcoming).

Renira Rampazzo Gambarato is currently Assistant Professor in the Faculty of Communications, Media and Design at the National Research University Higher School of Economics, in Moscow, Russia and teaches transmedia storytelling. Originally from Brazil, she has studied and worked also in Germany, Canada, Qatar and Estonia. Her Post-doctorate in Film Studies is from Concordia University, Canada and she holds a PhD in Communication and Semiotics from Pontifical Catholic University of São Paulo, Brazil and Kassel University, Germany; a MA in Communication and Semiotics also from Pontifical Catholic University of São Paulo and a BA in Industrial Design from São Paulo State University, Brazil. Her recent researches and publications are concentrated on transmedia story-telling analysis and complexity of transmedial experience. Visit her web page http://talkingobjects.org.

Steven Maras is an Associate Professor in Media and Communication at the University of Western Australia. He is the author of *Screenwriting: History, Theory, and Practice* (2009). He is also author of *Objectivity in*

Journalism (2013). He is on the editorial advisory boards of *Continuum: Journal of Media and Cultural Studies; Global Media Journal (Australian Edition)*; the *Journal of Screenwriting*; and *Communication Research and Practice*. He is also a Series Editor for the *Palgrave Studies in Screenwriting* book series.

Alessandro Nanì is a PhD candidate in Media and Communication at the University of Tartu where he is focusing on crossmedia audiences of television. He is as well the curator of the BA curriculum 'Crossmedia in Film and Television' at Tallinn University—Baltic Film, Media, Arts and Communication School where he teaches crossmedia and transmedia storytelling both at BA and MA level.

Felicity Packard is a Lecturer in Creative Writing in the Faculty of Arts and Design at the University of Canberra. She is also a screenwriter and producer. She was Lead Writer and Producer of the Screentime mini-series *ANZAC Girls* (2014) for the Australian Broadcasting Corporation and is one of the writers behind the *Underbelly* true-crime drama franchise: *Underbelly; Underbelly—A Tale of Two Cities; Underbelly—The Golden Mile; Underbelly—Razor; Underbelly—Badness*, and *Underbelly—Squizzy*, the last three of which she was also Associate Producer. She is currently writer and Associate Producer on *Wolf Creek*, the TV series.

Felipe Pruneda Sentíes is a PhD candidate in Critical and Cultural Studies at the University of Pittsburgh, where he is completing his dissertation 'Another Habitat for the Muses: the Poetic Investigations of Mexican Film Criticism, 1918–1968'. He has published articles in *Framework: The Journal of Cinema and Media*, the *International Journal of Cinema*, and contributed to *Women Screenwriters: An International Guide* (Palgrave Macmillan, 2015). He has been a Teaching Fellow at Hendrix College, where he now directs the Writing Center.

Eva Novrup Redvall is Associate Professor in Film and Media Studies and Head of the Research Priority Area on Creative Media Industries in the Department of Media, Cognition and Communication at the University of Copenhagen. She holds a PhD on screenwriting as a creative process and has published widely on screenwriting, film and television production and Nordic cinema and drama series. Her latest books are the monograph *Writing and Producing Television Drama in Denmark: From The Kingdom to The Killing* (Palgrave Macmillan, 2013), the edited collection *Cinema and Television: Cultural Policy and Everyday Life* (2015, with Ib Bondebjerg and Andrew Higson) and *The Danish Directors 3: Dialogues on the New Danish Documentary Cinema* (2013, co-authored with Mette Hjort and Ib Bondebjerg).

Jeff Rush is an Associate Professor and Chair of the Department of Film and Media Arts at Temple University in Philadelphia. He is the co-author of *Alternative Scriptwriting* whose fifth edition was recently published. He has written extensively on screenwriting, literature, video games, narrative theory and the philosophy of metaphor. He is on the editorial boards of the *Journal of Film and Video*, the *Journal of Screenwriting* and *Games and Culture*.

Ben Stubbs is a Lecturer in Journalism at the University of South Australia. He is a widely published travel writer; *Ticket to Paradise* was published in 2012 and *After Dark: A Nocturnal Exploration of Madrid* will be published in 2016. Ben is also a travel writing academic and his research focuses on exploring the plurality of the form; he has published on danger and travel writing, the history and humour of the genre and its continuing relationship with journalism.

CHAPTER 1

Ethics Beyond the Code

Steven Maras

This collection of essays on ethics in screenwriting seeks to open up new perspectives on a topic that is commonly discussed, but relatively neglected in academic research. It will be useful to begin with a clarification of this apparent paradox. For many readers, ethics and screenwriting will define a core research topic in cinema and media studies to do with public debate around the morality of screen works, including attempts to censor or regulate what we see on the screen. The demands of screen censorship in the early 1900s in the USA placed a huge moral burden on filmmakers, but the impact of this regulatory system on screenwriters, and screenwriting, has rarely been explored as a problem to do with ethics in screenwriting. It will thus be useful to reevaluate the operation of the production code from this particular perspective.

S. Maras (✉)
Media and Communication, The University of Western Australia,
Perth, WA, Australia
e-mail: steven.maras@uwa.edu.au

© The Editor(s) (if applicable) and The Author(s) 2016
S. Maras (ed.), *Ethics in Screenwriting*, Palgrave Studies
in Screenwriting, DOI 10.1057/978-1-137-54493-3_1

1

In the USA, as early as 1907, and through the 1910s, cities such as Chicago and states such as Ohio created boards of censors. Fuelled by puritans and 'yellow journalists' the trend continued into the 1920s.

> In 1921 alone, solons in thirty-seven states introduced nearly one hundred bills designed to censor motion pictures. The rules of the extant censor boards were mine fields. Women could not smoke on-screen in Kansas but could in Ohio. (Leff and Simmons 2001, 3–4)

As censorship states also had some of the biggest audiences, it was impossible not to engage with the boards, in what became a costly exercise of compliance for local exhibitors at first, and later producers. In the 1920s, off-screen scandals such as the 1921 Roscoe 'Fatty' Arbuckle case, but also others, fuelled the image of Hollywood as a modern Sodom, feeding a panic over Hollywood's moral standards.

Studio managers became concerned by the impact of off-screen scandal and on-screen immorality on financing, as well as the possibility of government regulation of the industry. In 1922, in an attempt to cool down hostility towards Hollywood, they moved to establish the Motion Picture Producers and Distributors of America (MPPDA), and appointed former Postmaster-General Will H. Hays to lead the Association (Doherty 1999, 6; Maltby 1995a, 5–7).

The approach pursued by the MPPDA was multipronged, including the registration of titles and advertising, and a process under which studios presented scripts to the Association for evaluation (Vaughn 1990, 44). Two other strategies stand out. Firstly, to persuade stakeholder groups that the industry took moral standards seriously. These groups included the various censorship boards, along with an estimated sixty other groups including the National Council of Catholic Women, the Boy Scouts of America, the YMCA, the American Federation of Labor, the National Congress of Mothers and Parent–Teacher Associations, and the US Chamber of Commerce (Vasey 1995, 65–66). One mechanism here was a Committee on Public Relations, which was seen as an advisory group on 'public demands and moral standards' (Leff and Simmons 2001, 5). Established as a Department of Public Relations within the MPPDA in March 1925, it promised a 'direct channel of communication between motion picture producers and the public' (Vasey 2004, 320–321; see Motion Picture Producers and Distributors of America Inc. 1929).

With demands for censorship continuing a second strategy saw the MPPDA engage the studios directly and convince them of the value of 'clean' pictures and self-discipline; even though box office success and public interest in salacious movies often suggested otherwise. The move to self-regulation was given concrete form in 1927, when the Studio Relations Committee (SRC) relocated its offices to the West Coast. It was organized by Colonel Jason Joy, who would advise producers of problems facing scripts and scenarios, and met with studio representatives fortnightly, with more frequent contact around specific projects (Vasey 2004, 232). Also, in 1927 a guideline known as the 'Don'ts and Be Carefuls' emerged. These guidelines arose to appease exhibitors concerned by industry practices and were developed out of an analysis of the activities of the censor boards across the country over several years (Vasey 1995, 66).

In 1929 only 20 % of scenarios were sent to Joy (Leff and Simmons 2001, 8). Studios further flaunted the code.[1] Alongside calls for control from civic organizations were those from small-town exhibitors who bore the brunt of decency concerns. Industry fears that anti-trust legislation would be applied to the film industry intensified. A new approach was needed, which localized around discussion of a new code (see Maltby 1995a, 15). For Will Hays,

> ...[the] goal was the formulation of a production ethic, capable of informing interpretation and based not on arbitrary do's and don'ts, but on principles. ... Hence a morality was necessary, a philosophy of right and wrong. The industry was growing up, and the list of "Don'ts" and "Be Carefuls" had served its day. (Hays 1955, 438–439)

The MPPDA used the coming of the sound film as a pretext for a new code (Maltby 1995a, 23; 1995b, 58). However, other powerful currents were at work, including the mobilization of Catholic groups. Several different versions and drafts of a new code were put forward: by Irving Thalberg, Colonel Jason Joy, and Father Daniel Lord SJ (Maltby 1995b). The 'Lord' code has received the most discussion. Devised by Lord and Martin Quigley, publisher of the *Motion Picture Herald*, this was an ambitious document, going beyond a statement of 'Don'ts and Be Carefuls'. It contained a statement of general principles alongside working principles addressing particular applications. A summary of the code was made public by the Hays Office in 1930, which contains a section on

General Principles, and Particular Applications, and was accompanied by a 'Resolution for Uniform Interpretation'. Although a compromise document (Maltby 1995a, 18) the new code had some impact, and story and screenplay submissions jumped from 48 in 1929 to 1,200 in 1930 (Leff and Simmons 2001, 13).

The full version of the Lord–Quigley code was published in 1934. It is the fusion of the earlier summary and the full document (see Leff and Simmons 2001, 285) that is normally referred to as the formal 'Production Code', although the simultaneous publication or private circulation of different versions of the code makes it difficult to pin down an authoritative version (Jacobs and Maltby 1995, 3). By 1934, federal legislation looked extremely likely (Doherty 1999, 324). Following action by the Catholic Legion of Decency, and spurred on by social science research (the Payne Fund studies)—which promoted the view that the movies were highly influential on the conduct of vulnerable members of the audience—the code formed the basis of a new, mandatory and enforceable self-regulation regime.

The key elements of this new regime were (1) compulsory submission of scripts for consideration by Production Code Administration (PCA), with appeals going directly to the MPPDA; (2) the replacement of the SRC with the PCA, under the authority of Joseph I. Breen; and (3) a $25,000 fine applied to any film shown without a Production Seal. This was seen as a response not only to religious groups and new research, but also the fear that the newly elected Roosevelt Administration would institute regulation of the film industry under the New Deal. As Thomas Doherty notes, 'The studios found themselves fighting a three-front war against church, state, and social science' (1999, 8).[2]

This sketch of the Production Code can only partly capture all of the forces at work in this period: fears over the rise of 'moral indifferentism' after the Great War (Quigley 1937, 27); technological change; the great depression and financing issues (Vaughn 1990, 57); changing patterns of cinema attendance; trade relations between distributors and exhibitors (see Vasey 2004, 321); all contribute to a fuller picture. Nevertheless, it serves to portray a research paradigm that will be familiar to many readers. This paradigm, I want to argue, can serve as a useful reference point for debates about ethics in screenwriting, but has also contributed to the neglect of broader questions and perspectives in ethics in screenwriting. In the absence of a well-developed approach to ethical analysis it forms a default way of thinking about key issues of morality and practice. While clearly the Production Code has specific origins in US screen culture it has wider discursive power in terms of how it frames or codifies discussion of questions of morality and practice, and restricts discussion of ethics. As a discourse it successfully forms questions of ethics and practice around morality, entertainment and compliance, to the extent that it articulates a key moment in discussion of ethics in screenwriting, without posing critical questions about the nature of ethics, or screenwriting. Thus the paradox with which I began this chapter: ethics in screenwriting remains both commonly discussed but neglected.

As a dominant framework and discourse through which ethics in screenwriting has been articulated the research on the code has some shortcomings. The first shortcoming to highlight is that its primary focus is on morals rather than ethics, and more specifically the project of how to establish 'a standard of morality independent of public taste' (Vaughn 1990, 41). While many readers and philosophers will find the words 'morals' and 'ethics' interchangeable, some scholars insist on a distinction between the two terms (see Rajchman 1986, 72), and I shall do the same. The articulation of morality spelled out in the Production Code has to do with sin and evil, moral standards, correct standards of life, natural and human law. This extends to prohibitions on representing homosexuality, childbirth and sexual relations between people of different races. Although there are instances where the Production Code is described as an industry 'code of ethics', on close inspection this is an injunctive, or negative ethics, one designed to expel offence and indecency rather than engage with the complexities or ambiguities of social ethics (Doherty 1999, 328).

When discussing morality and the Hays code, two caveats should be made. Firstly, the code is not a straightforward reflection of morality. Instead, it is the by-product of a series of moral panics and institutional negotiations (Jacobs and Maltby 1995, 3). Secondly, the sincerity of industry and the Hays Office, and its ability to wear a 'mask' of morality (Vaughn 1990, 45), was the subject of open debate (Maltby 1995a, 24; see 'Morals for Profit', *New York World*, 1 April 1930).

A second way in which the discussion of decency, morals and motion pictures, falls short in the discussion of ethics in screenwriting is that rather than focus on screenwriters, narrative craft and ethical choices, attention is primarily directed towards issues of regulation and compliance of a work to be exhibited under a code, or subversion of the code itself. In a rare consideration of the space of the writer, at a 1929 public relations conference Colonel Joy explained that, with the coming of sound, 'the picture had to be made almost exactly as the scenario had been written' (MPPDA 1929, 63). Furthermore, 'some of the continuity writers … felt a certain freedom as to what should go into their pictures', which meant discussion with the SRC could be beneficial. Another attendee suggested that the dominant 'menacing' force in moving pictures was the scenario writer who, because of the scarcity of people with writing skills, and the refusal of producers to challenge him or her, created material 'which should never have reached the screen' (MPPDA 1929, 79).

This is not to suggest that figures such as Breen ignored the artistic or creative dimensions of filmmaking. Indeed, it has been argued that Breen's 'intricate knowledge of film grammar and the production process allowed him to enforce his dictates' (Doherty 1999, 327). Accounts of the operations of the SRC reinforce the idea of a very engaged process. Staff members evaluated source materials, treatments and scripts, and were also available to review rewrites (Miller 1994, 52). Later, in the period of the PCA, the practice was to assign two members of staff to a script (Miller 1994, 84). Nevertheless, the 'space' of screenwriting remains narrow in discussions of the code.

Two aspects are worth highlighting here. The first is the limited formal participation of screenwriters in code matters. Doherty notes 'the correspondence between the Breen Office and the studio is typically addressed not to the director, still less to the lowly screenwriter, but to the producer or to a special liaison appointed by the studio to handle the PCA' (2006). This is despite the fact that story treatments and screenplays were central objects of this regime of control. The code is explicitly conceived as a discussion between the Association and production managers about scripts, and then prints. Daniel Lord may have sensed this marginalization when he observed that scenario writers were of a 'lower social caste' in Hollywood (1956, 204).[3]

The second point to make is that screenwriting practice itself is largely handled under the supervisory framework of 'script review'. As Doherty highlights,

> Censorship was best done in the preproduction "script-review phase" to eliminate the need for costly reshooting and reediting. Ideally, then, the final "print-review" stage undertaken by the Code staff was a pro forma ritual, all problem areas having been ironed out during the meticulous script-review phase. (Doherty 2006)

It is rare under this structure to see consideration of ethics as a question for screenwriting separate to approval under the code. The dominant focus is on the demands of compliance. As Miranda Banks notes: 'Overall, writers had to give producers what they wanted, no questions asked' (2015, 48–49).

Taken together, the narrow focus on morality, and restricted engagement with screenwriting limit discussion of ethics in screenwriting to a particular representational space. This space of representation is focused largely on the manifest or surface content of films and how it may, or may not, be transgressive of moral norms. Doherty has noted that 'What makes Hollywood's classic age "classical" is not just the film style or studio system but the moral stakes' (1999, 5). We can add that these moral stakes were played out in a representational arena that allows for a very limited construction of the relationship between ethics and screenwriting. This discourse continues to influence discussions today. What is needed in this context, I would argue, is a twofold approach. Firstly, we need a greater focus on screenwriting, not only as it operates under the code, but as a practice that engages with ethics and questions of representation on a number of different levels. Secondly, we need a more considered understanding of ethics as multifaceted and multidimensional.

MORAL STAKES AND REPRESENTATIONAL SPACE

To make way for a greater focus on screenwriting, as well as a more considered discussion of ethics, we need to understand how the 'code' is linked to a representational space in which morality became problematic in particular ways. Underpinning this representational space is the rapid diffusion of nickelodeons in lower socio-economic neighbourhoods in the early twentieth century. 'This sudden proliferation of "five-cent theaters" created what can at best be characterized as a moral panic among American elites in this period' (Phillips 2008, 4). This period in US history coincided with the era of progressive reform (1900–1920) which painted film theaters as breeding grounds for immorality (Black 1994, 8).

A full picture of how this climate of moral panic impacted on filmic representation is beyond the scope of this chapter. However, Tom Gunning has argued that moral discourse played an important part in the development of film narrative. He suggests that 'part of the transformation of

American cinema from its earliest period to the era we associate with the founding of narrative codes (roughly 1908–1913) lies in its ... conscious movement into a realm of moral discourse' (Gunning 2004, 146). Alongside this morally 'anxious' view of film and its 'moral lessons' arose the need to establish a 'moral pedigree' for motion pictures (2004, 146–148). This in turn gives rise to the 'articulation of a moral rhetoric within the narrative codes of the film' (2004, 149). In other words, the legibility of particular actions and behaviours on the screen are partly to do with film conventions and continuity, but also in moral terms of good and bad, right and wrong, virtue and vice. In other words, knowing who are the good guys and who are the bad guys helps drive narrative development.

This development in narrative occurs in a context in which the moving image is regarded as hugely influential and morally corrupting. Evidence for this can be found in regulatory and legal discourse. In the 1915 case *Mutual Film Corporation, Appt.* v. *Industrial Commission of Ohio*, US courts considered whether a state censorship board violated constitutional protections for freedom of speech. The judgement decided that no freedom of speech was violated because of the nature of moving pictures as a business, as well as its unique 'capability and power': 'a prurient interest may be excited and appealed to'. This view of the special powers of film informed the 1934 Production Code, especially its construction of film as entertainment. The code makes a clear statement of the possible harms of entertainment, which 'lowers the whole living conditions and moral ideals of a race' (Leff and Simmons 2001, 292).

Reviewing some of the key documents informing the redrafting of the code in the 1930s two distinct ways of articulating questions of morality and representation are evident. Drafts by Thalberg on the one hand, and Lord on the other, define different approaches to the same problem.

What has become known as 'Thalberg's Draft'[4] of the code begins with a critique of a 'tendency to over-emphasize' the moral influence of motion pictures. It suggests that 'To hold the motion picture chiefly responsible for the spiritual or moral tone of a community is greatly to overrate its social influence' (35). For Thalberg 'people influence people far more than pictures influence people'. As such, the motion picture is according to Thalberg 'bound to the mental and moral level of its vast audience'.

Usually a code of practice or ethics will define a clear role and responsibility. Interestingly, Thalberg's draft disputes the very discussion of morality and ethics, with concern that 'this tendency has developed until the motion picture is held wholly or in part responsible for every trend in manners and morals' (35). He counters this with a view that the commercial motion picture 'cannot be considered as a sermon or even essentially a moral or immoral force'. It is more like a news story, with our attention shifting from headline to picture. When he comes to define the purpose of motion pictures it is 'to entertain'. In Thalberg's formulation, education and morality are incidental to entertainment because ultimately entertainment reflects audience preferences: 'The motion picture does not present the audience with tastes and manners and views and morals; it reflects those they already have'. As such, a picture succeeds or fails on the extent to which it pleases audiences. If it does not reflect audience thoughts and attitudes, they reject it. Thalberg underlines this point in his draft text:

> *The picture may educate: all do to one extent or another. It may present moral views: no story lacks moral inferences. But both these are incidental. The picture is first and foremost a piece of entertainment.* That means it is presented because it pleases its audiences; *if it does not please it is a failure.*

From this statement, entertainment emerges as a field distinct from morality and education. Representation is first and foremost about entertaining, which is tied to enjoyment. There is no point, Thalberg argues, to raise moral standards if the audiences walk out.

In Thalberg's draft, the focus falls on standards of good taste, and motion pictures as a reflection of this taste. Morality cannot be ignored: 'The trend in every picture should be to uphold good and condemn evil'. However, Thalberg insists that this may be achieved non-censorially across an entire film rather than episodes or incidents. 'It often happens in the unfolding of a story of the most unquestionable moral worth that there may be phases in which evil is temporarily victorious'.

A focus on 'mode of treatment' becomes intertwined with an idea linked to Thalberg, to the importance of including 'compensating moral values'. 'Scenes will be included in these pictures which make a point of defending and upholding accepted moral and spiritual standards' (Maltby 1995b, 40; also 1995a, 18–19). This idea became an operative norm in the Breen Office (Miller 1994, 52). More cynical commentators saw the profit angle that allowed for 'five reels of transgression followed by one reel of retribution' (see Maltby 1995a, 24).

Thalberg's draft queries the connection between morality and representation, but also reestablishes it through concepts of entertainment and mode of treatment. This strategy has similarities but also differences to that adopted in an alternative draft of the code known as 'Lord's Draft'.[5] Lord's draft is similar to Thalberg's in stressing that theatrical motion pictures should be primarily regarded as entertainment. However, Lord's document seeks to reintroduce morality through a distinction of 'helpful' or 'harmful' entertainment, the latter being 'entertainment that tends to degrade human beings, or to lower their standards of life and living'. In this view, representations do not just reflect reality, but have an impact on it. If Thalberg's view of entertainment can be regarded as secular, Lord's is non-secular. The Lord draft states:

> *Hence* the *MORAL IMPORTANCE* of entertainment is something which has been universally recognized. It enters intimately into the lives of men and women and effects them closely. It occupies the minds and affections during leisure hours, and ultimately touches the whole of their lives. A man may be judged by his standard of entertainment as easily as by the standard of his work. ... So *correct entertainment raises* the whole standard of a nation. ...*Wrong entertainment lowers* the whole living conditions and moral ideals of a race. ('Lord's Draft', 41, emphasis in original)

Lord's draft advocates the idea of influence, and the link between morality, art and entertainment disputed in Thalberg's draft. Motion pictures 'reproduce' morality, and affect the moral standards of others. From this viewpoint, the motion picture, due in part to it being entertainment, and reaching wide, mass audiences in large and small communities, bears a moral obligation. In a variation to Thalberg's idea of compensating moral values, Lord's draft is more categorical: in the end the audience must feel that '*evil and good are never confused*, and that evil is always recognized as evil' ('Lord's Draft', 44). Lord's draft shares the focus on treatment or mode with Thalberg's draft, but the conditions are stricter: In the end 'the audience feels that *evil is wrong* and *good is right*'. 'The presentation must not throw sympathy with the crime as against the law or with the criminal against those who punish him' ('Lord's Draft', 44).

The two drafts seem to have been commissioned in late 1929 and were both considered by the Association of Motion Picture Producers in February 1930 (Maltby 1995b, 41).[6] Although it has been suggested that Lord's code was accepted 'almost without a whimper' (Black 1994, 42), the resolution that was recorded is in fact an amalgam of the two approaches we have been discussing, balancing the focus on entertainment with ideas of moral progress. The resolution reads: 'Whereas, though regarding motion pictures primarily as entertainment without any explicit purpose of teaching or propaganda, they know that the motion picture within its own field of entertainment may be directly responsible for spiritual or moral progress, for higher types of social life and for much correct thinking ...' (Maltby 1995b, 52). The general principles that were approved reflect Lord's focus on moral standards, without inflammatory terms such as 'moral importance' or harmful and helpful entertainment. A focus on correct standards of life is accompanied by 'the requirements of drama and entertainment'. These changes reflect what Stephen Vaughn sees as the main points of concern for producers with the Lord draft: 'At the center of this disagreement was the question of what responsibility Hollywood should take for public morality' (Vaughn 1990, 53). But they also represent a concession to religious interests by linking entertainment to theology. While a compromise text, the resolution helps demonstrate that at the same time as emerging as a significant narrative form in the early twentieth century the politics of that era helped shape this form in other ways by promoting anxiety around the influence and power of motion pictures, and the morally corrupting influence of entertainment.

WRITER RESPONSES

This tension between the presentation of correct standards of life, and the requirements of drama and entertainment, structures many of the responses we find from screenwriters who laboured under the code. A common theme in screenwriting accounts is the demand for changes to storylines due to the absence of a compensating voice or action, even for implied immorality. As Casey Robinson recalls of writing a love affair in *Kings Row* (Dir: Sam Wood; Wr: Casey Robinson 1942),

'I intimated rather than showed. I did everything to protect those scenes from the censors.... They said that we had not eliminated the sexual angles or the incest. ... As for our camouflage of saying it was instead a tendency toward insanity—they had decided the girl's insanity was nymphomania'. (in Greenberg 1986, 306)

Richard Maibaum gives another example in his account of working on *The Great Gatsby* (Dir: Elliot Nugent; Wr: Cyril Hume and Richard Maibaum 1942), where the PCA insisted on the voice of morality being inscribed in the plot, which took the form of a proverb inscribed on a tombstone. 'So we had to put it right in the opening where Nick and Jordan, now married, stop at Gatsby's grave and quote the chapter and verse from Gatsby's tombstone' (McGilligan 1986, 281).

Demands from Production Code officials could meet resistance. In response to concerns surrounding *High Sierra* (Dir: Raoul Walsh; Wr: John Huston and William R. Burnett 1941), John Huston wrote to the Executive Producer Hal Wallis warning not to take the spirit out the story by Burnett (Mate and McGilligan 1986, 52). Burnett outlines that 'we had twenty-seven pages of objections from the Johnston Office.[7] ... We had [the Motion Picture Code official] Geoff Shurlock from the Johnston Office on set with us practically every day.... But we got 'em through'. This was achieved 'Just by yelling. Our argument was that it was an absolutely integral part of the drama, which it was' (Mate and McGilligan 1986, 81).

Alternately, writers would comply but only up to a certain point, offering up sacrificial material. As Donald O. Stewart notes, '... if you sinned, you had to pay for it; and that payment had to be on the screen ... so you'd give the Hays Office five things to take out to satisfy them and you'd get away with murder with what they left in' (Stewart 1970, 53).

Screenwriter accounts often take the form of complaint or subterfuge, with one writer reportedly getting back at the censors for vetoing his description of a 'flimsy' negligee by adding a direction 'From off stage we hear the scream of a naked woman' (Miller 1994, 101). Another writer referred to 'a gown cut down to the Breen line' (Doherty 2007, 113). However, some writers reclaimed writing under the code as a challenge. Philip Dunne argues that it is 'possible to produce a great movie, a true dramatic delineation of life, without the explicit sex and violence' (1987, 8). W. R. Burnett writes of restrictions on sex and romance: 'Oh yes, you couldn't just do anything. That's not necessarily bad. ... Sometimes limitations on a writer are better than total freedom' (Mate and McGilligan 1986, 81).

For Dunne, good writing requires 'adroit indirection' (1987, 8), and the code made such cleverness or subtlety crucial. 'In the proper dramatic context, a touch of hands, a simple look, could be far more erotic than any of today's explicit tumbles in the hay' (1987, 10; see also Hays

1955, 444). He goes so far as to characterize some of the exchanges with Production Code officers as highly creative, bordering on a 'lively story conference' (Dunne 1987, 8).

From these statements it is apparent that screenwriters understood and learned to play the censorship game to achieve their goals. Nevertheless, as Vasey notes, 'An inevitable result of the SRC was the narrowing of the field of representation normally attempted by filmmakers' (1995, 79). As Richard Fine observes, 'the Code cut the movies off from many of the most pressing social and moral issues confronting American society, and it severely restricted the range of character and plot possibilities available to the screenwriter' (1985, 85). Critics complained at the way the Code seemed infallible and unchangeable (Doherty 2007, 294).

Evident in many statements by screenwriters is protest at narrowing of representational possibilities. Herman Mankiewicz highlights the absurd treatment of virgins and villains, virtue and vice in films as compared with novels (in Hecht 1954, 479). Hecht skewers the more bizarre aspects of this narrative space which privileges one basic plot, 'the triumph of virtue and the overthrow of wickedness', and treats sex in terms of sin. Audiences are taught daily 'that there are no problems of labor, politics, domestic life or sexual abnormality but can be solved happily by a simple Christian phrase or a fine American motto'. Characters 'must always be good or bad (and never human) in order not to confuse the plot of Virtue Triumphing' (1954, 468–469).

In passages such as these, it becomes evident that screenwriters were finely attuned to the moral stakes surrounding the representational space of the code. However, it is clear that a fuller discussion of ethics in screenwriting needs to move beyond this construction of representational space to entertain different kinds of practices and different ideas and activations of ethics.

ETHICS AND MORALS

In the discussion so far, I have suggested that engaging with 'morals' represents a restricted way of thinking about ethics. This may seem a difficult view to sustain from the point of view of etymology, since the Latin '*moralis*', the root of morals, is a translation of the Greek '*ethikos*'. Given the inter-relationship of the two terms it can be argued that the two terms are interchangeable (see Cohen 2004, 12). Nevertheless, it is possible to make a distinction. Indeed, differentiating between morality and ethics can help tease out new perspectives on ethics. Here, I turn to the work of Michel Foucault, which has itself been influential on thinking about ethics, and informed important work by Judith Butler on accountability (2005) and William E. Connolly on ethical sensibilities (1993).

Drawing on Foucault, I will call 'morality' a set of rules and values, usually formulated into a moral code that implies a social standard of wrong and right. The moral code is closely linked to a morality of behaviours in which the rules and values form prescriptive standards. These standards are recommended to us through what Foucault terms 'prescriptive agencies', which include family, educational institutions and churches. The agencies present to us, as a 'prescriptive ensemble', a moral code (Foucault 1987, 25). From this understanding derives an idea of morality as a code that demands more or less full compliance with a standard of conduct. An important dimension of the morality of behaviours is ethics, conceived as a relationship to oneself 'which determines how the individual is supposed to constitute himself [sic] as a moral subject of his own actions' (Foucault 2000, 263). Ethics in this sense is directed toward the problem of conducting oneself morally, viewed from the point of view of being an ethical subject rather than complying with a code. It constitutes a space of reflection, of judgement and decision-making. While often associated with a sharp distinction between ethics and morals, Foucault's work in fact provides a way to see the deep connection between ethics and morality. While morality might relate to absolute standards of right and wrong, ethics grapples with the experience of being good which may or may not draw on moral absolutes (see Rajchman 1986, 172).

Foucault's treatment of morality and ethics offers some important insights for research into ethics in screenwriting. Firstly, it provides a different perspective on the moral anxieties surrounding the influence of film. This can be framed as a concern that film was a new and powerful 'prescriptive agency' in apparently direct competition to families, schools and the Church. For Martin Quigley, co-drafter of the Lord Production Code, the influence of film in disseminating the moral code is a key concern.

Not only to youth but to the whole public the motion picture is an agency which assists in establishing ideals and standards. ... "There exists today no means of influencing the masses more potent than the cinema", declared Pope Pius XI. (Quigley 1937, 6)

Central to Quigley's argument is that film has radically upset the very sense of order on which the moral code is based (1937, 13).

While Foucault's approach helps us understand anxieties over the influence of motion pictures, his discussion of ethics helps open up a different space, which is that of how ethical subjects construct and form ideas of good conduct through reflection, judgement and decision-making about particular situations and roles. This, not coincidentally, is the domain of moral or ethical philosophy as formed through the work of philosophers such as Aristotle, Immanuel Kant, John Stuart Mill and myriad others.

Foucault's distinction between morality and ethics will be a useful reference point in the discussion that follows, not only because it validates the ongoing power of morality, but for the way it represents ethical decision-making and judgement as a dynamic space of invention. In a number of disciplines today, an 'ethical turn' is in evidence (see Garber et al. 2000, viii–ix; Hawkins 2001, 412). Without downplaying the importance of research in other areas, the area of media ethics is especially worth highlighting for its relevance to screenwriting research. Since the 1970s media ethicists have argued for a 'renewed emphasis on ethics as a discipline, as a normative science of conduct' in a manner relevant to practice and the professions (Christians 1977, 26). The idea is that moral philosophy can provide some foundation and coherence for media ethics. Consequently, a significant reworking of philosophical ethics through the lens of professional media ethics has been underway, represented in myriad studies and textbooks. The potential exists for a useful cross-fertilization between media ethics research, and those interested in screenwriting research, and practice (see an early attempt in Beker 2004, 109–122). The media ethics literature is vast, but two broad areas are especially significant to those interested in ethics in screenwriting.

The first area has to do with drawing on different philosophical ideas to tease out different forms of prescriptive ethics. Prescriptive ethics tackles the question of 'how someone *should* behave, what is the *right* thing to do' (Cohen 2004, 2, emphasis in original). Out of this discussion what becomes apparent is that different traditions in ethical philosophy construct the idea of 'the good' in different ways. Stephen Cohen suggests a useful initial distinction between consequentialist and non-consequentialist approaches: that is, between approaches that put consequences at the heart of their idea of the good, and those that draw on other reasons like duty (2004, 36). Immanuel Kant, for instance, was famous for being sceptical of any moral reasoning based on doing good work because he was suspicious of the motives for such actions (pleasing others, for example), and questioned the lack of basis in moral law and reasoning. John Stuart Mill, by contrast, felt that the consequences of an action mattered more than motive or temperament. While useful, this distinction doesn't say a great deal about the doing of ethics beyond consequences, so it will be useful to present just some of the different possibilities (see Table 1.1), drawing on a summary of ethical guidelines presented in well-known media ethics text books (Sanders 2003; Cohen 2004; Christians et al. 2005, 12–24; Patterson and Wilkins 2005; Black and Roberts 2011; Couldry et al. 2013). Readers interested in exploring these ethical philosophies further should consult those works.

A table of this kind can only be a starting point. There are philosophical trajectories such as existentialism, Nietzschean thought or situational ethics, which are barely represented. Scholars are actively fusing different approaches, such as the ethics of care and virtue ethics (Stadler 2008, 17). Philosophically minded readers might bemoan the reduction and simplification going on. Non-philosophically minded readers will feel there is too much abstract detail. They might follow a view promoted in documentary ethics that more empirical research is required (Sanders 2010). There is also a danger of introducing a requirement to choose a particular (Western) school of philosophy in order to follow it as some doctrine, rather than embrace ethical ambiguity and exercise ethical creativity and imagination (see Adams 2008, 178). As Judith Butler has noted, there is a

Table 1.1 Summary of ethical perspectives in media ethics

Philosopher	Ethical approach	Key concepts	Form of the good	Ethical focus
Aristotle	Teleology (from *telos* meaning end) Virtue ethics	Purpose Ends/Role Virtue	Flourishing Excellence Practical wisdom	Character
Immanuel Kant	Deontology (from *deon* meaning duty)	Duty Obligation Imperative	Good will Act according to the guide of Universal Law without conditions	The rational basis for Action

(continued)

Table 1.1 (continued)

William David Ross	Deontology	Duty Moral value Ethical decision-making	Consider competing duties to determine morally relevant differences Act to maximize justice and beneficence	Choice
John Stuart Mill	Consequentialism	Utility	Maximizing pleasure and minimizing pain or harm Greatest good for the greatest number	Outcome
John Rawls	Contractarian	Justice Fairness	Negotiate agreements in a situation of imagined equality behind a veil of ignorance Moral value arises out of agreement and obligations	Social relations
Carol Gilligan Nel Noddings	Relational ethics	Care Reciprocity Moral voice or advocacy Self-in-relation We-ness over individuality	We are caring beings first and foremost, embedded in mutually supporting relationships	Community and connection to others
Martin Buber	Dialogism	The Other Recognition Experience Relation	We should strive for an I-Thou rather than I-It relation to the world	Relationship to the world

danger that the turn to ethics is a return to moralism as well as an escape or a retreat from politics (2000, 15–17). Despite these reservations, as Jay Black and Chris Roberts suggest, these principles can form 'touchstones in our efforts to do ethics and to think critically about the media ethics environment' (2011, 305).

A second area of potential interest to those interested in ethics in screenwriting has to do with what are termed ethical decision-making models. These are designed to focus on the quality of our ethical decision-making on the assumption that this leads to more principled, considered and reflective actions. They encourage individuals to think through the different components of a decision. Marilyn Beker has summarized some of these and attempted to apply them to screenwriting, listing movies that illustrate her points (2004, 109–120). In one of the most famous models, the 'Potter box', developed by Dr. Ralph Potter of the Harvard Divinity School, the decision-maker is encouraged to walk through four steps towards a decision. The first step involves defining the facts of the case; the second involves consideration of cultural and professional values (and conflict or alignment between the two); the third involves the key principles involved (which may involve drawing on moral philosophy); and a fourth step involves consideration of loyalty (see Christians et al. 2005, 3–9; Patterson and Wilkins 2005, 90–94). While all of these steps are ethically significant, especially the definition of facts, for Patterson and Wilkins, 'most ethical decisions come down to the question "To whom (or what) will I be loyal?"' (2005, 84). In making this point, they are conscious of the fact that most media professionals live in a world of conflicting loyalties arising from family, professional ties, employment conditions, and citizenship (2005, 88–89).

Black and Roberts explore another ethical decision-making model associated with the philosopher William David Ross (Black and Roberts 2011, 340–341). Ross recognized that in many roles we are faced with a number of duties that may be relevant in any situation. These are called '*prima facie*' duties, or duties at first glance. From these we determine 'duties proper' or 'morally incumbent' duties. These are the duties that take precedence and guide our decision-making and action. Ross summarizes the duties at first glance as: non-maleficence, fidelity, reparation, justice, self-improvement, gratitude and beneficence. Using Ross, Black and Roberts walk the reader through a hypothetical case of a screenwriter under pressure to aim the script towards a kids' movie at a higher classification: leading to more swearing, killing and sex, and also make sure there is a marketing tie-in through a 'cartoonish' character (Black and Roberts 2011, 313).

> A different clash of duties occurs.... As a scriptwriter you would seem to have the prima facie duty of offering a film that is worth the price of admission: fidelity to the consumer. The same should hold true for the producer. Neither of you should set out to rip off your audiences: non-maleficence. In fact, both of you have an obligation to entertain without causing harm: non-maleficence, fidelity and perhaps justice. But you find yourself facing other duties: fidelity and gratitude to your producer, without whom your script will never become a movie. As you debate whether to convert your tame PG film into a spicier PG-13, yet still market it to children, the duty of self-improvement enters the equation. How do you prioritize these? Which prima facie duties become the morally incumbent ethical duties? (Black and Roberts 2011, 344)

There is not necessarily one answer to this question. Decision-making models place a strong value on the process of decision as a marker of integrity as much as the outcome. For Cohen, moral opinions and behaviours are 'principled', in the sense that the ethical subject searches for a *fit* between situations, behaviours, principles and opinions (Cohen 2004, 57). In the media ethics literature a greater understanding of ethical philosophies as well as a greater focus on reflective deliberation and decision-making are held to be core parts of ethical professional practice.

This focus on media ethics should not discount the importance of other areas such as literature and film ethics.[8] Film ethics, for example, seeks a unique meeting of film and ethics by focusing on the complex relationship *between* aesthetics and ethics, and the affective dimension of narrative (see Bergen-Aurand 2009). The situation of the viewer's relationship to, and separation from, the screen becomes a way to think through issues of presence, absence, recognition, ethical relation and responsibility and the complex nature of human reciprocity.

THE VIRTUOUS SCREENWRITER

A practising screenwriter who has just read the preceding section might feel some exasperation, possibly voiced through a question such as 'so just tell me what is the right thing to do'? The frustration comes not just from the idea that morals are not absolute, but also from the fact that competing ideas of what is right and wrong can emerge out of ethics. This is precisely the point of considering ethics in screenwriting—not to mention a great deal of ethical philosophy—that our sense of right or good emerges not just through moral codes recommended to us, but through the ethical cultures we commit to, the principles we hold ourselves accountable to, as well as the situations we encounter.

Underpinning this question of 'what is the right thing to do?' is a figure who has in a sense shadowed our discussion so far, but whom we should bring into the foreground now. This is the figure of 'the virtuous screenwriter'. We have already seen at least two versions of the virtuous screenwriter emerge in our discussion of the Hollywood Production Code: the first is the fully wholesome writer of 'clean' pictures; the second is the ingenious writer capable of writing with integrity despite the obstacles of the Code.

Many other versions of this figure exist. Conceptions of the virtuous screenwriter can emerge from within the community of writers. An example is Joe Eszterhas's view on Hollywood's responsibility for cigarette smoking deaths because of its glamorization of smoking (Eszterhas 2002; see also Watson 2004). Conceptions of the virtuous screenwriter can also arise from outside of the community of writers. Perhaps the most significant of these is the 'Entertainment-Education' movement (see Singhal and Rogers 1999). This is an umbrella term for a group of organizations that seek to provide services for screenwriters attempting to communicate information about particular health conditions and illnesses, including organizations such as the Johns Hopkins Center for Communication Programs (ccp.jhu.edu/entertainment-education/), as well as the 'Entertainment Education' program of the Centers for Disease Control and Prevention in the USA, who provide 'expert consultation, education and resources for writers and producers who develop scripts with health storylines and information' (www.cdc.gov/healthcommunication/ToolsTemplates/EntertainmentEd/). Other groups take entertainment education further by furnishing stories on particular themes (Glik 1998).We should also include pressure or advocacy groups who have a long tradition of 'targeting' Hollywood by evaluating scripts for sympathetic of offensive representations of gay civil rights or black, Hispanic, Asian, and women characters (Montgomery 1989, 78–80). In the 1970s Network 'standards and practices' departments engaged with key stakeholders. Disability activists worked directly with producers and story editors (Montgomery 1989, 183). Alcohol education lobbyists went further, producing their own version of an alcohol-related code and holding related 'sensitivity sessions' (Montgomery 1989, 187). Today, Participant Media, founded in 2004, maintains this focus on responsible media content that inspires social change (see http://www.participantmedia.com/about-participant-media). It continues and expands a concern around influence.

The US journalism and cultural critic James Carey takes a sceptical view on the virtuous practitioner, arguing that the discussion of ethics seems to be a 'cover' for deeper discussion of practice (1999, 39). Barbie Zelizer goes further to suggest that the complexity of practice can be undercut by ethics, which at the same time geographically favours ideas from the West and global North (Zelizer 2013).

The most fully-developed conception of the virtuous screenwriter in recent years comes from the work of Marilyn Beker, who has been a pioneer in promoting issues of ethics and screenwriting in her books *Screenwriting with a Conscience* (2004) and *The Screenwriter Activist: Writing Social Issue Movies* (2013). In *Screenwriting with a Conscience*, Beker outlines a vision for being an 'ethical screenwriter'. In the context of US first amendment considerations she advocates a philosophy of speaking one's mind and standing up for beliefs (despite the brutal commercial realities of Hollywood), but also resisting an 'anything goes' attitude.

> I'm tired of hearing that ethics for screenwriters is an oxymoron. I know there are lots of screenwriters who are ethical and believe that ethics should be an essential ingredient of how we treat each other, how we work, and what we choose to write. (Beker 2004, xvii–xviii)

Beker's plea comes out of exasperation with a lack of concern for social issues and responsibility and a 'seeming growing disinterest in humanistic standards on the part of entertainment executives' (2004, xix). Beker promotes a practical definition of ethics:

> I take ethics to mean a code of behavior (as it applies to screenwriters, a way of presenting material and ideas) that is fair, just, honest, and integrity-based; that intentionally hurts no one; that works toward the common good without destroying individuals in the process; that is honorable, consistent, and thoughtful, and that is life-affirming and humanistic. (Beker 2004, 6)

She outlines a number of ethical 'givens' guiding her book including anti-censorship; respect for humanity; a responsibility to contribute to peace; respect for audiences and self. Interestingly, she emphasizes that morality is different from ethics, and is more often linked to Church doctrine. Ethics by contrast is 'essentially humanistic' (Beker 2004, 9).

Influence is at the centre of her idea of the virtuous screenwriter, who must 'first examine their own values and philosophies and own up to them before they create works that will shape and/or influence the values, philosophies, and the lives of others' (Beker 2004, 10). Beker's approach seeks to overturn the idea of entertainment being merely shallow.[9]

From this analysis what becomes apparent is that the virtuous screenwriter is in fact a complex figure upon which to base ethics in screenwriting. What she or he looks like and how they perform their role depends on a number of different professional and regulatory factors and cultural expectations. In other words, the very idea of 'virtue' underpinning the virtuous screenwriter requires careful critical analysis around roles, and expectations. A purely abstract understanding of the virtuous screenwriter will fail to recognize situational factors to do with relationships with co-workers and with story material. In short, we need to deconstruct this mysterious figure as well as explore the ideals and discourses of ethical conduct embodied in the idea of the virtuous screenwriter.

BEYOND NORMATIVE THEORY

Aside from the historical and cultural contingency of the idea of virtue, two other issues come to the foreground in any critical examination of the virtuous screenwriter: the definition of the screenwriter and of screenwriting, and the complex nature of their responsibility.

In terms of the definition of the screenwriter and of screenwriting, a common approach in the media ethics literature is to pursue what is called a 'normative' theory of the role of the media (Christians et al. 2009). Distinct from a descriptive approach, a normative theory attempts to look at what the role of the media or a profession in a society *should* be. As such, 'normative theories are culturally bound constructs or paradigms rather than actually existing systems' (Christians et al. 2009, viii). By prescribing rather than describing roles, a supposed benefit of normative theories is that they support media autonomy and self-regulation (Christians et al.

2009, ix). Normative theories are used to construct 'ideal' expectations around professional responsibility and practice.

A challenge for normative theories, however, is that they are intended to cover a diversity of practices—they must work across the ideal and real level. This becomes important when discussing screenwriting, since normative definitions of the screenplay and screenwriting already form an 'orthodoxy' in the field (see Macdonald 2013, 36–61). An over-reliance on a particular normative idea risks marginalizing other forms of scripting practice that approach the writing of the script in different ways. In other words, a normative approach is arguably harder to pursue in relation to screenwriting because scripting occurs in a plurality of forms. A normative ethical approach built on the screenplay may not work for an approach based on improvisation (Millard 2014, 97–117), or in situations where the relation between script and moving image work is flipped, and the short film acts as a screenplay (Millard 2014, 75). Similarly, normative conceptions of narrative based on mainstream Hollywood may not work for independent cinema (Murphy 2007). The different contexts and genres for screenwriting represent a further challenge. What ethics looks like for a writer of animations may look different to an Indigenous screenwriter working on a drama in remote communities. A challenge for thinking about ethics in screenwriting, then, is to maintain an awareness of the limits of normative definitions of the script and screenwriting. Indeed, one could go so far as to say this in itself is part of the ethics of writing about the ethics of screenwriting. Bringing this back to the idea of the virtuous screenwriter, none of this is to deny that many screenwriters of different stripes can face similar problems. However, one needs to be careful of using this idea to institute or universalize a normative definition of the scriptor and of scripting that really only applies to one particular form of screenwriting practice.

One of the attractions of normative approaches to media ethics has to do with the way it bolsters a sense of journalism as an autonomous profession that is not solely beholden to the demands of one employer. Normative theories help delineate the responsibilities of journalists as ethical agents that go beyond those defined by their contractual employment with news organizations. This leads us into another area of difficulty to do with the virtuous screenwriter, which is that, as a profession, screenwriting has historically had very low autonomy. Aside from extremely successful screenwriters, or writers of spec scripts, or writer-directors working on small budget projects, the historical situation has generally followed what Janet Staiger has termed a 'division of writing' that segments or divides up the space of creation (1985, 190). This division of writing is further complicated by large-scale studio production, and also the relationship between the story, the script and the final moving image product. As Beker notes, in television writing, shows very often have their creative parameters very tightly delineated, so those who write for them 'have one ethical decision to make' (2004, 12): which is, whether or not to work on the show.[10]

This lack of autonomy in the system has historically made authorship for screenwriters a complex issue (see Maras 2009, 167–169), also giving rise to the idea that film is a director's medium (Beker 2004, 32). There exist valiant attempts to reclaim autonomy. As Beker declares: 'I believe screenwriters see themselves as writers, artists, and creative people first and as "workers" in an industry secondarily. I also believe that screenwriters' first allegiance must be to their own visions and not to the dictates of the marketplace' (2004, 45). While claims to autonomy are important, their normative basis is fragile, and screenwriting exists in a complex dynamic between the market, the general status of creative people, and the status of co-workers in moving image industries.

Historically, the low autonomy of the screenwriter had a direct impact on the debate around the Hollywood Production Code in the 1930s and the question of who should held be responsible. As Quigley notes: 'The responsibility for reasonably safeguarding the public interest rested with the producer' (1937, 49–50). One effect of this low autonomy is that the zone of responsibility of the screenwriter can be very fluid. It is possible for one screenwriter to have full responsibility over a script, especially if they are a 'hyphenate' producer-director or writer-director; but more than often this responsibility is shared with writers and producers, or even other writers. It is also the case that screenwriters may have a very narrow or diffuse zone of responsibility, focused on a rewrite of a script, or even just dialogue. This impacts directly on the idea of the virtuous screenwriter, since the screenwriter may indeed have no control over what aspect of their script finally appears on the screen, or the way it appears, or what is cut in the editing room. The issue of autonomy represents a challenge for the discussion of ethics in screenwriting, since, as discussed in the Preface, the exact space of 'screenwriting ethics' can be hard to fix and pin down.

CONCLUSION

While discussion of the morality of motion pictures was almost a constant during the twentieth century, ethics in screenwriting has remained a neglected topic. Research up to now has focused on questions of morality rather than ethics, and only occasionally placed the screenwriter and questions of screenwriting front and centre in the research. This chapter has argued that to rectify this we need a greater focus on screenwriting as a representational practice that engages with ethics on a number of different levels. Secondly, we need a more considered understanding of ethics as multifaceted and multidimensional. This chapter has begun this work, by seeking to understand the moral stakes surrounding the representational space of motion pictures, but also teasing out specific questions of ethics, new links to the literature of media ethics, and also calling for a critical analysis of the idea of the virtuous screenwriter, one that tackles key questions associated with normative approaches and autonomy. Once this is done, the hope is that new perspectives on, and questions for, ethics in screenwriting will begin to emerge. The rest of the chapters in this volume extend and expand upon this work.

NOTES

1. Hays attributes this to a new generation of Broadway writers who went to Hollywood and who did not always follow the Hays formula (1955, 436).
2. A fourth front has been implied, which is that while Breen was seen as a 'bulwark against the Legion of Decency' (Doherty 1999, 127), he 'encouraged and may even have stage-managed the Catholic march on Hollywood' (Leff and Simmons 2001, 43; Doherty 2007, 179).
3. Of the 17 member 'Production Committee' that hear appeals under the Production Code between 1930 and 1934—also known as the 'Hollywood jury' (Hays 1955, 452)—there are no well-known screenwriters, and only three members have minor writing credits, with the exception of John A. Waldron (who also worked as a production manager) with substantial writing credits (see Leff and Simmons 2001, 291).
4. In my discussion of the drafts I will draw on the versions compiled by Richard Maltby (1995b). For clarity of argument I will refer to the 'Thalberg draft' and 'Lord draft', which are both contained in Maltby's compilation. Subsequent quotes are from Maltby (1995b).
5. See note 4.

6. There is some uncertainty in the literature over whether Thalberg's draft was a draft or a memo about a draft or an extension of the Do's and Don'ts (See Vaughn 1990, 54–56). A full account of the drafting process is beyond the scope of this chapter (see Vaughn 1990, 56; Maltby 1995a, b).

7. The Johnston Office refers to the Hays Office. Eric Johnston succeeded Will Hays and served 1945–1961. Geoffrey Shurlock was Breen's successor (1954–1968).

8. For a discussion of the ethics of fiction see the analysis of Booth's work in the concluding chapter.

9. One way to think about Beker's work is in terms of the issues of representational space and moral stakes discussed earlier, since a big part of her work looks at who gets a 'black hat' and who gets a 'white hat', as well as depictions of good and evil, creating villains and heroes.

10. A number of factors contribute to the complicated autonomy of the screenwriter, especially in television. Production conditions are seeing the rise of the series producer/director. John Caldwell suggests that the 'written template is no longer sufficient to guarantee stylistic integrity throughout a series' (2008, 17). While a 'story bible' may introduce a level of control, it can also diminish the standing of writers to 'assemblers' (2008, 213). Authorship in TV in general is undermined by a conception of TV as a 'space trying to be filled' (Caldwell 2008, 202), for which storylines are perpetually churned (2008, 208).

REFERENCES

Adams, Tony E. 2008. 'A Review of Narrative Ethics.' *Qualitative Inquiry* 14 (2): 175–94.

Banks, Miranda J. 2015. *The Writers: A History of American Screenwriters and Their Guild*. New Brunswick, NJ: Rutgers University Press.

Beker, Marilyn. 2004. *Screenwriting with a Conscience: Ethics for Screenwriters*. Mahwah, NJ: Lawrence Erlbaum Associates.

Beker, Marilyn. 2013. *The Screenwriter Activist: Writing Social Issue Movies*. New York: Routledge.

Bergen-Aurand, Brian. 2009. 'Film/Ethics.' *New Review of Film and Television Studies* 7 (4): 459–70.

Black, Gregory D. 1994. *Hollywood Censored: Morality Codes, Catholics, and the Movies*. Cambridge: Cambridge University Press.

Black, Jay, and Chris Roberts. 2011. *Doing Ethics in Media: Theories and Practical Applications*. New York: Routledge.

Butler, Judith. 2000. 'Ethical Ambivalence.' In *The Turn to Ethics*, edited by Marjorie B. Garber, Beatrice Hanssen and Rebecca L. Walkowitz, 15–28. New York: Routledge.

Butler, Judith. 2005. *Giving an Account of Oneself.* New York: Fordham University Press.

Caldwell, John Thornton. 2008. *Production Culture: Industrial Reflexivity and Critical Practice in Film and Television.* Durham, NC: Duke University Press.

Carey, James. 1999. 'Journalists Just Leave: The Ethics of an Anomolous Profession.' In *The Media and Morality*, edited by Robert M Baird, William E. Loges and Stuart E. Rosenbaum, 39–54. Amherst, NY: Prometheus Books.

Christians, Clifford G. 1977. 'Fifty Years of Scholarship in Media Ethics.' *Journal of Communication* 27 (4): 19–29.

Christians, Clifford. G., Kim B. Rotzoll, Mark Fackler, Kathy Brittain McKee, and Robert H. Woods Jr. 2005. *Media Ethics: Cases and Moral Reasoning.* 7th ed. Boston: Pearson Education.

Christians, Clifford G., Theodore L. Glasser, Denis McQuail, Kaarle Nordenstreng, and Robert A. White. 2009. *Normative Theories of the Media: Journalism in Democratic Societies.* Urbana: University of Illinois Press.

Cohen, Stephen. 2004. *The Nature of Moral Reasoning: The Framework and Activities of Ethical Deliberation, Argument and Decision-Making.* South Melbourne, Victoria: Oxford University Press.

Connolly, William E. 1993. 'Beyond Good and Evil: The Ethical Sensibility of Michel Foucault.' *Political Theory* 21 (3): 365–89.

Couldry, Nick, Amit Pinchevski, and Mirca Madianou, eds. 2013. *Ethics of media.* Houndmills, Basingstoke, Hampshire: Palgrave Macmillan.

Doherty, Thomas Patrick. 1999. *Pre-code Hollywood: Sex, Immorality, and Insurrection in American Cinema, 1930–1934.* New York: Columbia University Press.

Doherty, Thomas. 2006. 'Hollywood and the Production Code.' Accessed 15 August 2015. http://microformguides.gale.com/Data/Download/3273000C.pdf

Doherty, Thomas Patrick. 2007. *Hollywood's Censor: Joseph I. Breen and the Production Code Administration.* New York: Columbia University Press.

Dunne, Philip. 1987. 'Blast it All.' *Harvard Magazine* September/October: 8–10.

Eszterhas, Joe. 2002. 'Hollywood's Responsibility for Smoking Deaths.' *The New York Times*, August 9. http://www.nytimes.com/2002/08/09/opinion/hollywood-s-responsibility-for-smoking-deaths.html

Fine, Richard. 1985. *Hollywood and the Profession of Authorship, 1928–1940.* Ann Arbor, MI: UMI Research Press.

Foucault, Michel. 1987. *The Use of Pleasure: Volume 2 of the History of Sexuality* Translated by Robert Hurley. New York: Penguin Books.

Foucault, Michel. 2000. 'On the Genealogy of Ethics: An Overview of Work in Progress.' In *Michel Foucault, Ethics: Subjectivity and Truth*, edited by Paul Rabinow, 253–71. London: Penguin Books.

Garber, Marjorie B., Beatrice Hanssen, and Rebecca L. Walkowitz, eds. 2000. *The Turn to Ethics*. New York: Routledge.

Glik, Deborah. 1998. 'Health Education Goes Hollywood: Working with Prime-Time and Daytime Entertainment Television for Immunization Promotion.' *Journal of Health Communication* 3 (3): 263–82.

Greenberg, Joel. 1986. 'Casey Robinson: Master Adaptor.' In *Backstory: Interviews with Screenwriters of Hollywood's Golden Age*, edited by Pat McGilligan, 290–310. Berkeley: University of California Press.

Gunning, Tom. 2004. 'From the Opium Den to the Theatre of Morality.' In *The Silent Cinema Reader*, edited by Lee Grieveson and Peter Krämer, 145–54. London: Routledge.

Hawkins, Gay. 2001. 'The Ethics of Television.' *International Journal of Cultural Studies* 4 (4): 412–26.

Hays, Will H. 1955. *Memoirs*. 1st ed. Garden City, NY: Doubleday.

Hecht, Ben. 1954. *A Child of the Century*. New York: Donald I. Fine, Inc.

Jacobs, Lea, and Richard Maltby. 1995. 'Rethinking the Production Code.' *Quarterly Review of Film and Video* 15 (4): 1–3.

Leff, Leonard J., and Jerold Simmons. 2001. *The Dame in the Kimono: Hollywood, Censorship, and the Production Code*. 2nd ed. Lexington: University Press of Kentucky.

Lord, Daniel A. 1956. *Played by Ear: The Autobiography of Daniel A. Lord, S.J.* Chicago, ILL: Loyola University Press.

Macdonald, Ian W. 2013. *Screenwriting Poetics and the Screen Idea*. Basingstoke: Palgrave Macmillan.

Maltby, Richard. 1995a. 'The Genesis of the Production Code.' *Quarterly Review of Film and Video* 15 (4): 5–32.

Maltby, Richard. 1995b. 'Documents on the Genesis of the Production Code.' *Quarterly Review of Film and Video* 15 (4): 33–63.

Maras, Steven. 2009. *Screenwriting: History, Theory and Practice*. London: Wallflower Press.

Mate, Ken, and Pat McGilligan. 1986. 'W.R. Burnett: The Outsider. Interview by Ken Mate and Pat McGilligan.' In *Backstory: Interviews with Screenwriters of Hollywood's Golden Age*, edited by Pat McGilligan, 49–84. Berkeley: University of California Press.

McGilligan, Pat. 1986. 'Richard Maibaum: A Pretense of Seriousness.' In *Backstory: Interviews with Screenwriters of Hollywood's Golden Age*, edited by Pat McGilligan, 266–89. Berkeley: University of California Press.

Millard, Kathryn. 2014. *Screenwriting in a Digital Era*. Basingstoke: Palgrave Macmillan.

Miller, Frank. 1994. *Censored Hollywood: Sex, Sin & Violence on Screen*. 1st ed. Atlanta: Turner Publications.

Montgomery, Kathryn C. 1989. *Target, Prime Time: Advocacy Groups and the Struggle over Entertainment Television.* New York: Oxford University Press.

Motion Picture Producers and Distributors of America, Inc. 1929. *The Community and the Picture: Report of National Conference on Motion Pictures held at the Hotel Montclair, New York City, September 24–27, 1929.*

Murphy, J. J. 2007. *Me and You and Memento and Fargo: How Independent Screenplays Work.* New York: Continuum.

Patterson, Philip, and Lee Wilkins. 2005. *Media Ethics: Issues and Cases.* 5th ed. Boston: McGraw Hill.

Phillips, Kendall R. 2008. *Controversial Cinema: The Films that Outraged America.* Westport, Connecticut: Praeger.

Quigley, Martin. 1937. *Decency in Motion Pictures.* New York: Macmillan.

Rajchman, John. 1986. 'Ethics After Foucault.' *Social Text* 13/14 (Winter-Spring): 165–83.

Sanders, Karen. 2003. *Ethics and Journalism.* London: Sage.

Sanders, Willemien. 2010. 'Documentary Filmmaking and Ethics: Concepts, Responsibilities, and the Need for Empirical Research.' *Mass Communication and Society* 13 (5): 528–53.

Singhal, Arvind, and Everett M. Rogers. 1999. *Entertainment-Education: A Communication Strategy for Social Change.* Mahwah, NJ: L. Erlbaum Associates.

Stadler, Jane. 2008. *Pulling Focus: Intersubjective Experience, Narrative Film, and Ethics.* New York: Continuum.

Staiger, Janet. 1985. 'Blueprints for Feature Films: Hollywood's Continiuity Scripts.' In *The American Film Industry*, edited by Tino Balio, 173–92. Madison, WI: University of Wisconsin Press.

Stewart, Donald Ogden. 1970. 'Writing for the Movies.' *Focus on Film* Winter (5): 49–57.

Vasey, Ruth. 1995. 'Beyond Sex and Violence: "Industry Policy" and the Regulation of Hollywood movies, 1922–1939.' *Quarterly Review of Film and Video* 15 (4): 65–85.

Vasey, Ruth. 2004. 'The Open Door: Hollywood's Public Relations at Home and Abroad, 1922–1928.' In *The Silent Cinema Reader*, edited by Lee Grieveson and Peter Krämer, 318–28. London: Routledge.

Vaughn, Stephen. 1990. 'Morality and Entertainment: The Origins of the Motion Picture Production Code.' *The Journal of American History* 77 (1): 39–65.

Watson, Mary Ann. 2004. 'Ethics in Entertainment Television.' *Journal of Popular Film and Television* 31 (4): 146–8.

Zelizer, Barbie. 2013. 'When Practice Is Undercut by Ethics.' In *Ethics of Media* edited by Nick Couldry, Amit Pinchevski and Mirca Madianou, 271–85. Houndmills, Basingstoke, Hampshire: Palgrave Macmillan.

PART I

Writers and Production
Environments

The Concept of 'Double Storytelling' in Danish Public Service TV Drama Production

Eva Novrup Redvall

What is the purpose of television drama? Is it to provide fleeting entertainment on the small screen or to raise larger ethical and social issues about society? From a public service broadcaster perspective, the production of expensive television fiction has often had to justify itself as more than 'just' entertainment in order to meet the demands of a public service mandate with certain inherent ideas of a quality product and of 'good television'. As defined in public service broadcaster remits such as the one for the BBC, public service broadcasting (PSB) is linked to ideas of serving 'the public interest' (The Royal Charter 2006, 2) and of promoting certain 'Public Purposes' (BBC 2013). Discussions of a certain 'public service ethos' is not unique to the field of television; it forms a 'benchmark against

E.N. Redvall (✉)
Department of Media, Cognition and Communication,
University of Copenhagen, Copenhagen, Denmark
e-mail: eva@hum.ku.dk

© The Editor(s) (if applicable) and The Author(s) 2016
S. Maras (ed.), *Ethics in Screenwriting*, Palgrave Studies
in Screenwriting, DOI 10.1057/978-1-137-54493-3_2

33

which public service workers and institutions should continually strive to measure themselves' (House of Commons 2002, 7). This chapter focuses on the understandings of the public service ethos in relation to a particular public service television production culture and explores whether this kind of framework for the development of new screen works leads to a 'public service screenwriting ethics': among commissioners spending the licence fee-money on new products for national audiences, as well as the creative practitioners who propose ideas for high-end TV drama series.

Using the work of the in-house drama unit (DR Fiction) at the Danish Broadcasting Corporation (DR) as a case study, the chapter analyses how, since 2003, DR Fiction has had specific production 'dogmas' as guidelines for their in-house productions, specifying among other things that the DR drama series need to contain ethical and social themes beside 'the good story'. The notion that 'society's historical-cultural discourses' should inform fictional stories is inherent to the concept 'double story-telling', which refers to an idea that fictional narratives should consist of ethical and social layers besides an entertaining plot. This concept has been influential in the development, writing and production processes of successful DR series such as *Forbrydelsen/The Killing* (Cr: Søren Sveistrup, 2007–2012) and *Borgen* (Cr: Adam Price, 2010–2013).

Based on ideas of media ethics and notions of PSB, the chapter outlines the different interpretations of how to create public service television fiction from the early monopoly years marked by a rather elitist approach to drama production towards the popular series of the 2010s, which have generally been regarded as a productive marriage between entertaining stories and the ethical undercurrents specified by the dogmas. Explicit statements on this kind of storytelling have been part of the production framework since the mid-1990s, when the development of long-running one-hour drama series was first linked to the need for them to have a 'philosophical layer'. Some writers and producers refer to this dual structure of the DR series as television fiction with a 'public service layer'.

Drawing on a major production study of the writing and production of series at DR from the mid-1990s to the 2010s (Redvall 2013), this chapter analyses how the concept of double storytelling has worked in DR since the development of the series *Taxa* (1997–1999), which was intended as a series with a strong ethical dimension that should stimulate discussions about Danish society heading into the new millennium. The developments of *Borgen* and *Forbrydelsen* are used as case examples of how their development processes were marked by discussions to ensure the right balance between an entertaining plot and ethical and societal layers in both series. The chapter ends by addressing what can be understood as a specific kind of 'public service screenwriting ethics' in relation to the production framework of DR Fiction and the value of having conversations about the ethical implications and desired impact of stories at an early stage in their development. The chapter thus considers what can be regarded as an institutionalized engagement with ethics through the concept of double storytelling.[1]

MEDIA ETHICS, TELEVISION AND ETHICS OF SCREENWRITING

As discussed in more detail by Steven Maras in the introductory chapter to this collection, ethics can be regarded as directed towards the problem of conducting oneself morally and is linked to principal considerations of how we justify our actions. One way to explore ethics related to the screenwriting of television drama is to explore the various discourses that are linked to the ethical dimensions of practice and reflective decision-making. What are the ideas of quality and ethical content in the institutional framework that circulate around the productions, as well as among practitioners? And how are these ideas expressed and negotiated during the making of a specific product? As highlighted by Maras, the history of film and television reveals numerous moral anxieties surrounding the influence of film and television products as a form of 'prescriptive agency', leading to discussions of 'prescriptive ethics' focusing on questions of how to behave and the right thing to do. These discussions take place on an institutional as well as individual level when the content of new screen works are considered.

In the context of broader discussion of ethics and mass media communication (for example, Couldry 2006; Couldry et al. 2013; Berry 2013), television, in particular, has garnered significant attention. John Hartley has described television's ability to communicate across demographics, allowing us to learn of others, for instance through different forms of 'democratainment' (1999, 154). Television programmes have the potential of reaching vast and varied audiences, and several studies have analysed what Stuart Hall has called their 'decoding' (1973), when audiences make sense of what they see on the small screen.

The majority of studies with an interest in ethical concerns related to media representation focus on factual and journalistic practices: for example, investigating whether news production or documentary practices can be considered as fair and balanced (see Knowlton and Freeman 2005). Less has been written on ethical issues related to the production of fiction, not least the production of television drama, even if the 'encoding' of fictional content naturally holds great power in terms of influencing audience perceptions of certain topics. As an example, Gary R. Edgerton's work on historical drama is based on the basic assumption 'that television is the principal means by which most people learn about history' (2001, 1). This assumption naturally leads to ethical questions about how historical events are portrayed; discussions are also recurring in the public realm when high-end series premiere to debates about whether their makers have been 'faithful' to historical facts or not.

The most expensive television drama production in Denmark ever, Ole Bornedal's historical war mini-series *1864* (2014), clearly demonstrated this, when it led to fierce debates about whether the series was too marked by certain political views by writer-director Bornedal and whether his way of 'mixing ethics and aesthetics' was acceptable (Maintz 2014). The eight-part series was the result of special funding where politicians decided to allocate money to the production of a series which could portray important events in Danish history. This unique funding arrangement led to numerous debates about the importance of the autonomy of artists and of the arm's length principle in cultural policy frameworks. Debate also focused on how the chosen historical events, and their framing through one storyline set in present-day Denmark, could be perceived as a critical commentary on the current political scene (see Redvall 2016).

The debates around *1864* point to what Downing and Saxton describe as cinema's 'ethical space of experience' (2010, 14) which is not just about how finished works are interpreted, but also the possible ethical considerations during their making. The debates illustrate what Jacqui Miller has outlined as the two main ways in which screen works engage with ethics (2013, 2). Firstly, film is an arena for the production of meaning, in which it is possible to explore what Miller calls the guiding 'ethical vision' behind a screen work (2013, 5). Secondly, screen works are part of a specific historical period, and while judgements might seem fixed at one point in time, these can be revised (2013, 3). As an example of this second point, my observations of a focus group audience test of *Bron/ The Bridge* (2011–) at DR pointed to how the reception of the series was marked by what was perceived by audience members as new norms for the portrayal of violence on national primetime TV. The test was partly intended to explore whether audience members with children of a certain age found the series to be too violent for Sunday nights at 8.00p.m. Their responses referred to the competing public service broadcaster TV 2 which had recently aired what was regarded as a violent crime series, *Den som dræber/Those Who Kill* (2011), in the same time slot. When audience members compared the two series *The Bridge* was found to be less violent and thus more acceptable, since *Those Who Kill* had changed their view of what can be shown in that particular time slot. Discussion of the ethics of screen works does not happen in a vacuum, and the specific time and context is of great importance.

While the field of audience studies has addressed the ethical aspects of finished television drama productions (for instance, with regard to screen violence), there are few studies of the ethical negotiations around their making. An obvious reason for this is the problem of getting access to reliable data on these work processes. As pointed out by David Hesmondhalgh and Sarah Baker, 'little research has focused in a sustained way, empirically or theoretically, on how cultural workers themselves conceive of the quality of their own output, and what this might mean for our understanding of cultural production in general' (2011, 396). They call for more work focusing on agency, reflexivity and value in order to explore the ethics of cultural work.

One exception highlighted by Hesmondhalgh and Baker is the work of British anthropologist Georgina Born who has put questions of how cultural production can be used 'responsibly, creatively, inventively in given conditions, and when not' on the research agenda (see Born 2000, 406; Hesmondhalgh and Baker 2011, 396). Born's study of the BBC explored 'the situated ethics and aesthetics' (2005, 84) in various in-house departments, one of them being the drama department. Her highly critical analysis illustrates how the everyday work and decisions of cultural workers in the television industry is inevitably linked to the institutional ideas of value and quality around this work. While public service remits and charters set the overall framework for an institution such as the BBC, Born demonstrates how it will always be individuals making specific creative choices in the everyday production framework. There may be more or less freedom to do so in a way that is perceived as original and creative for the programme makers involved. For Born, it is important to move beyond the official statements and explore what one could call the everyday ethics of different kinds of cultural work. Scholars can make a useful contribution here.

One interesting aspect of the everyday ethics of cultural work has to do with how larger ideas of quality and value will often be modified when meeting those aspects of production that might call for more pragmatic rather than ideological choices: deadlines have to be met, productions need to come in on budget, and there are considerations around the desired audience for the target time slot. There are many politics at play during these decision-making processes, and as researchers it is often hard to get access to these processes. Born's study explored the BBC at a turbulent point in time when negotiating access, according to Born, was like waging a military campaign (2005, 16), and her conclusions pointed to a number of troubles for the drama production of this particular 'value-imbued public institution' at the time of her study (2005, 372). In contrast, the case study of the fiction department at the Danish PSB DR in this chapter was conducted at a time of success for the national drama productions, and marked by commissioners as well as creative practitioners having a sense of working in constructive ('best practice') ways. While the overall climate for conducting the case study was thus remarkably different from when Born scrutinized the BBC, the case study similarly addresses how ideas of what constitutes 'good' public service television and the work conditions within a particular institution naturally influence the interpretations of what constitutes a 'good' screen idea and the way in which it develops from pitch to finished production.

PUBLIC SERVICE BROADCASTING AS A SYSTEM FOR SCREEN IDEAS

As discussed in the extensive literature on PSB, questions about how to create an informed and cultured modern society, and how mass media might help in that task, have marked PSB since its formal, institutional birth in the 1920s. Media scholar David Hendy has stressed how these notions are, among other things, related to certain conceptions of enlightenment, cultivation and enriching audiences. One senior BBC producer has described the attempt to live up to the public service task in moral terms as not only making 'the good popular', but also as making 'the popular good' (Hendy 2013, 50). According to Hendy, this two-way engagement still survives in what public service broadcasters produce 'to justify their persistent claim to have a special cultural role in the modern world' (2013, 50).

The Royal Charter of the BBC states that '...[T]he BBC exists to serve the public interest' with the main object being 'the promotion of its Public Purposes' (2006, 2). These public purposes are outlined by the BBC as part of their mission to 'enrich people's lives with programmes and services that inform, educate and entertain' (BBC 2015). While there can be differences in the character of public service media across different countries and continents, most public service charters 'include requirements for diversity, innovation and quality' (Debrett 2010, 19). Mary Debrett has highlighted how a classic PSB system, being 'freed from the need to return a profit', 'enables risk-taking in programme content and form, providing scope for extending the creative boundaries of the medium and thereby also serving industry development' (2010, 19). Richard Collins has labelled European PSB as marked by certain 'oughts' (a term borrowed from moral philosophy) in terms of which role to perform in society as such (2004, 41). There can be different kinds of 'oughts' between national public service television cultures, but most share fundamental principles with the ideas of serving the public interests as outlined by the BBC.

In Denmark, DR is the equivalent of the BBC as an independent, licence fee-financed public institution comprising television, radio and online services. Founded in 1925, it is the oldest and largest electronic media enterprise in Denmark with the purpose, as described in the Law on Radio and Television, of ensuring the existence of a wide variety of programmes and services for the Danish population based on notions of quality and diversity (DR 2015). As I have previously analysed in relation to writing and producing Danish television drama, the public service mandate of DR creates a certain framework that can be regarded as a particular form of 'Screen Idea System'(Redvall 2013). The Screen Idea System is a conceptual framework for understanding how 'screen ideas' come into being (see Macdonald 2003). Screen ideas are conceived and negotiated in a particular context at a specific point in time as part of a complex interplay between creative individuals proposing new ideas; the existing productions and ideas of best practice in the domain of television drama; and the field of experts or commissioners having a certain mandate and certain managerial idea of what they are put into the world to produce. The following analysis of the concept of 'double storytelling' within this particular Screen Idea System illustrates how certain ideas of what characterizes 'good' public service television drama have been highly influential in terms of what kind of screen ideas to commission and how to go about writing and developing them when looking for ethical and social connotations, as well as an entertaining plot.

TELEVISION DRAMA FOR THE PEOPLE

DR Fiction is the in-house production unit at DR. According to the Danish Media Agreement, the unit is to produce a minimum of 20 hours of new television drama annually (DR 2014) to national audiences consisting of 5.6 million Danes. This normally means producing two seasons of high-end drama of ten one-hour episodes per year, and the traditional primetime family advent calendar of 24 episodes in December every second year. The production output is thus rather limited, but it is highly popular with national audiences. The Sunday night drama series are often the most viewed content on national television. Audiences rate the quality of these series highly, and they are widely discussed in the national press. In an international TV landscape marked by time-shifting and binge-watching, the Danish drama series are still very much 'appointment viewing' and regarded as potentially agenda-setting television content.

In the history of DR, the notion of what constitutes 'good' television drama has changed dramatically from the days of monopoly when DR functioned as both the creator and mediator of a shared national experience and consciousness (Hjarvard 2006, 8) to the current media landscape marked by fierce competition and a wide range of attractive offers to national audiences within many different media.

As in many other countries, the early years of television saw the TV medium becoming an element in the welfare state project. The approach to television was marked by what Ib Bondebjerg has called an ideology of cultural unity, building on the notion that all Danes have the same sense of culture and quality as the cultural elite (1991, 151). This gradually changed as the concept of public service television became more about securing the existence of a plurality of expressions and cultural diversity as well as about public enlightenment and educating citizens for the common good. Mirroring the BBC remit, the current DR mandate is to 'serve the people' and to assume a number of societal and cultural obligations.

A main obligation is to provide what the market-driven players are not providing, yet DR is also expected to compete on creativity and quality within all kinds of programmes.

It has sometimes been difficult for television fiction to find its place in a public service mindset where ideas of enlightenment and entertainment have often been regarded as two very different things (Agger 2005, 146). To illustrate this sense of a divide between enlightenment and entertainment, DR's scripted fiction was produced in two different departments up until 1989; the Theatre Department (*'Teaterafdelingen'*) produced plays and more serious content, while the Entertainment Department (*'Underholdningsafdelingen'*) produced comedies and lighter fare. When analysing the 'paternalist' heritage of Danish PSB, Henrik Søndergaard has addressed what was sometimes perceived as a 'patronizing elitism' (1992, 47). Focusing particularly on DR television drama production, Peter Schepelern has argued that the productions of the 1980s were 'all-penetratingly boring' (1986, 57), often marked by a stereotypical or didactic approach. With the establishment of a TV Fiction Department in 1989 there was an ambition to try to move away from thinking of television fiction as either 'theatre' or 'entertainment'. As the analysis of the emergence and use of the concept of 'double storytelling' during the 1990s will now explore, the ambition of the in-house drama unit to produce series that are entertaining as well as containing ethical and societal connotations can be regarded as an explicit attempt to formulate guiding 'institutional ethics' for what to produce, naturally having a great impact on the work of screenwriters and discussions of 'screenwriting ethics' in this particular production framework.

DOUBLE STORYTELLING IN TELEVISION DRAMA

The concept of double storytelling grew out of a deliberate attempt to change the DR approach to television drama production during the 1990s. The early 1990s were marked by widespread criticism of the quality of DR productions such as the historical series *Gøngehøvdingen/The Gønge Chieftain* (1992). Film director Ole Bornedal, who briefly held the position of Head of Drama from 1993–1994 (before going to Hollywood to direct his Danish 1994 hit *Nattevagten* as the 1997 film *Nightwatch*), publicly announced that the DR productions lacked 'bloodthirstiness' (Nordstrøm 2004, 15) and called for the DR production to become more popular and less elitist (Rasmussen 2007).

Film director Rumle Hammerich, who followed Bornedal as Head of Drama in 1994, shared his predecessor's critical thoughts on the in-house productions in what he described as an organization with a weak identity (Redvall 2013, 60). His strategy for changing this was to focus on producing 'flagship series', which could be in the public awareness week after week, aiming for what he called 'quality within a genre' and targeting original material written for television rather than adaptations of existing works from other media (2013, 60). The inspiration was American quality television series of the time and the idea was to make popular series that respected but renewed a well-known genre in a specific Danish context.

The idea for the first attempt to create this kind of series grew out of an open call for pitches where a journalist proposed a sitcom with a small taxi company as the main setting. Hammerich liked the idea of a taxi company as an arena for a TV series, but thought it was better suited for more dramatic content. He wanted a series that could run for 100 episodes, into the 2000s, and the development of the idea centred on questions of what Danes ought to bring with them into the next millennium. Together with the main writers Hammerich decided that the theme of the series should be the notion of charity or of caring for others. The taxi setting provided a range of opportunities for having the drivers come into contact with all sorts of ethical dilemmas and having to decide whether to just drive by or whether to get involved. In the research interviews around the DR productions, *Taxa* is highlighted as the first series where this sense of what Hammerich calls 'a philosophical layer' underneath the entertaining plot was discussed in this manner (Redvall 2013, 68).

Taxa ended up as a 57-episode series. Gunhild Agger argues that the series' melodramatic storylines raise questions about a number of different moral issues and about the values in Danish society (2005, 417). Storylines dealt with topics such as how to survive with fair play as a small company in a competitive international corporate market; and of how to be a good colleague in a work environment where individual interests often collide with the expectations of community solidarity. Other storylines addressed conflicts related to aspects of immigration that challenged both the personal and professional lives of the characters.

Taxa was successful with Danish audiences and regarded as a new kind of Danish television drama marked by visual and storytelling strategies familiar from popular US productions, while being firmly set in a Danish everyday context, with engaging personal and societal problems at the core of the story. The next high-end series from DR, the crime series

Rejseholdet/Unit One (2000–2004), similarly found critical and audience appreciation, and when the series won an EMMY for best international drama series in 2002 this led to new Head of Drama Ingolf Gabold (from 1999–2012) deciding to put the guiding principles behind what was perceived as a successful new approach to production down on paper. This resulted in the formulation of 15 in-house 'dogmas', with the word dogma being used to reflect the influential Dogma '95 Manifesto in Danish cinema.

The dogmas outline what are regarded to be the defining principles of DR drama productions, such as putting the writer at the centre of the production framework based on the notion of 'one vision' and deliberately working with 'crossover' between the film and television industry (Redvall 2013). For the purpose of discussing the ethics of screenwriting, this chapter will only focus on the concept of 'double storytelling' from the second dogma, which is the only dogma that addresses what sort of content to aim for in the series by stating the following:

> DR's public service status demands that our productions contain—besides "the good story"—an overall plot with ethical/social themes. In other words, we must always have a dual narrative. The weight of each of these two narratives in relation to one another will always depend on society's historical-cultural discourse. (Dogma 2 in the DR Production Dogmas, Redvall 2013, 69)

Dogma number two thus explicitly relates the DR Fiction drama productions to the public service remit of DR stating that what can be perceived as mere entertainment, or 'the good story', is not enough. Series are expected to also contain ethical and/or social themes.

My research interviews and observations of writers' rooms and meetings at DR showed how this concept was not only a managerial term in a mission statement for the drama unit, but a concept that was used and discussed among commissioners and executives as well as creative practitioners. As an example, when the family series *Arvingerne/The Legacy* (2014–) was pitched to the DR executives who were to greenlight the series, one executive enthusiastically responded that the series proposed was a perfect example of double storytelling. This concept was at the top of the executive's mind when responding to the pitch, and it seemed to be an important part of being greenlit that the head writer was able to explain how the series had an entertaining story with the inheritance family drama of who gets what as the motor for the plot, while containing larger ethical/societal layers about issues such as modern family constellations, and consequences of the liberal attitudes of 1970s art-world parents on their children's 'social inheritance'.

Similarly, most of the series produced by DR since the early 1990s are presented by DR executives as examples of series based on double storytelling. In the DR framework, *Unit One* was thus not 'just' another crime series, but a story based on the premise that 'one hunts a criminal and catches a human being', meaning that the series, among other things, tried to focus on ethical and societal issues of what drives ordinary human beings to commit crimes. Former Head of DR Fiction Nadia Kløvedal Reich (from 2012–2014) has described the concept of double storytelling as crucial to creating series which can stir debate, mirror relevant issues of our times and create insights into different values, cultures and ways of living (Redvall 2013, 68). In what can be regarded as the 'corporate storytelling' of DR (Caldwell 2008, 5) there are obvious reasons for executives to justify all licence fee-financed series as more than mere entertainment, but the interviews with writers also point to how discussions around having multilayered stories with ethical and social connotations have in fact been influential in the development processes of most series. Moreover, my observations of the so-called 'TV term' in writing and producing for students at The National Film School of Denmark—partly taught by creative practitioners from DR—illustrated how double storytelling was presented as an important element in the production framework and part of the evaluation of the proposed series pitched by the students at the end of the term (Redvall 2015). Already at an educational level, writers and producers are encouraged to think in terms of ethical and social connotations in their stories if they want to write series for DR.

Some writers at DR discuss double storytelling as 'the public service layer' of their series (Redvall 2013, 68), but they do so with an emphasis on the value of having a multilayered approach rather than as a complaint of the potentially patronizing effect of working in a framework with an emphasis on creating series with a certain kind of public service ethos. However, several of the writers in the DR framework insist that as screenwriters they will always be looking for stories with several layers. As Marilyn Beker comments in her book *The Screenwriter Activist*, 'at its core, every screenplay is "about" something and has a theme and sensibility that drives it. This "about" is deeper than the surface story. It's the ultimate message of the movie—its essential theme and sensibility' (Beker

2013, 1). It is rare to find writers arguing that there is nothing more to their screenplays than superficial entertainment. While most screenwriters would argue that they are always looking for stories with several layers, having an institutional concept like double storytelling does, however, ensure having explicit discussions around the possible ethical and social layers in a proposed screen idea during the development and commissioning process that can have major consequences in terms of how these ideas are shaped from the original idea to final series.

BORGEN AND THE KILLING AS DOUBLE STORYTELLING

Some screen ideas contain what can be regarded as an obvious premise for marrying PSB purposes of entertainment, information and education and for raising ethical and social concerns in contemporary society. In hindsight, *Borgen* seems like the perfect PSB double storytelling series with female politician Birgitte Nyborg at the centre of a story on the political life in Denmark based on the premise of whether one can hold on to power and still hold on to oneself. The series' portrayal of the troubles of marrying a difficult professional life with a demanding family life encourages reflections on work-life balance and gender roles, while each episode has the possibility to dive into a specific political case, ranging from large foreign policy issues to smaller domestic affairs.

However, when creator Adam Price pitched the original idea for the series, Ingolf Gabold, then Head of Drama, found the idea of a political series to be too elitist to attract the wide audiences expected for the Sunday night DR drama series. Who would want to see a series about politics? The screen idea contained plenty of opportunities for informing and educating audiences, but how could this be done in an entertaining way? Adam Price was inspired by US series such as *The West Wing* (1999–2006), but this kind of very talkative material with a focus on the professional arena would never be able to attract the large shares wanted for the expensive national series. In this case, the subsequent discussions between Adam Price, his co-writers, the DR Fiction executives, as well as the DR in-house commissioners centred on how to give fiction based on the national political scene broader appeal. As pointed out by Hendy, PSB discussions often focus on how to make difficult material into accessible programmes (2013, 50). With *Borgen*, developing the premise of focusing on the challenging relationship between people and power, with a female politician at the core of the story, led to a sense that this could be a popular mainstream series while also addressing the various ethical dilemmas that are inevitably part of many political cases. These dilemmas range from universal foreign policy questions of how to legitimize going to war, to the way in which personal ideals are challenged when trying to reach pragmatic compromises in everyday politics. By having a journalist and a spin doctor as the two main characters next to Birgitte Nyborg, *Borgen* also had the opportunity to explore the complicated relationship between politicians and the press, as well as the many behind-the-scenes intrigues where considerations of what would ethically be the right thing to do compete with considerations of what would be the strategically right move for future success.

My observations of the writers' room of *Borgen* during the development of episode 25 in the series' third season pointed to how issues of ethics were continuously discussed when creating a storyline where Birgitte Nyborg has to address the controversial topic of whether to legalize prostitution. This discussion focused not only on the ethical standpoints of the different characters when taking a stand on the topic, but also in terms of the overall 'message' of the episode and how it might be decoded by national audiences. Before the first episode of *Borgen* even aired in 2010, there was great concern among some national politicians about how this new series would portray right- versus left-wing politicians, and whether it was possible to make a non-biased fictional story about contemporary political life. Because of the constant scrutiny of whether the series was fair and balanced, discussions of ethics and an awareness of the public decoding of the written material seemed to be at the forefront in this particular writers' room, but the writers were able to make their own decisions about how to approach even potentially controversial issues addressed during the three seasons.

All observations and research interviews pointed to only one instance of executives raising concern about a scene which could perhaps be interpreted as ridiculing a right-wing politician, but the creatives won the battle over the choice of shoes (!) for that particular character. The pitch meeting of episode 25 in the writers' room revealed how producer Camilla Hammerich would question the creative decisions around the material, but always leave it to the writers to make the final choices. While the call for ethical and social connotations implicit in the concept of double storytelling could potentially lead to controversial material for the broadcaster, the *Borgen* writing process pointed to a trust in the writers in terms of them being able to navigate producing quality PSB content, once the initial concerns about whether politics could actually be made entertaining were off the table.

The development of *The Killing* points to other PSB concerns regarding how to create a crime series that is not 'just' about finding the murderer, but also contains other layers based on the concept of double storytelling. When creator Søren Sveistrup originally pitched the series it was a mini-series in eight episodes about the murder of a young girl. Then Head of Drama Ingolf Gabold wasn't keen on producing more crime at that point in time, since DR had just produced *Unit One* and was developing the crime series *Ørnen/The Eagle* (2004–2006). Based on the idea that DR should produce material that the market is otherwise not providing and work with diverse genres, Gabold asked Sveistrup to rethink the idea of doing a crime series. Moreover, DR was looking for material for longer series rather than mini-series.

Sveistrup held on to his idea of writing a series about a crime, but returned with a pitch about what the murder of a girl does to a number of people around the crime when interweaving their destinies. He used the chaos theory metaphor of the butterfly effect where the flapping of butterfly wings in one place can set off a snowstorm somewhere else, and rather than being 'just another crime series' Gabold and DR producer Sven Clausen now saw the screen idea as based on an interesting 'theory of interdependence', and on how one crime has an impact on people from many different layers in Danish society, from a whole school to the career of one politician (Clausen in Gemzøe 2010, 202).

All three seasons of *The Killing* have a crime as the inciting incident and the solving of the crime as the motor that drives the story forward through police detective Sarah Lund's investigative work. However, all three seasons also have what can be regarded as a three-plot structure with the crime plot being accompanied by a family plot and a political plot. This structure mirrors the structure of *Borgen* having the political arena at the core, but also having the press arena and the personal lives of the main characters as crucial story elements. One could argue that having to think along the lines of double storytelling and ensuring the existence of a multilayered story with social and ethical connotations from the outset encourages writers to create arenas with the possibility to come into contact with many different layers of society in a natural way. Indeed this challenges some aspects of more traditional goal-oriented storytelling where one character neatly wraps everything up, allowing instead for more ventures into everyday life in all its ethical and existential messiness. This does not mean that classical 'protagonist-antagonist' storytelling strategies are ignored, since they are crucial to creating entertaining stories with a wide appeal, but having to think about ways to create certain public service layers from the very beginning of the development process can attune writers into thinking about different kinds of characters, plots or subplots, beyond those they might otherwise have considered.

In the case of *The Killing*, the series gained widespread attention for keeping the crime plot of who killed the young girl going for 20 episodes. The remarkable length grew out of the DR wish for a longer series, while the three-plot structure was a consequence of trying to rethink traditional crime stories. Sveistrup has explained how the murder of the girl is 'just an excuse for telling a lot of other stories' (Redvall 2013, 173), and from a PSB perspective executives have repeatedly stressed how the series is 'not just about finding the murderer' (for example, Piv Bernth, in Jane 2012). In the corporate self-representation of DR, *The Killing* is a perfect example of double storytelling. Audiences might primarily see it as an entertaining crime series, but when former Head of Drama Nadia Kløvedal Reich reflected on the second season it was not just a crime story, but a story about the killing of civilians in Afghanistan, about how far to bend democracy in the attempt to defend it and about what it means to be a nation at war (Redvall 2013, 173). This interpretation helps legitimize the production of popular crime fiction as quality PSB content, and it shows how, rather than only being a creative tool during discussions of screen ideas, the concept of double storytelling has also gradually moved into the public sphere to be part of the institutional explanations of what marks a series as coming from DR.

Having a dogma about double storytelling creates a certain framework for how to think about screen ideas, and while the concept seems to have led to many fruitful discussions about how to create series that are more than 'just entertainment', it is worthwhile noting that some writers oppose trying to force concepts like this on the creative process. As an example, Søren Sveistrup describes how he instinctively wants to rebel against executives presenting any kinds of concepts for series in the name of public service storytelling. However, he respects how DR executives have tried to explain and frame the series produced and how specific conceptions of quality drama on the management level naturally influence the choices of content and can, later on, be used to interpret the series in the public realm (Redvall 2013, 176). Both *Borgen* and *The Killing* were shaped in the meeting between the original screen ideas of their creators and the institutional ideas of the 'public purpose' of a television series from DR, and they can both be considered as interesting examples of the constant PSB tensions of making the popular good and the good popular while trying to raise issues of ethical and social concern in an entertaining TV fiction framework.

PUBLIC SERVICE SCREENWRITING ETHICS?

Since the beginning of PSB, issues of how radio and television can enlighten, cultivate and enrich audiences have been crucial in the understanding of this particular framework for media production. When regarding PSB as an important institution in modern society, these issues are naturally linked to questions of ethics. Most often ethical debates about television fiction address questions of representation, for instance in terms of how violence or sex is portrayed or focusing on issues of gender and race related to the presence (or absence) of certain kinds of characters. While these questions about representation are important to address, it is also worthwhile thinking about what can be regarded as the more philosophical layers in the fictional content on the small screen. What kind of society is presented? How are characters treating each other? What is presented as right and wrong while the entertaining story is moving along? Topics like these are harder to address, but both their encoding and decoding are important to explore when thinking about ethics of screenwriting and the possible impact of television drama. Addressing these questions becomes more important in the context of one of the few examples of an institutionalized engagement with ethics in PSB, enacted through the dogma of double storytelling.

This institutional engagement cannot be separated from wider historical, and cultural factors however. In the 2010s, DR series such as *Borgen* and *The Killing* found a somewhat surprising international success as subtitled, niche content on BBC4, building on the success of Scandinavian crime exports such as Stieg Larsson's 'Millennium Trilogy' and the Wallander books, films and series. Framed as 'Nordic Noir', the noir label links the Nordic series to a genre which has often been analysed in terms of its ethical ambiguity (Skoble 2007, 42). The 'noir' label relates to the stories told, but is also fundamentally derived from the darkness of the Nordic winter and from portraying what can be perceived as the darker sides of the Scandinavian welfare societies. An important part of the series' international appeal thus seems linked to their take on a challenged welfare state model, by their approach to gender roles and by their portrayal of the constant tensions between professional and family life. Series such as *Borgen* and *The Killing* might have emerged without a concept like double storytelling in the production dogmas behind their making, but as I have attempted to show their development with DR Fiction has been intertwined with an explicit concept defining how series should be more than 'just' entertainment, leading to an awareness of how new screen ideas should contain different layers that make them qualify as quality public service content among in-house commissioners and executives as well as creative practitioners.

Exploring how practitioners engage in negotiations of how to create television drama in a public service context allows for a nuanced understanding of what ends up getting commissioned and produced. For screenwriters, proposing series and writing content for a small national public service broadcaster will always be marked by certain constraints, and the managerial ideas of quality and purpose in these processes will inevitably influence how ideas are shaped during the screenwriting process. This chapter has analysed how the concept of double storytelling can be regarded as a special kind of institutional public service screenwriting ethics that creates a certain framework for developing and talking about new screen works.

The 'influence', for want of a better word, of this public service screenwriting ethics, is still being played out. In Danish media culture, the national TV series bring together huge audiences on Sunday nights and influence what is on the press agenda as well as in the many private conversations about what we encounter on screen. A series such as *Borgen* is an excellent example of 'democratainment', and, following its Danish run, researchers from the Copenhagen Business School studied whether votes had been moved while watching the fictional Birgitte Nyborg's political endeavours (Jessen 2013). The study concluded that this was not the case. However, people had generally become more interested in politics. A recent study of the historical series *1864* showed that almost half of the population claimed to have followed the press debates around the series, and surveys of the audience perceptions of the reasons for the 1864 war showed how the series had changed these over the course of the eight episodes (Brunbech 2015). As argued by the historian conducting the study, 8.2 % of the population read Tom Buk-Swienty's historical bestseller behind the series, while 65 % of the population watched one or more episodes of the TV series.

We can suggest that national drama series have the potential to influence audience perceptions of national heritage as well as contemporary society. As an example, the European crime series *The Team* (2015, co-produced by DR and shown in the Sunday night time slot) was criticized in the press for possibly being EU propaganda (Thiemann 2015a)—an accusation immediately denied by the screenwriters, not least since the encoding of the series took place long before the critical points raised by the sceptical decoding were even relevant to consider (Thiemann 2015b). The studies and press debates around DR series show how television drama is a potentially powerful media product but also a significant aspect of the cultural and ethical landscape.

In a time when national public service broadcasters are facing still more competition and the traditional licence fee-financing is under pressure, it is worthwhile asking whether public service television drama in fact offers a different kind of television drama product that would otherwise not see the light of day. Head of DR Fiction Piv Bernth has argued that public service broadcasters from the outset attract other kinds of material than the commercial broadcasters (Bernth 2015). The question is, however, how these ideas are perceived and developed when the public service ethos is interpreted in different countries and contexts, and how the institutional and managerial ideas of good public service fiction influence the concrete decisions of what to produce. Does a certain kind of institutional public service ethics of screenwriting ensure the existence of a particular kind of series that might be hard to finance under purely market-driven circumstances? DR is developing a new Sunday night drama series on faith and religion by *Borgen*-creator Adam Price. That series will most certainly raise interesting debates in the national sphere, and one can rest assured that its making will be marked by many writers' room discussions about how to approach this topic in an entertaining as well as enlightening way based on a wide variety of ethical considerations.

NOTES

1. This chapter was written as part of the HERA-financed joint European research project Mediating Cultural Encounters Through European Screens (MeCETES). I would like to thank my colleagues in the project for interesting discussions on issues of ethics in European film and television.

REFERENCES

Agger, Gunhild. 2005. *Dansk tv-drama: Arvesølv og underholdning*. Frederiksberg: Samfundslitteratur.

BBC 2013. Purpose Remits—March 2013. Accessed 10 May 2015. http://downloads.bbc.co.uk/bbctrust/assets/files/pdf/about/how_we_govern/purpose_remits/2013/purpose_remits.pdf

BBC. 2015. 'Mission and values'. Accessed 10 May 2015. http://www.bbc.
co.uk/corporate2/insidethebbc/whoweare/mission_and_values
Beker, Marilyn. 2013. *The Screenwriter Activist: Writing Social Issue Movies*.
New York, NY: Routledge.
Bernth, Piv. 2015. Presentation at the Creative Europe conference *TV Series Now*
in Copenhagen on June 18.
Berry, David. 2013. *Ethics and Media Culture: Practices and Representations*.
Oxford: Focal Press.
Bondebjerg, Ib. 1991. 'Dansk tv-fiktion: Indenfor rammen og udenfor.' In
Analyser af tv og tv-kultur, edited by Jens F. Jensen, 149–171. Copenhagen:
Medusa.
Born, Georgina. 2000. 'Inside Television: Television research and the sociology of
culture.' *Screen* 41: 68–91.
Born, Georgina. 2005. *Uncertain Vision: Birt, Dyke and the Reinvention of the
BBC*. London: Vintage.
Brunbech, Peter Yding. 2015. 'DR og Bornedal har ændret vores syn på 1864.'
Historie og Kulturarv, 11 March. Accessed 10 May 2015. http://historieog-
kulturarv.ucl.dk/dr-og-bornedal-har-aendret-vores-syn-paa-1864/
Caldwell, John T. 2008. *Production Culture: Industrial Reflexivity and Critical
Practice in Film and Television*. Durham: Duke University Press.
Collins, Richard. 2004. '"Ises" and "Oughts": Public Service Broadcasting in
Europe.' In *The Television Studies Reader*, edited by Robert C. Allen and
Annette Hill, 33–51. London: Routledge.
Couldry, Nick. 2006. *Listening Beyond the Echoes: Media, Ethics, and Agency in an
Uncertain World*. Herndon, VA: Paradigm.
Couldry, Nick, Mirca Madianou, and Amit Pinchevski, eds. 2013. *Ethics of Media*.
Basingstoke: Palgrave Macmillan.
Debrett, Mary. 2010. *Reinventing Public Service Television for the Digital Future*.
Bristol: Intellect.
Downing, Lisa, and Libby Saxton. 2010. *Film and Ethics: Foreclosed Encounters*.
London and New York: Routledge.
DR. 2014. *Media Development 2014*. Copenhagen: DR. http://www.dr.dk/Om_
DR/About+DR/articles/20130502122501.htm
DR. 2015. 'Public Service'. Accessed 10 May 2015. http://www.dr.dk/Om_
DR/Fakta+om+DR/Artikler/02092932.htm
Edgerton, Gary R. 2001. 'Television as Historian: A Different Kind of History
Altogether.' In *Television Histories: Shaping Collective Memories in the Media
Age*, edited by Gary R. Edgerton and Peter C. Rollins, 1–16. Lexington, KY:
University Press of Kentucky.
Gemzøe, Lynge Agger. 2010. 'Vi har førertrøjen! Interview med producer Sven
Clausen i DR om den danske tv-krimi.' In *Den skandinaviske krimi*, edited by
Gunhild Agger and Anne Marit Waade, 195–203. Göteborg: Nordicom.

Hall, Stuart. 1973. *Encoding and Decoding in the Television Discourse*. Birmingham: Centre for Cultural Studies, University of Birmingham.

Hartley, John. 1999. *The Uses of Television*. New York: Routledge.

Hendy, David. 2013. *Public Service Broadcasting*. Basingstoke: Palgrave Macmillan.

Hesmondhalgh, David, and Sarah Baker. 2011. 'Toward a Political Economy of Labor in the Media Industries.' In *The Handbook of Political Economy of Communications*, edited by Janet Wasko, Graham Murdock and Helena Sousa, 381–400. Malden: Blackwell.

Hjarvard, Stig (ed.). 2006. *Dansk tvs historie*. Frederiksberg: Samfundslitteratur.

House of Commons. 2002. *The Public Service Ethos*. Accessed 15 June 2015. http://www.publications.parliament.uk/pa/cm200102/cmselect/cmpubadm/263/263.pdf

Jane, Emma. 2012. 'BBC News—The Killing and Borgen: Danish drama wins global fanbase.' bbc.co.uk, April 27. Accessed 10 May 2015. http://www.bbc.co.uk/news/magazine-17853928

Jessen, Catarina Nedertoft. 2013. '*Borgen* flytter ikke stemmer.' *Information*, 15 February. Accessed 10 May 2015. http://www.information.dk/451260

Knowlton, Steven R. and Karen L. Freeman, eds. 2005. *Fair and Balanced: A History of Journalistic Objectivity*. Northport, AL: Vision Press.

Macdonald, Ian W. 2003. 'Finding the Needle. How Readers see Screen Ideas.' *Journal of Media Practice* 4: 27–40.

Maintz, Jan. 2014. '1864'. *Information*, 20 December. Accessed 10 May 2015. https://www.information.dk/moti/2014/12/1864

Miller, Jacqui. 2013. *Film and Ethics: What Would You Have Done?* Newcastle upon Tyne: Cambridge Scholars Publishing.

Nordstrøm, Pernille. 2004. *Fra Riget til Bella*. Copenhagen: DR Multimedie.

Rasmussen, Anita Brask. 2007. 'Succesens farlige nabo.' *Information*, 26 July. Accessed 10 May 2015. http://www.information.dk/118399

Redvall, Eva N. 2013. *Writing and Producing Television Drama in Denmark: From* The Kingdom *to* The Killing. Basingstoke: Palgrave Macmillan.

Redvall, Eva N. 2015. 'Craft, Creativity, Collaboration, and Connections: Educating Talent for Danish TV Drama Series.' In *Production Studies II*, edited by Vicki Mayer, Miranda Banks and Bridget Conor, 75–88. London: Routledge.

Redvall, Eva N. 2016. 'Kulturpolitiske kampe og public service-slag: 1864-seriens vej til de danske tv-skærme.' In *1864: Tv-serien, historien, kritikken*, edited by Kim Toft Hansen. Aalborg: Aalborg University Press.

Schepelern, Peter. 1986. 'Det uendeligt små: En vis tendens i moderne dansk tv-dramatik.' In *Sekvens 1986: Dansk TV*, edited by Lene Nordin, 53–66. Copenhagen: University of Copenhagen.

Skoble, Aeon J. 2007. 'Moral Clarity and Practical Reason in Film Noir'. In *The Philosophy of Film Noir*, edited by Mark T. Conrad and Robert Porfirio, 41–48. Lexington, KY: University of Kentucky Press.

Søndergaard, Henrik. 1992. 'Fra programflade til kontaktflade: Det "moderniserede" public service-koncept i DR's TV'. *Mediekultur* 17: 45–60.

The Royal Charter. 2006. *Broadcasting: Copy of Royal Charter for the continuance of British Broadcasting Corporation*. London: Department for Culture, Media and Sport. Accessed 10 May 2015. https://www.gov.uk/government/uploads/system/uploads/attachment_data/file/272348/6925.pdf

Thiemann, Per. 2015a. '*Mord uden grænser* anklages for propaganda.' *Politiken*, 11 April. Accessed 10 May 2015. http://politiken.dk/kultur/filmogtv/ECE2624287/mord-uden-graenser-anklages-for-propaganda/

Thiemann, Per. 2015b. '*Mord uden grænser*'s forfatter: Fiktion skal ikke opdrage.' *Politiken*, 10 April. Accessed 10 May 2015. http://politiken.dk/kultur/filmogtv/ECE2624288/mord-uden-graensers-forfatter-fiktion-skal-ikke-opdrage/

FILM AND TELEVISION REFERENCES

1864. 2014. Cr: Ole Bornedal, produced by Miso Film for DR, Denmark, 58 mins. x 8 eps.

Arvingerne/The Legacy. 2014–. Cr: Maya Ilsøe, DR, Denmark, 58 mins.

Borgen. 2010–2013. Cr: Adam Price, DR, Denmark, 58 mins. x 30 eps.

Bron/The Bridge. 2011–. Cr: Hans Rosenfeldt, Filmlance and Nimbus Film for SVT and DR, Sweden/Denmark, 58 mins.

Den som dræber/Those Who Kill. 2011. Cr: Elsebeth Egholm and Stefan Jaworski, Miso Film for TV 2, Denmark, 55 mins. x 10 eps.

Forbrydelsen/The Killing. 2007–2012. Cr: Søren Sveistrup, DR, Denmark, 55 mins. x 40 eps.

Gøngehøvdingen/'The Gønge Chieftain'. 1992. Wr: Bjarne O. Henriksen and Gert Henriksen, Dir: Peter Eszterhás, DR, Denmark, 30 mins. x 13 eps.

Nattevagten. 1994. Wr: Ole Bornedal, Dir: Ole Bornedal, Denmark, 107 mins.

Nightwatch. 1997. Wr: Ole Bornedal and Steven Soderbergh, Dir: Ole Bornedal, US, 101 mins.

Ørnen/The Eagle. 2004–2006. Cr: Mai Brostrøm and Peter Thorsboe, DR, Denmark, 58 mins. x 24 eps.

Rejseholdet/Unit One. 2000–2004. Cr: Peter Thorsboe, DR, Denmark, 60 mins. x 30 eps and 90 mins. x 2 eps.

Taxa. *1997–1999*. Cr: Stig Thorsboe, DR, Denmark, 45 mins. x 56 eps.

The Team. 2015. Cr: Mai Brostrøm and Peter Thorsboe, Network Movie Film, und Fernsehproduktion and others for ZDF and other broadcasters, Austria/Belgium/Denmark/Germany/Sweden/Switzerland, 60 mins. x 8 eps.

The West Wing. 1999–2006. Cr: Aaron Sorkin, NBC, USA, 42 mins. x 156 eps.

CHAPTER 3

Ethics, Style and Story in Indigenous Screenwriting: Warwick Thornton in Interview

Steven Maras

For Pauline Clague, 'Indigenous storytelling can in some way have its own unique formulas to follow when Indigenous filmmakers put their stories onto the page or the screen' (2013). This observation applies to Warwick Thornton, born in 1970 in Alice Springs, Australia. Thornton is best known for his 2009 debut feature, *Samson and Delilah*, which was selected for the 2009 Cannes Film Festival where it won the *Caméra d'Or*. A multifaceted filmmaker, he was trained at the Central Australian Media Association of Australia and the Australian Film Television and Radio School. As a cinematographer, Thornton has worked on successful Indigenous features such as *Radiance* (1998) and *The Sapphires* (2012). As a writer and director, as well as his feature film work, his résumé includes several acclaimed short

S. Maras (✉)
Media and Communication, The University of Western Australia,
Perth, WA, Australia
e-mail: steven.maras@uwa.edu.au

© The Editor(s) (if applicable) and The Author(s) 2016
S. Maras (ed.), *Ethics in Screenwriting*, Palgrave Studies
in Screenwriting, DOI 10.1057/978-1-137-54493-3_3

films such as *Payback* (1996), *Mimi* (2002), *Green Bush* (2005), and *Nana* (2007), that collectively represent an extended reflection on Indigenous cultural production. These works are at the same time evidence of effective film policy from the Indigenous Branch of the (then) Australian Film Commission (Thornton and Shelper 2012, 36). It is a body of work supported by successful long-term collaborations and developmental processes, and part of a wider cultural moment in which a range of Indigenous image-makers, such as Rachel Perkins, Ivan Sen, Wayne Blair, Darlene Perkins, and Beck Cole, are finding success across film and television in what has been called (after a 2009 Australian Centre of the Moving Image (ACMI) exhibition) the 'Blak Wave'.

Thornton's work, in *Samson and Delilah* especially, has drawn strong critical interest (see Davies 2009). The interview below focuses on ethics and writing. In respect to ethics, discussion of Indigenous film-making has long focused on questions of cultural sovereignty and cultural protocols (see Janke 2009). However, while these concepts are essential parts of the ethical landscape, we do not often hear individual Indigenous filmmakers speak about their own personal relationship to ethics. In respect to writing, Thornton has, in a number of interviews, drawn out a complex approach to issues of ethics, style and story in relation to Indigenous screenwriting. Beyond being a vehicle for promotion of his films, the interview is an important form for Thornton because, as he explains, 'I actually don't like writing, the physical side of it. I don't type. I write with a pencil and a pad. And it's quite painful for me to do that 'cause I can't spell very well. I left school in Year 6 and I didn't learn that stuff very well' (Thornton 2009b; see samples of Thornton's scripts at http://samsonanddelilah.com.au/behind-the-scenes.php).

This relationship to writing impacts on his approach to screenwriting.

So what I do with films is I think about them for bloody years until I've got beginning, middle and end, all the characters, their journeys—you know, not incredibly succinct but just the real scene one, scene two, kind of thing, this happens, that happens. So I'll think all of that in my head and then I'll sit down for three or four days and actually write the whole thing. Twenty pages a day. Twenty pages of my handwriting translate into about 12 or 13 typed pages. And this script I think was about 60 pages long. So that whole idea of a page a minute never works with me. (Thornton 2009b)

The process by which Thornton's approach is 'normalized' into a typed script consists of sitting with his frequent collaborator, producer Kath Shelper, or director Beck Cole, in a process characterized as a 'redrafting' whereby 'we'll discuss the scene and flesh it out as we are going' (Thornton and Shelper 2012, 38). This includes working with script editors, such as Keith Thompson (see Boukabou 2007).

In his reflections on writing Thornton returns to several specific themes. These include the impact of cinematography on his thinking about performance, scripting with sound and the role of the Indigenous filmmaker today.

In terms of the impact on cinematography on his scripting practice, Thornton's work can be situated in a longer tradition of using the camera as a tool for scripting, as well as an 'iterative' style of project development in which short dramas feed into a larger process of development (see Millard 2011).Thornton has acknowledged that the success of *Samson and Delilah* is directly linked to his short films (Thornton and Shelper 2012, 44).Thornton does not feel he has to write in order to communicate images. 'I come from a cinematography background, and because of that, that's all happening in my head. I don't need to write it. … If you ever read a page that I've written is incredibly slim on visual action or concept' (Thornton 2009d).

Thornton's training as a director of photography also impacts directly on the way he relates to performance. This is certainly a feature of the way the actors 'dance' with the camera in *Payback*. In terms of *Samson and Delilah*, Thornton explains what could be seen as a kind of 'writing' with the camera in company with the actors:

> I wanted to create this sort of, this one-on-one with them. Have the camera on my shoulder, those two kids in front of me and be able to just have this sort of eye contact when we were actually shooting. It was fantastic for me, because I was there, you know, they're only eight feet away from you, you've got the camera on your shoulder, it's sort of this really personal one-on-one kind of film making with the actor. And I really, really enjoyed that part of it. Some other films I've done, you walk onto set and you walk past the video split and it's, you know, 600 metres from the actual place you're shooting … [and] your actors are a mile away. (Thornton 2009a)

It could be argued that his background in cinematography contributes to Thornton's antipathy towards lame dialogue. As he notes in his discussion of *Samson and Delilah*: 'Cos we didn't have that classic kind of "I'm angry" dialogue, or "I'm happy" kind of dialogue, just to wash over a scene whether it was good or bad. We actually had to get every scene exactly perfect to the script because of the lack of dialogue' (Thornton 2009a). For Thornton a bad approach to dialogue results in a spoon-feeding of emotion and motivation. 'I also think that audiences should work as well. It's easy for a writer to have his characters say "I'm happy", "I'm sad", write that into a script and then have an actor say it. It's much harder when you have to play it without words' (Thornton 2009c).

Thornton's approach to scripting encompasses writing with sound (see Gallasch 2009), as well as with images, words and places, and repetition of these elements.

> In most of my films I write the music into the script. I'm listening to songs and lyrics that empower the themes of the film. There's a lot of Indigenous music that has not been heard widely and I love the idea of giving that music to the rest of the world. I love music more than language: it's the best, it's universal. Like the Anna Gabriel song that Delilah listens to in the film. ...You don't actually have to understand the song to be emotionally moved and uplifted, whereas with language it becomes quirky and analytical. (Thornton 2010)

Thornton is sceptical of an approach that relegates sound design to the post-production phase. For him, sound is an important dimension of the scripting process:

> They weren't songs that we went and found after we cut the film, which I think is a big mistake in cinema. Australians do it a lot, they finish a film and they go, "OK, how much money have we got left? And we've got 10 cents left, so let's go and buy some songs that we can fatten up this film with". (Thornton 2009a)

Finally, Thornton's views on writing are noteworthy for the way he sees his practice on a continuum with traditional approaches to storytelling, and weaves in consideration of traditional communities, morality and law. Thornton's relationship to story is mediated by his identity as an Indigenous person.

> Kind of the reason why I make films is it's just an extension of storytelling for me. Traditionally our mob used oral history and storytelling to teach in the

way of morals, to do with law or to do with our dreaming. For Aboriginal people cinema is a very new thing. We haven't sort of understood it and we haven't learnt the craft up until probably thirty or forty years ago. So by having development for Indigenous people we can actually take all those stories of ours and we can create a new, almost like a new dreaming. I love filmmaking because it's an extension of that. It's us taking our oral histories but now putting them in celluloid and on screen to keep teaching, to keep our culture in a sense live. (Thornton 2009d)

Thornton resists any attempt to keep storytelling static, formulaic and unchanging. He insists that it constantly moves, and because culture is constantly changing practitioners must adapt and learn new approaches.

> ... Indigenous culture needs to move; it can't be chiselled into rock. Aboriginal law and everything has to change, and I think our culture will keep changing and with that so should our storytelling and our cinema because we'll always have issues and ideas that will move with our culture. ... As writers and directors we have to adapt and keep changing with our culture. And I think it's really important to keep an open mind like that. And not shut ourselves down into, you know, a format, or three-act structure, or any of that kind of stuff. We need to keep pushing ourselves and keep developing ourselves until we, across the board, have this amazing concept of storytelling. All the directors, all the writers, all the web-page designers, all of us need to keep a really open mind as blackfellas about our culture; and keep an eye on how it's changing and how we are changing, and how we need to take control of that. (Thornton 2009d)

Underpinning Thornton's argument is a wider view of the purpose of cinema and the human dimension of story.

> I truly believe that cinema has to tell real stories. It needs to work that way. There is the financial side of it—making money and being in business—but its existence lies in its story-telling abilities. If you go right back to the times that pre-date writing, communication was through images and story-telling; the old man under the tree, not just in Central Australia, but in Europe and everywhere else. Movies have to tell stories—moral stories, stories of change, stories that kids and everyone else can take into their lives and make them better human beings. (Thornton 2009c)

The following interview took place between Steven Maras and Warwick Thornton in Sydney, Australia on 25 May 2015.

Q: You spent part of your youth in New Norcia in Western Australia, in a Benedictine mission for Aboriginal boys. Did you get much moral or ethical education in your schooling there? I grew up a free-range child in Alice Springs where I did whatever the hell I wanted. There was no pecking order. Suddenly you are in a college where there is a pecking order and you soon learn your place. There was mass every day. It was drummed into you. It was enjoyable in a strange kind of way. Where I was in my life as a kid I needed stability and a regimented life. They gave it. You need a little bit more … when you are a kid.

Q: Would you say you think or reflect a lot about ethics and morals? Good and bad, right and wrong? Yes, absolutely. That's why I do like religion. All religions are based on pretty simple ideas: don't go killing each other, and try to look after each other. But when religions get oppressed they tend to get distilled in a bad way, and more self-centred. When religion gets oppressed they get more violently, rigidly connected to what they believe in—because that's all they've got by the end. This cuts across Judaism, Islam, Christianity; and also Indigenous religions, which can become more secretive. The more you know about the secret parts of that religion the more powerful you become.

Q: Is there anything that gets you ethically and morally fired up in terms of justice or fairness? Everything! Whether it is the state or federal government, to religion. My idea of life is pretty basic. I run amok. But, on my deathbed, if I truly believe that I gave more than I took I think I will have had a good life and have done the right thing. The idea of giving more than you take is really important to me. You want to fight for the people who have nothing and you want to take that from people who have everything.

Q: Where did you get your sense of right and wrong, good and bad from? What are your big moral or ethical influences? Just being really poor. I'm pretty bullet proof and an emotional mute in life. But you see bad things happen to other people and you just want to stand up, and especially when you get to a point when you can make a film or take a photo that represents what's pissing you off at that time, or, what's really making you happy at that time.

Q: How influential is love on your moral voice? I'm thinking of ideas of devotion and sacrifice. And women. It is all important. It is more devotion rather than love in general—I've actually never written a sex scene— a kind of *Samson and Delilah* love; which is a love out of necessity. Survival, more so, than just a chemical reaction where a boy or a girl just completely besots you, and you fall in love. That film, them two kids, they needed each other more than they actually needed to love each other in a way.

Q: I'm interested in what might be called your moral or ethical voice or eye? It's a hard one, the moral or ethical, when you write. Because, a lot of it is contradictory, as well. Something like *Samson and Delilah* ... The only thing that got me through writing that film is that everything in that film I had seen personally. And I was asked by funding bodies as well as communities to, not negotiate, but, to talk to Elders, to make sure everything is kosher in a way. And I said no. Because I knew it would just be watered down. And the truth, the moral and the ethics of that film, and how I wrote it, was actually that personally I had seen it. So there was a truth to me. I wasn't making anything up. Over the 44 years of living in Alice Springs I had seen everything in that film. So morally and ethically the truth was there. And I had to tell the truth. And I knew that morally and ethically I couldn't negotiate or bring in a council of Elders, because it would have just been watered down.

Q: What's your fear? What would have happened? They just go, 'do we really want to show our dirty laundry?' The thing is we do, we have to. So morally and ethically I kind of did something that morally and ethically I shouldn't do. Half of my point is to put a mirror in front of Indigenous people more so than opening a door for non-Indigenous people to see a place they might not have access to and get knowledge of stuff they might not understand.

Q: So when you feel that obligation… … It's an obligation to those kids who had no voice, not to the Elders who are more worried about Indigenous perspective being put on a screen. Morally and ethically those kids don't have a voice, and I have seen what happens to them. They need a voice and that was my job at that point.

Q: Do you think that the system of approval can work as a form of censorship? Totally. I've said this a couple of times. Indigenous people today are going through a phase. The people in control are much more missionary based. They come from the stolen generation.[1] A lot of mission mob. With a really placid perspective, like 'We had it really bad, but you have it really good now so you shouldn't be complaining'. But it's actually really bad out there at the moment. They are in a place of power.

They don't really want to upset the applecart because they really do think it was really bad back then. And it was. But they think it's much better now, which is not true. An interesting dynamic will happen when this generation will be replaced by a much more angrier and educated community that rises up; a younger generation that will become older, that didn't go through that missionary experience where the priest gave out flour, sugar and tea.

Q: There seems to be a strong moral dimension to your films but not a lot of moralizing or pontificating? And giving an answer. There are no answers, just questions. If two people sat down to watch *Samson and Delilah*, they could be friends since they were in pre-school, and they're 80 now, they'll come out with different points of view because it's actually their humanity that creates their answer to what the film is. Which is kind of nice. It's not the clear-cut Hollywood concept of storytelling—'Once upon a time and then they lived happily ever after'. That doesn't really happen. Though with *Samson and Delilah* they were at a point where they could live happily ever after at the end. Which I needed. I needed that personally. You write about these two kids. And when you are writing these two characters, you are dragging them through hell. And they, as characters, looked back at me and said, 'You need to make sure we are ok'. Even though they are in an outstation, there's food, but what does life bring now the federal government will probably shut down the outstation and they'll be dragged back to the city.

_Q: In_ Samson and Delilah _there seem to be a lot of ethical themes. And it seems to be a balancing act. On the one hand you could see Samson as indolent, but on the other hand Delilah is surrounded by duty and obligation. And there is a bit of retribution when Delilah is beaten by her female relatives because she didn't look after her grandmother, even though she did. What are the challenges of writing and filming these scenes?_ Just an honesty. A real honesty to what actually would happen. And then juxtaposed with what the character would actually do. Would they break that cycle or would they not? Just keeping their mind space. But also the natural progression of community life. And then asking what kind character that person is. How would they deal with it? Would they just accept it? That all comes from building the backstory of the character.

Q: When you are thinking about that honesty and the backstory, where does the ethics mainly happen for you, in the writing or in the directing or in the shooting or editing? The writing. Everything has to come from the writing. It all has to be built there. You can't rely on ... You know directing is very much nuts and bolts. It's like building an engine. You have all the parts and you just have to put the thing together. Whereas writing is designing the engine, in a way. And you have to design it properly or else it won't be put together properly. So writing is the most important thing. That's why I'll think about a film for a very, very long time, before I even write a single page. And I have to have a beginning, middle and an end.

Q: There was a scene in Samson and Delilah _that wasn't written before the shoot_ [_see Thornton and Shelper 2012, 41_]. _So you had spent all this time thinking it through but there was one more. What was that scene and how did it come about?_ That scene was when she gets to the car and she plays the music. I never had a scene where she actually found anything interesting in him; a little glimmer, a little sparkle in her eye going 'He's incredibly mad, but I think I might like him'. You know what I mean? So she gets in the car and he does the dance.

Q: Why did she have to get in the car? She needed a form of escapism, some respite. And that piece of music that she played was respite. He already had a tape player so I didn't want another tape player. But then there was this car that is not going anywhere because it had no wheels, but it works fine. So I thought 'that's perfect'. It's like a little cocoon. She jumps in the car, plays this music and can drift off to a foreign land.

Q: And that is the scene where she sees Samson dancing. Was that scene there or did you create it with the car scene? We kind of created it. Him dancing, and her watching. There was none of that in the film that was funded, or the version we were shooting. But we felt she needed to find some connection to him. A spark. So we kind of wrote that scene in the first week of shooting the film and put it in.

Q: You've talked about how storytelling in traditional culture has a role in teaching morals. Do your films work in this way too? Yeah, I like moral storytelling. The thing with me now is that you become so blinkered about being a filmmaker and making films, and you have so many ideas but they just don't connect with cinema. And then you realize that not everything is a movie. It could be a poem. It could be a novel. It could be a photograph. It could be a chair, or a table that tells a story. Or lyrics to a song. That freed me up a lot. We get so blinkered in being auteur filmmakers that we forget that there are so many wonderful ways of telling a story. A journey through a story should always have some form of outcome. It doesn't have to be an answer. It could be a question that can be answered later.

Q: So just so I get this right, so it's not just giving information out through the story. It's about taking the viewer somewhere or into something. And a personal, moral point of view. Whether right or wrong—that is the audience's perspective and answer. Good cinema does that.

Q: Are you pushing a point of view in Samson and Delilah *or your short films. Or, are you creating situations which make the viewer think?* I have a point of view. But I am very careful it is not the only point of view. I love it when people say, 'the film's about this'. They tell me what the film is about. And, you know what, they are completely wrong but they are completely right. It's their point of view and they are allowed to have that point of view. And that is special.

Q: It seems to me that when you look at Samson and Delilah, *along with your short films, that there are some themes that recur in your work...* There's always strong women. And slightly useless men.

Q: Culture and community seems to be a big theme for you. I'm interested in this because an aspect of your films is that community seems strained or stretched thin. Which they are, that is just reality.

Q: But at the same time there is a strong sense of cultural maintenance. Is that something you are aware of? Yes, totally. There always needs to be light. Even if the communities are dysfunctional. There is always light at the end of the tunnel. You cannot just write them off. You cannot just shut them down.

Q: So, thinking about your 2005 short film Green Bush, *there's a lot of meaning in that cup of tea. The cup of tea keeps on coming back.* Yes, it's a nurturing and a respite. In the 1980s, the federal government decided to create a thing called BRACS [Broadcasting for Remote Aboriginal Communities Scheme]. So every community got a little radio station that could chop between TV [channel]s or could play tapes. They weren't cheap, and a lot of communities did not have health clinics, but they suddenly had a radio station. The communities turn what they get into what they need, so a lot of them were turned into clinics, with a radio station. It was more important to have a clinic, and I kind of liked that. So that is what *Green Bush* is about. He's playing music to people in jail and that but at night, when people are drinking and fighting, all the Elders come there. So it almost becomes the safe house, more so than a radio station. There is always tea and biscuits.

Q: And at one point the announcer has had jack of it and says I don't want to be part of this, doesn't he? And the Elder says, 'you're a good part of this'.

Q: What is the 'this'? The 'this' is our existence. The way it is. You accept that people are going to drink and fight and you accept that when that happens you go to the radio station and turn it into a safe house, rather than a radio station. He's wanting to change everything about everything. And actually, he doesn't realize that the little bit he is doing is powerful stuff.

Q: On a similar theme, and focusing on your other short film Payback *(1996), there is something deep going on here. A man is released from the Western prison system and faces traditional punishment. It is a confrontation enacted as a ceremony. He faces a traditional system of morals and laws, alongside the morals and laws of the media. So my question is Who's dancing with who? Which media system is the dominant one? Old media or new media? Which idea of justice prevails? Which idea of freedom?* And the dancing and spearing is that really for him? Or is that to prove to a Western world that our law is still alive? And is it just a dance for them, or is it *really* a payback? Did it have to happen out the front of the jail? It could have happened in the bush. Is it a political statement by the Elders and by the law, the Indigenous law?

Q: So you are pointing to the fact it may have been/is staged. When you are setting that up are you wanting to put a whole load of things in play, or are you trying to make a point? Obviously you start with a fire inside you. And at that time, I think *60 Minutes* had gone into a community to witness a payback. They went with the man who was getting speared and didn't set up any ground-work with the people who were spearing him. So the people who were spearing him felt that justice had already been decided that he was right because the cameras were coming with him. The dynamic was completely obscured; that was actually their power. He had done very bad things. And he needed to be speared traditionally, because that is the law. But then suddenly they did not want to spear him because he was bringing a camera crew; and it felt like he was in the right and they were in the wrong. That was the fire that started inside me with this story. I wanted to write about that, keeping those dynamics open, including the sideshow that it is.

Q: You seem quite interested, even in your 2002 short film Mimi, *in this theme of traditional culture or representation co-existing with different worlds: the art world or the media world. Is* Payback *an example of you exploring that co-existence?* There was a scene that is not in *Payback* where one of the young men after he says 'You're speared now', he says to the camera crews 'You happy now, you can all f-off'. But then he turns to our camera and says 'Yeah, you happy? You should f-off'—looking straight down the lens at the audience watching the movie. There was a lot of kerfuffle over it, so I got rid of it, because it created a political statement in a sense, and that's not what I am about. That scene came from the anger in me, and it is something I have to be very careful with when I write—that it doesn't become a complete piece of propaganda.

Q: So that would have turned the media into intruders, yes? Yes. And us as part of that circus.

Q: Because you are using those tools as well. Yeah, I am doing exactly the same thing. You are looking at the media and they are in the way, and they are in their faces. There's people trying to do something. And we're actually there as well. We forget that. What I have created, we are partisan to that concept, as well. We're watching for entertainment.

Q: Exploring more about the way you work. Do you think it would be possible for a non-Indigenous filmmaker to make a film like Samson and Delilah? Yes, for sure. Absolutely. That is a really interesting dynamic. I have never ever had a problem with non-Indigenous people making Indigenous stuff. Just like I might go to Hollywood and make *Star Wars*. If I think non-Indigenous people should not make film about Indigenous people then I should not be allowed to make *Star Wars*. It's all very hypocritical.

Q: It's quite controversial what you are saying. There is a lot of focus placed on non-Indigenous filmmakers following cultural protocols. ... But it's about getting it right. And about respect. The thing I do know that a lot of non-Indigenous people don't think about is that when I walk into a community, my community, if I stuff up I can't go back to my community. And that ostracization of my community and my culture is pretty well one of the most horrific things that could ever happen to me. I can't get back onto country. I can't visit my ancestors. I can't do these things that make me stronger. It is like purgatory, for the rest of your life. Especially my language group, the Katish [also known as Kaititja, Kaytetye, Kartetye, Kartiji, Kaytej, and Keytej]. There is a lot more responsibility in a sense. But you have got to have respect and understanding to get it right, whether you want to take on the hard yarns and put that mirror up. Or whether you want to open a door for other language groups and other cultures to see a world that they won't have access to. Now you get a non-Indigenous person: they can walk into a community and make a mess, it doesn't matter if they don't come back. There is that dynamic.

Q: In the case of Samson and Delilah, *How did you make sure the community was on board?* Well, we had a free screening in Alice Springs. And we basically bussed in 50 buses worth of people from all the communities around. At the telegraph station we had around 15,000 people and we just screened it on a big projector. I sat there and crapped myself. And everyone loved it, thankfully. That's the other part of it too. You make a film in a community and then it goes on the ABC [the Australian Broadcasting Corporation, a national public broadcaster] and you never see it again? No, you make a film in a community take it back to the community and show it to them *before* it gets on ABC. And nut it out; punch it out. You have to have the arguments. And be truthful. And my argument for *Samson and Delilah* was, hey, you can't tell me anything about this because this actually personally I've seen. You can't say that's not true, because it is true. Because I've seen it. That's why I could make that film. You can't just walk into a community and do a film about drug addicts unless you've been in that community and done a lot of drugs. Or spent a lot of time with the drug addicts. It can be that simple.

Q: Going back to this question, could a non-Indigenous filmmaker make Samson and Delilah, *could they get the performances?* Yeah, for sure. That's casting. We have a saying, there is no such thing as a bad actor, there are just bad directors. Because it boils down to the fact that you should not have cast those people in the first place. If you put an actor there who can't act or is really bad, it is your own fault. It's not because they can't act; it's because you can't direct.

Q: You've worked with a range of producers and filmmakers, Indigenous and non-Indigenous. Have you ever faced professional challenges yourself around ethical or moral treatment? You've got to be super-wary of co-directions. I've done it a couple of times and some of them have been awesome. Some of them have been absolutely atrocious. And you ask 'why the hell did you get involved?' And 99.9 % of the time it was financial; where you do it for the money. They are the ones that stuff you up. You are doing it for all of the wrong reasons.

Q: So just to clarify, does co-direction refer to a segment film in which different directors contribute? Because I am a director of photography I will shoot and direct with another director, who is generally non-Indigenous. But those are so dangerous. It is usually their idea and they are using you to help fund it.

Q: Is that ethical dilemma about being Indigenous, or is it about professional respect? No, it's about the way they want the story to go. The stuff that they think is needed. The stuff that you think is needed. It is just those clashes. Anything is up for grabs unless it's secret or sacred. There are places I'll refuse to go to. There is a line drawn in the sand. Whereas I've been with co-directors who don't see that line and they want 'that' because it 'makes' their film.

Q: So the danger seems to be around mediating between that community and a project? And getting caught in the middle. What's the secret ingredient to make it all go well? I don't know. But you're there ethically just as much as financially. You have to be bad cop. They are going into your community. Or a community that you have friends in and you know you want to go back to. You can get caught in the middle. And you know what side I'll take. I'll take the side of the community. I have to. That's part of my existence. It's more than filmmaking. Law and culture is much more than cinema.

Q: I'm interested in the way you work with actors. Your scripts are not over-written but you talk about the importance of nailing what is in the script at the same time. And then there is the interpretation that can come from an actor, especially when you are casting non-professional actors. There are two ways you can do it. You write a film about a community. You can actually use someone from that community who is just going to go 'this is easy, because this is just my life'. Or you can cast around Australia (and this is a detriment to Indigenous actors around the world) and you can get an actor from Sydney and they're going to have to go on this cultural journey into this community. They might have grown up on a mission in Queensland, they can act fantastically, they can perform amazingly, but they are always going to be on this journey. You have to seriously look at that, and the pros and cons of either approach. You cast a non-actor from the community and in the end you get this complete method acting: they know it, they've seen it, they've done it. But then again, is that what you want? Do you want a different kind of journey happening through the head of the character? So if it was an Aboriginal policeman working for the first time in the community, well I would seriously consider casting someone from Sydney who is going to be on that journey. If it's a Samson, I'd be casting from the community, not from outside. And it's survival as a director—you try and look after yourself and make it as easy as possible.

Q: So do you drill your actors or do you let them improvise? Well, if it was an external actor I would drill them. If it's a first time actor from the community I would let them improvise because they will give me more than I actually know. It's their community. They'll give me stuff that will probably be a thousand times better than I have written; as long as I am 'nailing' or getting what I need out of the scene. The way they do it; I'm not worried if it's better.

Q: Do you see actors as full collaborators? Do you take changes from actors in the script? Yes, totally. I'm always open to any perception or point of view but I am always basing everything back into the script, and the journey that the character takes in the script, so you have to keep that close to your heart. You don't want to go off on these tangents.

Q: So you have stated in an interview that Marissa and Rowan, who played Delilah and Samson, 'took over the writing process' and demanded a happy ending. We have touched on this, but how did they do this? Did they demand a happy ending? It was the characters. That comment is out of context because it is Samson and Delilah who took on what they wanted to do in the script while I was writing it. They were going 'hey, hey, hang on' in my head. And they demanded a happy ending, because I had dragged them through the wringer. And rightfully so.

Q: And what does happy ending mean? Well, they lived. They're not dead. They are washed; there is food in their stomach. There's light at the end of the tunnel, but tomorrow is another day. They're out in the middle of nowhere and have got no friends. Will he keep sniffing, or not? It is up for grabs.

Q: Looking at the making of Samson and Delilah *documentary on the DVD, there were complicated moments in the making of the film it seems. There were moments of shame on the part of the young actors, for example. How did you deal with that?* It is really just propping them up to feel important. And empowering them to be able to do it.

Q: Do you feel like a bit of a parent in that context? I used to call myself a grumpy uncle. That dynamic worked because that is the dynamic they are used to. They can accept a grumpy uncle but they have never met a grumpy filmmaker before. They understand a grumpy uncle. Part of it too, is that with Rowan [MacNamara], who I think is a brilliant actor, and could do anything he ever wanted to, I started recognizing on the second day that if we did more that three takes of something he really felt that he failed. He really felt that it was his shame. So what I learnt to do was after the third take I would actually go and change the angle, even if I was not happy with the third take and I still did not have the scene. I would just change the angle. It was more important to nurture him and keep that confidence than it was for me to get the 'perfect scene'. This idea of the 'perfect scene' is full of crap—there is no such thing. So I changed the angle, did a close up, and if that's all I got at least I got what I wanted but he walked away empowered that he gave what he thinks I wanted, which is awesome. I would never do more than three takes with him, and with Marissa [Gibson] and Scott [Thornton] (my brother) as well, just to ensure they kept feeling empowered. That is part of directing, the nurturing.

Q: There were also moments in the 'making of' documentary when Mitjili Gibson, who plays Nana, felt 'Samson' was the wrong skin group for 'Delilah'. From an anthropological perspective [see Michaels 1989], *this would be a big deal and you would have to cast according to skin group and traditional moieties.* It is always a consideration but if you find Rowan McNamara, and he is prepared to do it, you have to throw the actual skin group connection out the window. It's more important for a great actor to play that role than it is to say 'they are the wrong or right skin group'. There is a point of make-believe in everything that needs to be kept.

Q: Does that pop up often for you in casting? If it is two people who are in love, and in the script they are the right skin, well then it is important, but it is not the defining point. It does, it pops up everywhere. You want two people to sit next to each other, and then one of them says, 'she's my grandmother'. And you are not allowed to sit next to your grandmother. So that is where the make-believe has to be stopped and the true laws of that community have to be respected. Especially with mothers-in-law, sisters and brothers.

Q: In the film there is an allusion that Samson has a disability. Can I tease this out? How conscious was this in your thinking? Or is it tied in with the petrol sniffing? There are multiple reasons why he doesn't talk. As a generation, traditionally, these kids weren't allowed to talk. They are not in that position yet to talk. They are also a silent generation in a sense, because they haven't been allowed to talk on behalf of themselves to a government. But then again, Samson has a speech impediment, he stutters. At the same time, he doesn't say anything because no one actually asks him a question.

Q: So you are not necessarily trying to push one point of view about him having a disability, or a stutter. It's a device that let's you ask questions? Yes, there are different reasons why he is not talking, and you choose which one you want as an audience member. At the same time, actions speak louder than words. In so many films nowadays, a person walks in and they say 'I'm angry. I'm angry about this, and I'm angry about that'. But that is so boring and painful, when it is spoon-fed to an audience. Whereas if you can find something that means what they are wanting to say, and if they can do it without speaking, that is so much more powerful. And it makes the audience work, it makes them think, it makes them question and find answers in their brain rather than being spoon-fed.

Q: It is interesting that it is not just a question of Samson not talking, but that Samson's world tends to fall apart when he is not listening. And hearing difficulties are common in community. Yes, there are massive problems with hygiene issues with babies leading to perforated eardrums contributing to deafness. There are so many kids like that in community. And—he is high too.

Q: As a screenwriter, did you decide that I am going to give Samson a speech impediment? Yes, and he is going to be deaf. Remember, him playing with his ears.

Q: Where did you get that idea from? Just finding an alternative to him saying so. And using the tools of the cinema but also the community to tell the story in a different way.

Q: There is always a temptation to fall into the moral eye. But as a screenwriter and director or cinematographer you seem to think a lot about the audio, and the ear. As Keith Gallasch [2009] *has noted, at times we only hear what Samson's hearing when the rest of the world is going to pieces. And you envelope us in Samson's 'aural oblivion'.* That's my radio upbringing. I was a DJ before I started as a camera assistant. I spent years and years thinking about sound, way before I began thinking about the image. The film I just did, *The Dark Side* [2013], I wanted to make a film where you could just switch the picture off and you can still understand the whole film. And you can, it's a radio show with pictures. I wanted it to be simulcast on radio, but it never happened.

Q: You've said that in Samson and Delilah *a sign language takes the place of dialogue in the script? Talk us through a scene of this kind and what appears on the page.* There is one simple one right at the beginning where Samson is hanging out at the front of the shop. She has to go to the shop. He asks her for some money. And she says no, but she comes out with chips. And then the second time he asks her again and she says no, and then she buys him a packet of chips. So this is an inkling that she might like him. So then he follows her home and she has to throw rocks at him. So those gestures are what I mean by sign language. Traditionally, in the desert, if you were in another language community or area out of respect you would not speak your language. So there is a universal sign language that would be used if you did not know their language and could not speak it, because you would not use your language in their country. But this is part of the reality, I didn't play that very much.

Q: And what appears on the page? Just that. She walks past. He gestures. And because Samson is a non-professional actor from community, he knows how to gesture properly.

Q: Returning to the theme of getting it right. Any advice to non-Indigenous filmmakers? It is just understanding. And being truthful. If you are going to walk in and hold a mirror up to the community, you tell them that. And you have to create that argument. See this is why I am hypocritical. Because I say that, but I then didn't do that with *Samson and Delilah* because I knew it would get watered down. But there are times when you decide you are going to put a big mirror up. You at least tell them. My community knew I was going to put a big mirror up to them, and I wasn't going to talk to them about what I was actually going to do, but at least they knew in Samson and Delilah's case. As long as people know, and you are truthful.

NOTE

1. The Stolen Generations refers to generations of Indigenous children in Australia forcibly removed from families from the late 1800s up to the 1970s.

REFERENCES

Boukabou, Ruby. 2007. 'Warwick and Kath.' *Inside Film* 103 (October). Accessed 26 October 2015. http://samsonanddelilah.com.au/uploads/IF.pdf

Clague, Pauline. (2013) 'The Five Beats of Indigenous Storytelling.' *Lumina* 11. Accessed 26 October 2015. http://www.aftrs.edu.au/media/books/lumina/lumina11r-ch3-1/index.html

Davies, Therese. (2009) 'Love and Social Marginality in *Samson and Delilah.' Senses of Cinema* 51 (July). Accessed 29 November 2015. http://sensesofcinema.com/2009/feature-articles/samson-and-delilah/

Gallasch, Keith. 2009. 'The Seeing Ear, the Hearing Eye.' *Realtime* 90 (April/May): 23. Accessed 29 November 2015. http://www.realtimearts.net/article/issue90/9404

Janke, Terri. 2009. Pathways & Protocols: A Filmmaker's Guide to Working with Indigenous People, Culture and Concepts. Accessed 29 September 2016 https://www.screenaustralia.gov.au/about-us/doing-business-with-us/indigenous-content/indigenous-protocols

Michaels, Eric. 1989. *For A Cultural Future: Francis Jupurrurla Makes TV at Yuendumu.* Sydney: Art & Text.

Millard, Kathryn. 2011. 'The Screenplay as Prototype.' In *Analysing the screenplay*, edited by Jill Nelmes, 142–157. London: Routledge.

Thornton, Warwick. 2009a. Interview by Fenelle Kenerbone, Sunday Arts, ABC1, 10th May. Accessed 9 February 2015. http://www.abc.net.au/tv/sundayarts/txt/s2567721.htm

Thornton, Warwick. 2009b. 'The Making of *Samson & Delilah.'* Interview by Keith Gallasch. *Realtime* 90 (April/May): 24. Accessed 14 January 2015. http://www.realtimearts.net/article/issue90/9405

Thornton, Warwick. 2009c. 'Warwick Thornton discusses Samson and Delilah with the WSWS.' Interview by Richard Phillips. *World Socialist Web Site*, May

14. Accessed 14 January 2015. https://www.wsws.org/en/articles/2009/05/inte-m14.html

Thornton, Warwick. 2009d. 'Interview with Warwick Thornton.' *Australian Centre for the Moving* Image. Accessed 14 January 2015. http://generator.acmi.net.au/gallery/media/interview-warwick-thornton

Thornton, Warwick. 2010. 'An Interview with Warwick Thornton.' Interview by Will Owen. *Aboriginal Art & Culture: An American Eye*, 12th October. Accessed 14 January 2015. https://aboriginalartandculture.wordpress.com/2010/10/12/an-interview-with-warwick-thornton/

Thornton, Warwick, and Kath Shelper. 2012. 'A Distinctive Voice.' Interview by Rachael Turk. *Lumina* 1: 35–44.

FILM REFERENCES

The Darkside. 2013. Dir: Warwick Thornton, Australia, 94 mins.

Green Bush. 2005. Wr: Warwick Thornton, Dir: Warwick Thornton, Australia, 13 mins.

Mimi. 2002. Wr: Warwick Thornton, Dir: Warwick Thornton, Australia, 13 mins.

Nana. 2007. Wr: Warwick Thornton, Dir: Warwick Thornton, Australia, 6 mins.

Payback. 1996. Wr: Warwick Thornton, Dir: Warwick Thornton, Australia, 12 mins.

Radiance. 1998. Wr: Louis Nowra, Dir: Rachel Perkins, Australia, 83 mins.

Samson and Delilah. 2009. Wr: Warwick Thornton, Dir: Warwick Thornton, Australia, 101 mins.

The Sapphires. 2012. Wr: Tony Briggs and Keith Thompson, Dir: Wayne Blair, Australia, 103 mins.

CHAPTER 4

On Morals, Ethics and Screenwriting: An Interview with Jimmy McGovern

Steven Maras

Over a long and extraordinary career, Jimmy McGovern (born in 1949) has worked on some of the most celebrated British television of the last 30 years, including single dramas such as *Hillsborough* (1996) and *Sunday* (2002), and series such as *Cracker* (1993–1996) and *The Street* (2006–2010), to name only some of his works (BAFTA 2015). Often writing in a social realist mode, his writing is grounded in an empathy with working-class morality; and at the same time tackles serious issues surrounding the judicial and political system (see Blandford 2013, for an important overview of his work). McGovern's work is well-known for its exploration of religion, morality and ethics (see Maras 2015). In the final chapter of this collection I draw on an analysis of the script for *Common* (2014) to explore how scripts can perform 'ethical work'. This edited interview between Steven Maras and Jimmy McGovern took place via email between March and December 2015.

S. Maras (✉)
Media and Communication, The University of Western Australia,
Perth, WA, Australia
e-mail: steven.maras@uwa.edu.au

© The Editor(s) (if applicable) and The Author(s) 2016
S. Maras (ed.), *Ethics in Screenwriting*, Palgrave Studies
in Screenwriting, DOI 10.1057/978-1-137-54493-3_4

Q: To clear up an issue of terminology at the outset: Do you draw a distinction between ethics and morals? Is the distinction one you would make or are concerned about?

Well, I'm no intellectual—as you're about to discover—and, till now, I've never thought there WAS a difference between 'moral' and 'ethical'. I'm about to reach for my Collins Dictionary but before I do I'll have a stab at it.

I'd say we're all born with 'morals' (the odd psychopath apart). They're what make us human. They force us to treat other human beings with respect and dignity. They're the things that make us feel pity or sympathy. The things that make us rush to another person's aid. Or support another person under attack. They're instinctive. I'd guess that 'ethics' are learned. I'm almost tempted to say that *Guardian* readers have 'ethics', *Daily Mirror* readers 'morals'.[1]

I'll now look them up in the dictionary...

ethics:
    1) a code of behaviour considered correct, especially that of a particular group, profession or individual.
    2) the moral fitness of a decision, course of action, etc.
    moral:
    adj. 1) concerned with or relating to human behaviour, especially the distinction between good and bad or right and wrong behaviour.
    n. pl. 2) principles of behaviour in accordance with standards of right and wrong.

I wasn't too far off.

I told you that, till now, I'd never thought there was a difference between them but I now realize that I once wrote an entire BBC film precisely *about* that difference. It was *Priest* (1996).

In *Priest* a teenage girl tells Father Greg—in the secrecy of the confessional—that her father is sexually abusing her. Later her father confirms the abuse, even tries to justify the abuse and, again, it is in the secrecy of the confessional. Thus, ethically, Father Greg is bound by the seal of the confession. Morally he desperately needs to end this abuse.

Without divulging anything specific, Father Greg asks an older, more experienced, priest for advice. The older priest says he'd 'drop a hint'. In other words, 'you can tamper with ethics as long as it is to serve morals'. Father Greg drops that hint but it achieves nothing: the abuse continues.

Later Father Greg conducts a meeting at which the abused girl's mother is present. Greg asks after her daughter. The mother replies that the girl (Lisa) is with her Dad. The meeting continues but Father Greg can hardly function; he is seeing in his mind's eye exactly what the incestuous father is doing to that child. Ethically Father Greg should carry on as if nothing is wrong. Morally he cannot. He abandons the meeting and the mother goes home early and catches her husband in the act of sexually abusing their daughter. A miracle is wrought, the sexual abuse is ended, because morally he was unable to do what ethically he should.

Similarly, at the climax of *Priest*, Father Greg and the older priest stand at the altar, preparing to give communion to the congregation. But by this time Greg has been caught by the police having sex with another man in the back of a car in broad daylight. He is in disgrace and not one member of the congregation will take communion from his hands. After all, who knows where those hands have been? Parishioner after parishioner walks past Greg to take the host from the older priest's hand. Suddenly footsteps are heard. Lisa, the abused girl, the girl whom Father Greg failed so spectacularly, is approaching him. He gives her communion. He starts to sob. She takes him in his arms.

It is Lisa's working-class morality, her working-class decency, that propels her forward. She has suffered so much herself that she cannot see another human being suffering too. Greg's ethical dilemma is totally forgotten when confronted by Lisa's working-class morality.

I think I write about that a lot. It's not *morality*, it's *working-class morality*. *Banished* (2015), is a seven-part drama series about the First Fleet [sent to Australia]. Nearly all the drama stems from two basic principles, two *morals*, to which the convicts adhere: they will not grass on a man and they will not hang a man. They're a million miles away from the moral choices facing middle-class people today but *they are still moral choices*.

Britain being such a class-ridden society, can I say something about ethics/morals/class? There's an episode of *The Street* (2006–2010) in which a man comes across a house that's ablaze. He sees a young girl in an upstairs window. He sprints to the front door, kicks it in, runs up the stairs, fights his way through the flames, takes the girl in his arms and carries her to safety. Once outside, he gives the girl to his friend and says, 'You did it. I'm on invalidity.' (That is, he's getting benefits because of an injury or illness that he has invented.) British working-class people found this moral dilemma (winning acclaim versus losing your benefits) funny and true. Middle-class journalists, however, thought it a 'ludicrous premise on which to base a story.'

There's an episode of *Accused* (2010–2012) in which a young man is killed in an accident at work. His mother, played by Juliet Stevenson, expects to receive an explanation, a bit of sympathy and an apology from her son's boss. But, when they meet, the boss is flanked by a lawyer and the explanation is vague, the sympathy guarded and she gets no apology whatsoever. Juliet Stevenson won't let the matter drop and she pursues the boss through the usual legal channels. She gets nowhere and eventually burns the boss's warehouse down. But, for me, the climax comes a little earlier when she asks the boss why he simply didn't say sorry. She says something like, 'People say it all the time: sorry. They bump into someone in the supermarket. Sorry. Even when it's not their fault. Sorry...'

To this the boss replies, 'My lawyer won't let me.'

That poor man. He is an extremely *moral* person. He desperately wants to tell her everything and go down on his knee and beg forgiveness but the law won't let him.

That *Accused* (jointly written with Alice Nutter) is not too distant from *Hillsborough* (1996).[2] I'm sure that, some time after Hillsborough, the people responsible for the disaster wanted to confess and apologize. To carry on denying it, living a lie, must have been horrendous for them. But they weren't allowed to confess. Or to apologize. So they carried on living a lie. Meanwhile the Hillsborough Family Support Group (HFSG) pursued them. The HFSG went through every legal channel open to them. There was the original inquest. There were judicial reviews of that inquest. There was a so-called 'scrutiny' led by a senior judge. There was a private prosecution. And now there is a new inquest. But, you know what, the more law the HFSG got, the less chance they had of justice. Law and justice, they learned, are incompatible. Most people here [in Britain] think of law as a route to justice. It's only when they get caught up in the legal process that they realize it is no such thing.

Q: It's often been remarked that you are a writer who specializes in moral dilemmas facing characters as well as moral choices in your stories, but this comment is rarely explored in depth. Does your screenwriting have an ethical dimension? If it does, how would you characterize the moral/ethical impetus, power or dimension in your work?

I suspect that every single story ever told has had a moral/ethical dimension. Otherwise it would not work as a story. It would not survive through the years.

We root for David, for example, when he takes on Goliath because David has right on his side and he is small and Goliath is huge. David doesn't have to WIN for the story to work. He could lose and it would be a tragedy. But we have to be on David's side and he has to face over-whelming odds. Similarly Gary Cooper in *High Noon*, Clint Eastwood in the spaghetti westerns, Paul Newman and his shabby little outfit in *The Verdict*, Stanley Baker in *Zulu*, even that old reactionary John Wayne in *The Alamo*...

This championing of the underdog with right on his side is, I think, inherently moral. I'm not arguing that we Brits DID have right on our side when we fought the Zulus. Still less am I arguing that Davy Crockett and his gang had it at the Alamo. But they were *portrayed* as having it and that is why the audience rooted for them.

My first job in television was *Brookside* (1982–2003), a twice-weekly soap opera set in Liverpool. I was there from 1982 to 1989, a time of great political unrest in Britain generally and in Liverpool specifically. Mrs Thatcher was in the process of using North Sea Oil to close down British Industry and smash the trade union movement. She was also slashing the budgets of local councils throughout the country. As far as I remember, not one single drama on British television tackled this subject but we on *Brookside* featured it regularly. While trade unionists and local council-lors were vilified by the media for resisting Thatcherism we on *Brookside* portrayed them sympathetically. It was not a fashionable thing to do but we believed it was the *right* thing to do, the *moral* thing to do, so we did it. I'm proud of my time on *Brookside*. That approach to life we had back then has stayed with me ever since. '*Who are they all knocking this time? Right, let's fight that poor bastard's corner.*'

Not long after *The Sun's* front page vilifying the Liverpool fans at Hillsborough, I attended a *Brookside* storyline meeting. I argued for a story about one of our characters organising a mass burning of *The Sun* newspaper on the first anniversary of the Hillsborough Disaster. A few locally born writers supported me but other non-Liverpool-based writers (a majority) opposed it. I left *Brookside* shortly afterwards and never went back.

A few years later, still burning with resentment over the disaster and *The Sun's* front page in response to it, I was commissioned to write *Cracker* (1993–1996), starring Robbie Coltrane as Fitz, a boozy, brilliant psychologist. The first series was a huge hit and ITV [the UK based Independent Television] gave me virtually free rein for the second so I decided to write a story called 'To Be A Somebody' in which Albie, a man traumatized by the Hillsborough Football Disaster, seeks revenge by going on a killing spree that ends with the murder of a journalist on *The Sun*.

(Where does 'righteous anger' fit into this morals/ethics debate? It has a place surely?)

Liverpool, despite a population of over 600,000, is a village and the HFSG soon got wind of the fact that I was writing this story. A few months after that I came back from a walk to find Doreen Jones and Jenni Hicks waiting for me on my front step. Doreen had lost her son Richard at Hillsborough and Jenni had lost her daughters Sarah and Vicki. They said (and I'll never forget their exact words), 'We'd like you to tell our story, Jimmy.'

And that is why I wrote *Hillsborough*: because the families of the dead asked me to write it.

Q: What is the moral/ethical impetus?
I think a lot of it is down to the fact that British newspapers are so bad. Especially the tabloids.

Immediately after Bloody Sunday[3] the British Army spoke of 'gunmen and nail bombers' getting shot. The British media reported it as fact. The people of Derry and their priests were adamant that the people killed were all unarmed. But very little of what they said made it into our newspapers.

I've already described what *The Sun* said about Liverpool fans. Other media outlets repeated it.

The Liverpool Docks dispute[4] was virtually ignored by the British media. Those who did report it often described the dockers as 'dinosaurs'—implying that the dispute was some sort of throwback to the industrial unrest of the seventies. In fact the dispute was fundamentally about the creeping casualization of work, something that has continued apace throughout our country. The dockers were bang up to date.

I've often said that if our press was better, I'd be out of work. I do the work I do because our journalists get it so wrong in the first place. But then those same journalists pronounce judgement on my work. Ludicrous.

Common (2014) was a work of fiction, loosely based on lots of joint enterprise cases and it came about in a similar way.[5] There was a notorious murder in Liverpool. One boy got life for it and seven others got long prison stretches averaging about six years each. The local paper (*The Liverpool Echo*) described them all as scumbags. That was not the truth. Nearly all of them had full time jobs and four of them weren't even at the scene when the murder (a stabbing) occurred. There was an even more notorious murder in nearby Warrington when Gary Newlove was punched and kicked to death outside his own home. Three boys got life for this. One of them was Jordan Cunliffe. He did not participate in the attack in any way. He COULD not; he was technically blind at the time, awaiting a cornea transplant. None of that was reported in the papers. He was found guilty, therefore he, too, was scum.

Incidentally, prior to *Common* scores of people convicted of murder under the joint enterprise principle had appealed against their conviction. Not one appeal had been upheld. The first appeal to be heard *following* the screening of *Common* resulted in one boy being freed and another having his sentence drastically reduced. When I say 'one boy was freed' I mean his sentence was reduced to something like two and half years and he had already served more than that so he was released.

Q: Has your approach to ethics stayed the same, become more simple, become more complex?
I'll take that to mean my approach to campaigning films such as *Hillsborough* rather than fictional stuff like *Cracker* or *The Street*. Yes, it's changed in so far as I know how hard it is now. It's no coincidence that *Common* was fictional. Had I not been through *Hillsborough* and *Sunday*, I might have taken a real life case (the murder of Gary Newlove, for example) and written a blow-by-blow account of that. But that would have meant having my script scrutinized by everyone at the BBC (up to the Director-General) and then scrutinized again by an army of lawyers. That would have meant rewrite upon rewrite upon rewrite—not to make the script better but to make it legal. Also making it fictional meant that it was almost certain to get made. That is not the case with a docudrama.

Also, with docudrama you often have to write badly, you often have to write appalling lines simply because the lawyers tell you to. In *Hillsborough*, for instance, Chief Superintendent Duckenfield has allowed a dangerous crush to develop outside the stadium at the turnstiles. Another officer asks him if he is going to open a gate to relieve this crush. In all early drafts

I then cut to the gate opening. That's standard screenwriting. We don't need to hear Duckenfield say yes when we can SEE that he has said yes. But the lawyers told me I had to write Duckenfield's answer in full. It was something like: 'If there is risk of serious injury to anyone outside the ground, I have no option but to open the gate.' I argued that no one, not even a robot, would say something like that at that time. They said, 'Tough. That's what he says he said so write it.' I said, 'He only says he said that because a lawyer has told him to say he said that.' They agreed with me on that but still made me write it.

I didn't know any of this when I threw myself into *Hillsborough*. But I'm older and wiser now and I'd tell a story as docudrama only if it could not be told in any other way.

I should say something about energy here. When you're telling other people's stories, their stories about their dead children, for example, the responsibility you feel drives you on. When I was writing *Hillsborough* I felt overwhelmed at times. Drained, in fact. So I put photographs of the victims all around my word processor and those photographs kept me going. I was about 46 years old when I wrote *Hillsborough*. I was probably close to my peak as a writer. But I'm 65 now and I doubt I'd be able to muster the energy to do anything like it now.

People get bored of you as well if you're always banging the drum about one injustice or another. In fact I met a few boyhood friends the other day and one of them cynically called me a 'working-class hero'. It's because of stuff like that that I've always maintained the right to tell a story simply because it's a great story. No politics, no moral dilemma, no tub-thumping; it's just a great story. *Banished* for the most part falls into that category. There's a vicar so desperate for a church that he betrays a young woman in order to get one built. That sort of twisted logic, that perverted approach to Christianity, has always fascinated me.

Writers should be able to make mischief. *Dockers* (2009), for example, was never going to get the sacked men their jobs back. It was never going to 'write' a wrong. But, my God, it was going to make a hell of a lot of mischief for Bill Morris, head of the Transport and General Workers Union (as it then was). I wouldn't say that about *Hillsborough*. That was a genuine attempt to right an enormous wrong. But other times I have set out to make mischief, to discomfort the comfortable. No matter how old one gets, I suspect, no matter how much gravitas one displays, the child lives on in every writer.

I'm a bit worried about being seen as some sort of moral crusader. I suspect I do only what it is necessary to do. I know that if I pick a moral issue I'll be able to generate the energy needed to write the bloody thing. Other writers will generate the energy in other ways. Also, I'll be just as energetic attacking my cause as I will be in championing it. If I'm not, the story won't work. There's a scene in *Common*, for example, in which Johnjo's family sit down in the court canteen and realize they have sat opposite Mrs Ward and her daughter. Johnjo's Mum tells Mrs Ward that Johnjo is innocent. Mrs Ward replies, 'Innocent? Then why didn't he go to the police immediately?' Johnjo's Mum says, 'Because his head was...' and she gestures something to the effect that Johnjo just couldn't think straight. Mrs Ward comes back with 'His head? What about mine?'

I think it's one of the best scenes in the film and I very nearly left it out. I thought it was too damning of Johnjo, you see. Also, this hesitation in going to the police is extremely common in joint enterprise cases. It is something of which many otherwise innocent people are guilty: not going to the police and telling them everything. I didn't want to give our enemies—a right-wing press and bone idle, uncaring barristers—a stick with which to beat us. It would have been a huge mistake to have left it out, of course. And it would have been immoral too. If you care about your writing you have to be every single character's *best barrister* so to have a great point to make on behalf of a character and then fail to make that point—and fail because you are biased towards another character—would be very wrong, I think.

Q: If the proposition was put to you that there is a kind of moral philosophy in your work, that through your screenwriting you are doing a kind of moral or ethical philosophy, what would you say to that? And if you agreed with this proposition, what would be the key concepts or terms that you would want people to focus on? What are some of the key ethical questions raised or tackled by your work?

I don't think I have a philosophy. I think I have an instinctive grasp of what would make a good story and because of that instinctive grasp other people might think me philosophical but I'm not.

I watched *High Noon* for the first time when I was about ten years old. 1959 or thereabouts. It had a tremendous effect on me. I identified so strongly with all the people who had excuses NOT to help. The guys in the saloon and the decent people in the church who wanted to avoid a shootout because a shootout is bad for business. But, overwhelmingly, I identified with the man who was prepared to help as long as others helped as well. When he found out, of course, that there was NOBODY else, he left Gary Cooper to fight alone. I also identified with the man who hid in his own house whilst his wife answered the door to Cooper. I mention this because I think I simply mine/explore/exploit my own failings—and cowardice is one of them.

I think we are quick to see in others what we know is within us.

Hypocrisy is another trait of mine. I'm a typical old British leftie, for instance, and old British lefties always want other people to pay more tax, never themselves. I vote for parties that will increase other people's taxes and I employ an accountant to keep mine down.

Q: Is this a good way to talk about character in your work, people striving to do their best but held back or constrained by their own struggles and contradictions?

I'm very fond of saying that you have to be able to afford integrity. Charlie has plenty of money. The barman undercharges him. Charlie tells him he's been undercharged. Peter, on the other hand, is practically skint. He too is undercharged but Peter pockets the money. Charlie, I argue, doesn't have more integrity than Peter. He simply has more money. THAT is what I write about all the time, I suspect. We all want to do the right thing but the cost (in money, in effort, to our security, to our very lives) is simply too great.

I love *High Noon* (1952). Gary Cooper is told the baddies are coming so he hightails it out of there with his new bride. But, on the edge of town, he decides to go back. He weighs the cost of running (to his reputation, to his self-esteem) against the cost of going back (death). For Cooper, the former outweighs the latter and he returns. It is a decision born totally of character. There is nothing external stopping him. No Indians on the warpath, no raging torrent, no broken bridge. It is totally internal.

Of course I doubt I'd ever write a character like Cooper's in *High Noon*. I'd write the characters who refuse to help Cooper, yes, but not Cooper himself. Penny Chapman (the Australian producer) once told me that I write about weakness and, at my best, I make weakness interesting. An alcoholic man, for example, (Stephen Graham in *The Street*) unable to open the front door to his Down's Syndrome son. Or a gay man (Stephen Graham again, this time in *Accused* (2010–2012)) murdering his wife because he lacks the courage to reveal his sexuality to her. A soldier (in *Accused*) unable to return fire when under attack.

I think writers understand weakness because we are full of it ourselves. Writers, for example, find it hard to say no. I do not know of any other profession that finds it so hard to turn people down, to disappoint people—particularly if those people are producers. I think it might be because we're so good at walking around in other people's shoes, imagining what it is like to BE other people, imagining what disappointment would DO to those people.

Q: Your identification with Gary Cooper is interesting as it points to the powerful effect writing can have on the viewer. I would like you to turn this on your own work. In Accused *it seems to me that you put a character in front of the viewer, but also invite them into a particular situation of judgement?*
Yes! 'There, but for the grace of God, go I.' I think THAT is what I want people to feel at the end of an *Accused* episode. 'If I had started off from where this character started off and if I had experienced the things that this character experienced, would I have acted any differently?'

Q: I want to push you on this to say something more generally about your reasons for bringing the viewer into these stories of crime and punishment, justice and judgement. Why it is important for viewers to ask the question 'would I have acted any differently?' Will this lead to more compassion or understanding? A better justice system? A better world?
The primary duty of any storyteller, I think, is to tell good stories and to tell them well. I think the answer to your question lies in the definitions of 'good story' and 'well'.

I remember as a kid I read a comic strip about a working-class man who saw a narrow, dismal room and was told that he would end his days there. He stole money to avoid that fate. And, of course, the narrow, dismal room turned out to be the cell in which he ended up. I remember being deeply affected by that story. I remember thinking how unfair it was. At the time I didn't realize that I was learning about 'tragedy', that I was learning that tragedy can strike the poorest of men just as easily as it can strike the likes of Oedipus.

It was a good story about a person with whom I could easily identify and, being a comic strip, it was told with great clarity and economy. At the end of it I'm sure I said, as kids throughout the ages have said, 'It's not fair!!!'

So maybe you're right: it's all about justice. But it's not necessarily 'justice' in the legal sense. It's justice in the sense of 'just deserts'. Did he deserve to (fill in the blank: win the woman, win the trophy, get away with the crime, lose his life)?

Q: So justice amounts to fairness. And is also linked to punishment. Can you tease out an example for me? The example is Johnjo in Common, *and especially the letter to the victim's mother. Was that about justice? Why was the admission of guilt important?*
I don't think there IS an admission of guilt. Okay Johnjo says that had he not been born he would not have been able to drive them that night but that hardly constitutes an admission of guilt. I think what Johnjo is doing is searching for ANY kind of guilt that will allow him to think—over the next four and a half years of incarceration—that he is there for a reason. I think Johnjo is doing it for himself here. But what for me (and for Johnjo's mother) is truly crucial is for Margaret Ward to believe that letter, to believe that he really did think he was going for a pizza, he really was ignorant of the other boys' plans for a showdown with an enemy.

Q: In the opening of Common *multiple characters say different things exploring different perspective on the same point. They speak over one another in a very choreographed way. I first noticed this kind of scene in* Hearts and Minds *(1995) when some key characters are in the pub debating whether or not to grass on (another) Johnjo, and the mate keeps on interjecting by saying, 'bollocks'. It's a really interesting way of representing discussion and debate. Not calm and cool, but passionate and anarchic. Are you conscious of this technique? Does it have a particular origin or has it just developed?*
Before I start on this topic, I'm not obsessed with class, honestly. But the British are.

In the fifties and sixties we played cricket in the street. We'd have a piece of wood for a bat and three bricks for the stumps. When the ball went anywhere near those stumps people would scream their appeals and you, the batsman, had to be equally as passionate when you screamed back at them: too high, too wide, whatever. The working-class trust passion far more than they trust reason. They know when passion is genuine and they know when it is artificial. But reason...

You'll remember I talked about middle-class critics thinking that a man saving a child from a burning house and then fearing he might lose his benefits because of it was 'ludicrous'. That's reason for you. It was 'reason' that, in the hungry 1930s here, introduced the means test. If you had, say, a fancy clock inherited from your parents and you also had hungry mouths to feed, you should sell that fancy clock before asking the state to help you. In David Cameron we have the most right-wing prime minister since Thatcher. He is slashing vital benefits and it will cost vulnerable people their lives but he is 'reason itself' every time he announces them.

I'm not saying that the British working-class cannot respond to 'sweet reason'. I'm saying they never actually hear it. All they get is the dominant ideology of the day—from newspapers, from the BBC, from the council official, from the copper, from the doctor, from the social worker...

Working-class people (Scousers particularly) never sit back and simply listen. Take a group of women, for instance. If one woman is talking the others will interject with 'yeah, yeah'—in other words 'carry on, we're following what you say'. Or they'll offer an occasional 'go 'way!'—in other words, 'That's amazing. Please carry on.' They support the other person in the telling of her story.

More so when they're not supporting but opposing. I have never in all my life heard an argument in which one person listens patiently and answers only when that other person has stopped. Never. Except on TV, of course. People talk across each other all the time. Particularly working-class people. And particularly in heated discussion.

This presents a problem to the writer who wants to write realism. It is absolutely essential to make your script as readable as it can possibly be—yet to render working-class speech realistically—with all its interruptions and hesitations, with all its passionate interjections and supportive comments—is to make your script unreadable.

You might get away with SOME of it if, like me, you've got a bit of a track record so readers might think it worthwhile to expend the effort but if you don't have a track record and you're writing like that, you have no chance of getting your script read properly.

Q: I'm interested in truth-telling as an ethics and as a practice of writing. Your commitment to truth-telling has taken numerous forms, most famously in terms of cases like the Hillsborough disaster and Bloody Sunday. In the context of Hillsborough *you formulated three rules of drama-documentary (McGovern 2004): (1) you don't write drama-docs to further your career. You write them because the victims or their families have asked you to write them; (2) the process of writing a drama-doc is as important as the drama-doc itself. It must empower the powerless; (3) those in power hate drama-docs, because the camera goes to places where they do not want it to go.*

But at the same time there are different kinds of truths. Emotional truths, historical truths, political truths—those you can live with and those you can't. And of course the deception and lies that go with them. And you need to bring the audience with you rather than adopt a dogma.

As a writer do you have to decide what kind of truth lies behind the story, and shape the story around it? Or does the truth come out of the story?

That's a difficult one. If you take Hillsborough and Bloody Sunday, you'll see that both events precipitated appalling lies. With Hillsborough the police said that the fans were pissed and riotous and what not and, with Bloody Sunday, the victims were said to be gunmen and nail bombers. In truth, only ONE of the Hillsborough victims was above the drink-driving limit (and he wasn't driving of course) and only one of the Bloody Sunday victims could be linked with a nail bomb (and even this was a very tenuous link).

Why did the police and the military lie to that extent? I think it was because the truth was so horrific (an 'appalling vista' to paraphrase Lord Denning). The truth, in the case of Hillsborough, was the police were so uncaring and reckless that 96 people were allowed to die—in full view and begging for help—with hardly one copper lifting a finger. In the case of Bloody Sunday the truth was even worse: that highly trained British soldiers murdered people on their streets.

The greater the atrocity, the greater the chance of public outcry, the greater the chance of people blatantly lying about it. So I think the first duty of a drama-doc is to set the record straight. And because the truth is so hard to take (our soldiers murdering people for no good reason save for the fact that they could—and our judiciary absolving those soldiers) the drama-doc itself is hard to take and often dismissed as 'polemic'. It is not polemical; it is not absurd, it is, as far as possible, the stating of the brutal truth.

Looking at *Hillsborough* again now and knowing what I know now, I would argue it is extremely restrained, extremely balanced. Similarly when *Sunday* was shown, people got upset over our depiction of the killings. Later Saville[6] vindicated us totally.

Q: I wonder when you write about the importance of a drama-doc stating the brutal truth, is this where dignity lies for you? In being able to live with the consequences of what has happened, of characters accepting the emotional truth as well as the truth as history will tell it. Is this why the families and victims are important, that it's not some truth 'out there'?

A journalist (I think it was Robert Crampton of *The Times*) said of the Hillsborough drama-doc that all involved in it seemed to accept that they had a duty to the dead, and that they carried out their duties extremely well. I think he got it right. We all felt an overwhelming sense of duty. More so because the dead had been so besmirched—'all drunk' in the case of Hillsborough, 'all gunmen' in the case of Bloody Sunday. The dead are no longer able to defend themselves so others have to do it for them.

The other thing to mention is LOVE. Yes, the families of the dead are dedicated to TRUTH and JUSTICE and the NEED FOR ACCOUNTABILITY, all those huge abstract nouns and phrases but, in truth, the Hillsborough campaign has been an outstanding demonstration of enduring love. Those people whom the media condemned ('hooligans' at Hillsborough, 'bombers' on Bloody Sunday) were no such thing. They were good people from good, loving families and the longer the campaign goes on, the more that goodness is exhibited, the more that love is demonstrated.

Another thing about TRUTH—the Hillsborough families have fought for almost 30 years now. Because of their fight there is a new inquest taking place as I write this. Do you know that in the last month or so, at this fresh inquest, many families heard for the very first time what exactly happened to their loved ones in the minutes leading up to their deaths? For the very first time! After almost 30 years of digging. And this truth was not covered up to spare the families pain (though it was painful for many of them to hear this truth at last). No, it was covered up to spare the authorities' embarrassment. And money…

Q: At the beginning of the interview you spoke of your commitment to working-class morality. At the same time, in your BAFTA screenwriting lecture you mention you occupy something of a privileged position with the broadcasters, because you have done this so well for so long. I'm interested in the responsibilities that come with writing that tries to give expression to working-class morality. You mentioned earlier that you were a bit worried being seen as a moral crusader. In your BAFTA screenwriting lecture you talk about witnessing a period in which working-class males were especially targeted by the left. How have things changed? Are there clichés to avoid? Or risks in this kind of writing? Is there too much focus on crime? On troublesome youth? Is there a risk of misrepresenting the working classes? Are there certain kinds of stories that simply aren't being told today? Or have things improved and are we seeing more diversity on the screen?

Turning the focus towards the broadcasting system and film industry, could they be doing more to support writers. Both those trying to maintain a position of ethical integrity. But also those trying to explore their class experience?

Only certain sections of the left attacked the white working class in the eighties. Not all of them.

I live in Liverpool but a lot of my stuff has been set in Manchester (35 miles away). I've been happy with that because Scousers are very sensitive about the way they and their city are portrayed and over the years I have taken plenty of criticism over it. However I'm getting less and less happy. Media City (in Salford, Greater Manchester) has had billions spent on it and is now the source of lots of very well-paid jobs. Nothing, however, has been spent in Liverpool. I think there is a huge moral issue here. Kirkdale in Liverpool (where we produce *Moving On* (2009–2015)) is one of the poorest communities in Western Europe. Don't I, therefore, have a duty to bring work to Kirkdale if I possibly can? Nothing to do with theme or content, this, I know, but it's always bothering me…

The big thing to avoid, of course, is sentimentality. It's too easy to put the working class on a pedestal. Proportionately there are just as many scumbags amongst the working class as there are amongst the aristocracy, I'm sure. But when a badly educated, skint, unemployed, working-class man rails against, say, asylum seekers and immigrants I find that more understandable than, say, well-educated, well-healed members of parliament passing racist laws.

Stories not being told today? I think drama doesn't tackle the so-called 'underclass'. Reality TV shows tend to do that—with predictable consequences. I think there is not enough attention paid to the financial consequences of decisions made by working-class characters. In my experience money often determines exactly what decisions are made. There would be no scabs if we all had enough money of our own. And the way working-class characters speak exercises me too. I personally make them just as articulate as anyone else. Because (in my experience) they ARE. One of my all time favourite scenes is that one in *Kes* (1969) in which the boy describes the way he has trained his hawk. It's wonderful.

I see a fair bit of a man called Tony Mulhearn. He was one of the driving forces on the Liverpool City Council that took on Margaret Thatcher in the eighties. The council lost, of course, and all its 47 members were thrown out of office. So much for local democracy. Anyway Tony said to me one day that I was one of the few writers in Britain today prepared to discuss politics. I told him he was wrong. I hardly ever discuss politics in drama but I am prepared to portray working-class characters in my drama, proper working-class characters, and this makes the drama SEEM political whereas, in the old days of Jim Allen [a socialist television writer, 1926–1999], etc., it would not have been considered political at all.

'Supporting writers'—I'm not sure about that. I think the main thing is to support storytellers and you do that by helping them to tell their stories in the best way possible. I'm getting more and more jealous of the American model: lock a load of writers in a room, let them map out every single beat of a story and then have them offer that storyline to an experienced writer and say to him/her, 'Now take this away and make it even better. Astonish us.'

Q: But I can see here a potential ethical dilemma: Which comes first, writing the good story or writing good working-class characters? Do you feel the pressure to give one up for the other? Or is the idea to find the balance between the two?
The story comes first. Always. I always say I reserve the right to tell a story simply because it's a good story. If it's a good story, to hell with the politics. I kept writing and rewriting Mary Queen of Scots and there was very little socialism in that but it WAS a great story.

Q: You have done quite a bit of mentoring of writers. From Dockers *to* The Lakes *(1997–1999) and* Redfern Now *(2012–2013). Is this an ethical commitment?*
I don't want to blow my own trumpet. Nobody bats an eyelid when a plumber/bricklayer/joiner passes on his knowledge to someone younger or less experienced. That passing on of knowledge has been part and parcel of working-class life since time began. How to hunt. How to farm. How to build. How to stay safe whilst doing it. I like to think that when I do my little bit I'm simply following a noble tradition.

I mentor other writers because I enjoy doing it. If I didn't enjoy it, I wouldn't do it. But to be honest I do see it as an ethical commitment as well. *Redfern Now* had an ethical dimension to it and—even though the British working-class have suffered nowhere near as much as Australia's Indigenous people—*The Street* and *Accused* had it too. It's great when an untutored, raw working-class person comes into the room with a great story to tell. You know you are in with a chance of changing someone's life for the better AND you'll end up with a great drama at the end of it all. Again the same proviso applies however: if a little rich kid entered the room with a great story, I'd help the little rich kid to tell it. The story must come first. The ethics and politics second.

NOTES

1. *The Guardian* is a politically left of center daily UK newspaper published with an intellectual tenor oriented to the professional middle class. The *Daily Mirror*, also a UK daily, casts itself as a tabloid and working-class paper.
2. What has become known as the Hillsborough disaster occurred in 1989, at a football game between Liverpool and Nottingham Forest, at Hillsborough Stadium, Sheffield, UK. A crowd crush resulted in the deaths of 96 fans and injury of countless others (see www.bbc.com/news/uk-19545126). A failure in police crowd control was seen as the main contributing factor, however, Liverpool fans were vilified by *The Sun* newspaper as hooligans who pick-pocketed the dead and obstructed police and aid workers.
3. 'Bloody Sunday' refers to an incident on 30 January 1972 in Londonderry, Northern Ireland, when British paratroopers opened fire on unarmed civilians during a protest march killing 13 and wounding 13 others. (see www.bbc.co.uk/history/bloody_sunday).
4. The Liverpool or Mersey Docks dispute lasted for two years and began on 28 September 1995 when 329 dockers were locked out of the Port of Liverpool after they refused to cross an unofficial picket line in solidarity with men from another company who had lost their jobs (see news.bbc.co.uk/2/hi/uk_news/50779.stm).
5. 'Joint enterprise laws' refer to laws in which criminal liability for an action can be extended to any member of a group involved in that enterprise.
6. Namely Lord Saville of Newdigate, who headed an inquiry into Bloody Sunday in 1998 and which reported its findings 12 years later.

REFERENCES

BAFTA. 2015. 'Jimmy McGovern delivers his Screenwriters' Lecture', 30 September. http://www.bafta.org/television/features/jimmy-mcgovern-delivers-his-screenwriters-lecture

Blandford, Steve. 2013. *Jimmy McGovern*. Manchester: Manchester University Press.

Maras, Steven. 2015. 'Jimmy McGovern through an Ethical Lens', *Journal of Screenwriting* 6 (2), 203–220.

McGovern, Jimmy. 2004. 'The Power of Truth'. *The Guardian*, 10 June. http://www.theguardian.com/film/2004/jun/10/features.features11

FILM AND TELEVISION REFERENCES

Accused. 2010–2012. Cr: Jimmy McGovern; UK, RSJ Films for BBC; c. 60 mins 10 eps.

Banished. 2015. Cr: Jimmy McGovern, UK, RSJ Films, See-Saw Films for BBC2; 60 mins 7 eps.

Brookside. 1982–2003. Cr: Phil Redmond & Colin McKeown; UK, Mersey Television for Channel 4; c 30 mins 2915 eps.

Common. 2014. Cr: Jimmy McGovern; Dir: Davis Blair, BBC1, UK, 90 mins. Script available at http://www.bbc.co.uk/writersroom/scripts/common

Cracker. 1993–1996. Cr: Jimmy McGovern; UK, Granada Television for ITV; 100 mins 24 eps.

Dockers. 2009. Wr: Jimmy McGovern, Irvine Welsh, et al., Dir: Bill Anderson, UK, 100 mins.

Hearts and Minds. 1995. Cr: Jimmy McGovern; UK, Alomo Productions/ WitzEnd Productions for Channel 4; 65 mins 4 eps.

High Noon. 1952. Wr: Carl Foreman, Dir: Fred Zinnemann, USA,

Hillsborough. 1996. Wr: Jimmy McGovern. Dir: Charles McDougall, UK, 101 mins.

Kes. 1969. Wr: Ken Loach, Tony Garnett. Dir: Ken Loach, UK, 110 mins.

Moving On. 2009–2015. Cr: Jimmy McGovern; UK, LA Productions for BBC. 45 mins 42 eps.

Priest. 1996. Wr: Jimmy McGovern, Dir: Antonia Bird, UK, 98 mins.

The Lakes. 1997–1999. Cr: Jimmy McGovern; UK, BBC and Company Pictures; 14 eps.

The Street. 2006–2010. Cr: Jimmy McGovern; UK, Granada Television for BBC; 60 mins 18 eps.

Sunday. 2002. Wr: Jimmy McGovern. Dir: Charles McDougall, UK, 109 mins.

Redfern Now. 2012–2013. Pr: Darren Dale and Miranda Dear; AUS, Blackfella films for ABC; 55 mins 12 eps.

PART II

Actuality and History

CHAPTER 5

ANZAC Girls: An Ethical Auto-analysis

Felicity Packard and Ben Stubbs

In the late thirteenth century William Wallace led the Scottish people in the First War of Independence against England, now an episode of pride and legend in Scotland. In 1995 Mel Gibson's *Braveheart* dramatized the events around William Wallace's journey to liberate Scotland. The film won commercial acclaim and five Oscars, however the historical liberties taken by the screenwriter Randall Wallace have left an indelible mark on the production. The *Braveheart* screenplay invented characters, relationships, customs and resolutions alongside material which is part of the historical record (McArthur 1998). It is from a cautionary tale such as this that our chapter finds its inspiration to discuss the ethical responsibilities of writing the historical screenplay.

F. Packard (✉)
Faculty of Arts and Design, University of Canberra, Canberra, ACT, Australia
e-mail: felicity.packard@canberra.edu.au

B. Stubbs
Journalism, University of South Australia, Adelaide, SA, Australia
e-mail: ben.stubbs@unisa.edu.au

© The Editor(s) (if applicable) and The Author(s) 2016
S. Maras (ed.), *Ethics in Screenwriting*, Palgrave Studies
in Screenwriting, DOI 10.1057/978-1-137-54493-3_5

This chapter uses the Australian series *ANZAC Girls* (2013), of which Felicity Packard was the lead writer and producer, as our case study. *ANZAC Girls* is a six-part drama series made by Australian production company Screentime for the Australian Broadcasting Corporation (ABC) which explores the important, but under-represented role of nurses in World War I. It dramatizes the lives of real people and is based on *The Other ANZACS—The Extraordinary Story of our World War I Nurses* (2008) by Peter Rees as well as on a variety of other historical sources. This auto-analysis offers an intimate understanding of the ethical responsibilities of the screenwriter in the representation of history. Of course, there are many understandings and versions of the screenwriter's responsibilities towards history. Some are focused on synthesizing archives and historical material, others on staying true to the broader themes at work and the process of creating a plausible, dramatic rendering of these. The case of *ANZAC Girls* provides a particular insight into the use of historical source material against the dramatic purpose of the screenplays and the framework which was used to navigate between the various ethical and historical questions raised during the process.

'ANZAC' is the acronym given to the Australian and New Zealand Army Corps who were among the Allied invasion force who landed on the Gallipoli Peninsula in Turkey on 25 April 1915. In Australia and New Zealand, the ANZAC landing is widely seen as a pivotal moment in the formation of a national identity distinct from their British colonial heritages. The term 'ANZAC' continues to have considerable social power in both countries, embodying the positive (moral) qualities of mateship, humour in the face of adversity, duty, endurance, sacrifice and courage. As a result of this social power, the representations of 'ANZAC' are held under much scrutiny and interest.

This chapter examines how concepts such as truthful representation, the double story and refraction can inform the writing of a screenplay that is both dramatically and commercially appropriate. It offers a particular perspective on the narrativization of history (see White 1973) from a screenwriting perspective. The screenwriter has the opportunity to represent history in new and valuable ways by virtue of the screenplay form's particular stylistic and aesthetic qualities. In our analysis of *ANZAC Girls* we draw on studies of ethics and representation in complementary disciplines to provide context and comparison. We also observe how, within this particular project, the screenwriter balanced considerations of truthful representation of historical events against the dramatic needs of the project by utilizing a four-part framework comprised of truthful representation, subjectivity, the double story and ethical dramatic construction. This essay introduces this framework and then uses *ANZAC Girls* as a case study in its application. We suggest that by writing within this framework, the *ANZAC Girls* screenplays offer insights into ethical representation of a particular history.

THE FORM OF HISTORY

In order to begin an analysis of screenwriting as a legitimate and ethical contributor to history, it is necessary to observe how the discipline of history has been challenged in the recent past. Much depends in this analysis of the responsibilities of the screenwriter on the form of history presumed to be most appropriate, as well as the model of historiography being proposed. In both areas, the terrain is complex and shifting, and we can only offer a partial view. In this section, we focus on the work of Hayden White, primarily because recent commentary on White's idea of history as a narrative form opens up useful links to screenwriting as a practice. We also draw on the work of Keith Jenkins, a contemporary British historiographer, to elaborate on a view of history writing as refraction.

Georg Iggers, Edward Wang and Supriya Mukherjee write that up until well into the twentieth century, 'historians shared the optimism of the professionalized sciences generally that methodologically controlled research makes objective knowledge possible' (2008, 1). This scientific conception of truth gave rise to the idea that it was possible to understand history as it had actually happened. As the perspectives of history broadened to include 'from below' analysis, subaltern studies and focus beyond the 'Great Men of History', historiography began to move away from the previous insistence on objectivity and empiricism (Iggers et al. 2008). In the second half of the twentieth century, and intertwined with these developments, the narrative and narratological practices of the discipline came into sharper focus. Hayden White with his 1973 work *Metahistory: The Historical Imagination in Nineteenth-Century Europe* stressed the plotmaking choices inherent in history writing. White's theory of the narrative quality of all historical works was a significant contribution to this focus on the plurality of history.

White noted that history writing contains 'a deep structural content which is generally poetic, and specifically linguistic, in nature, and which serves as the precritically accepted paradigm of what distinctively "historical" explanation should be' (1973, ix). Despite the resistance of many historians, this alerted practitioners in other fields such as ethnography, travel writing and film studies to the possible value of their 'poetic' and textually focused interpretations of history. Recently there has been a move towards the recognition of these alternative forms within 'post post-modernism' (Ankersmit et al. 2009), a term coined to suggest the future narrative and creative interpretations of history writing. Post post-modernism broadens the possibilities of what history is by acknowledging a plurality of voices and interpretations.

According to Frank Ankersmit, Ewa Domanska and Hans Kellner, White gave historians and writers new 'technical implements' with which to interpret history writing and it led to the discovery of a new intellectual universe of historical narrative (2009, 3). For Jenkins, history writing must rethink and expand its mode of representation. Jenkins insists that we 're-think that which we call a historical fact so that we understand that it is only a description of things that happened and which, therefore, cannot have an intrinsic meaning' (2003, x). Jenkins says that history writing should now focus on the new ways to construct its representation. The idea of construction here refers to the narrative structure (the organization of the plot) used to give the history meaning for the reader.

Just as with White's critique of the narrative structure of history, Jenkins' celebration of values of plurality and inclusiveness in history open up new possibilities for the screenwriter as historian. Jenkins asks for an openness with history that provokes 'radical readings and rereadings, writings and rewritings of the past' (2003, 3). Jenkins writes of the plausibility of artistic interpretations when he says that it is often expected that words or texts be 'true', though there is not the same expectation of a painting. He asks us to imagine the different interpretations of 'Gainsborough, Turner, Picasso, Warhol, Hockney—all painting the same people against the same, scenic backdrop' (2003, 55). We expect five very different points of view and stylistic interpretations. He then asks us to imagine asking five historians writing a history and asks why there is resistance to accepting these same differences in style and point of view within history.

Jenkins argues that our attitude towards new history writing should be 'refractive'; our view (from where we sit in time, culture, profession, etc.) will always give the past a sense of dislocation which we should embrace. Refraction is thus a key component to the ethical dramatization of history within a screenplay. This concept invites us to consider the negotiation which occurs between the research material and supplementary sources and dramatic needs of the project. Refraction furthers the understanding that a diversity of narratives presented to a reader can provide more complex and creative, and ultimately illuminating, versions of history.

Refraction is not just a question of perspective, but can also concern the medium with which history is constructed. In his 1995 article 'The Historical Film as Real History' Robert Rosenstone observes that many professional historians view the historical film with caution, highlighting the lack of control the historian has over the telling of history in film as a major reason for their unease: 'They (film makers) fictionalize, trivialize, and romanticize important people, events, and movements. They falsify History' (1995a, 1). Rosenstone contests this view in *History on Film/ Film on History*, suggesting that we 'who are called "postmodernist historians" … want our deep interest in and caring for the past to be expressed in forms congenial to both a contemporary sensibility and to intellectual forms consonant with our own era' (2012, 3).

Rosenstone examines genres such as history films, mini-series, documentaries and docudramas and asks why these forms cannot offer valid representations of history: 'To leave them out of the equation when we think of the meaning of the past is to condemn ourselves to ignore the way a whole segment of the population has come to understand the events and people that comprise history' (2012, 4). By way of an example, the 1981 film *Gallipoli* directed by Peter Weir, is a representation of history which uses research material, subjective interpretation and immersion to create a narrative that is intentionally shaped for its original late twentieth century audience. The film depicts the Australian experience leading up to the Battle of the Nek, where the 3rd Light Horse Brigade charged the narrow stretch of land on the Gallipoli Peninsula. *Gallipoli* not only examines issues of World War I and Australian soldiers, it refracts them through the style of a well-known director who implores us to question the on-going significance of these historical events.

Rosenstone argues that film 'emotionalizes, personalizes, and dramatizes history' (1995b, 59) and that this should not be seen as a restrictive practice, but rather as one that can broaden history. The diversity represented by different forms of histories are an important form of refraction. If someone gains their first understanding of the important role women played in World War I through watching *ANZAC Girls*, this is not necessarily a negative attachment. If this 'creative' history then prompts a reading of additional histories or women's roles in war to gain a broader understanding of a specific era or topic, then it has enriched their historical understanding. If a film is 'inspired by events' or 'based on real events', it is not necessarily a threat, as some historians would see it, but can be a further contribution to the mosaic of a particular history.

A Framework for Screenwriting as History

Rosenstone's claims for the director as the 'creator' of a film history, can, we believe, also be made for the screenwriter constructing the framework of the story, but this raises some key questions. What are the standards that screenwriters as historians should strive for? What are the criteria by which we should evaluate our work? How should we define, and then work within, our ethical, historical and creative responsibilities? Arising out of the experience of working on *ANZAC Girls*, we suggest that careful use of a framework of truthful representation (Berkhofer 1997), subjectivism (Ankersmit et al. 2009), the double story (Grafton 1997) and ethical dramatic construction (Beker 2004) can be used to evaluate and inform historically oriented screenwriting. This framework covers a variety of issues and subjects which articulate some of the key responsibilities of the screenwriter, on both ethical and dramatic levels.

Truthful Representation

The acceptance of the truthful representation by the reader is crucial to the recognition of a screenplay as a legitimate and ethical contribution. Robert Berkhofer (1997, 66) states that no work of history conveys only literal truth through factuality, and few fictional narratives depict only fantasy. Berkhofer says that historians claim the accuracy of their subjects and a fidelity to the past on the basis of documentary evidence—they do not create motivations or allude to acts without this evidence. Because of the selection and ordering of material it could be said that this is also a form of subjective history and it suggests that any narrative expression—such as a screenplay—that adheres to a conduct of truthfulness can make claims to validity. In other words, it is possible to believe in the 'truth' of a work if it adheres to this conduct. This also suggests that the truth of a work is dependent on the conduct of a subject (the screenwriter) much more than the qualities in an object, thus highlighting the responsibilities of the screenwriter if they hope their screenplay is regarded seriously.

Subjective Perspectives

Subjective perspectives acknowledge the place of the constructor within the work. Scholars have now come to accept the narrative nature of history, which can be subjective, against the notion of a singular 'truth' which previously clouded accounts of the past and the claim of objectivity. The key here is the conduct of the writer and the production team representing this truthfulness. Ankersmit argues that by accepting that there are different notions of 'truth' we can observe the validity of a subjective perspective in history writing: 'a political history of France in the eighteenth century does not contradict, but complements, an economic history of France in that same period' (2001, 78). Ankersmit continues, 'What is objective truth to one historian may well be a mere value judgment in the eyes of another historian' (2001, 80). He says there are three variants to be taken into consideration with the writing of history:

> First, it presents us with a *representation* of the past; second, this representation will consist of *true statements* embodying its cognitive pretensions; and third, though this may take different forms and may be more prominent in some cases that in others, *ethical rules and values* will codetermine the historian's account of the past. (2001, 95)

This provides clear suggestions for the writing of a particular history. The elements of representation, truth and adherence to certain ethical values offer different points of intersection for all writers of history, whether they are traditional historians, filmmakers or screenwriters and these ethical values, such as responsibility, reaction and fidelity to sources will differ depending on the medium.

Ankersmit affirms multiple representations of a history: 'If we were to possess only *one* representation of part of the past, we would be completely helpless to judge its scope' (2001, 96). From this statement it is possible to suggest that the screenwriter's account can be both an ethical and valuable addition to the narrative while extending the reach and perspective of a particular history.

The Double Story

A further aspect to consider when constructing a historical screenplay is the 'double story', a term coined by Anthony Grafton in *The Footnote*. The double story is the trust forged with the audience through the visibility of the research. 'Like the high whine of the dentist's drill, the low rumble of the footnote on the historian's page reassures' (1997, 5). It is not enough to recount months or years of archival work, it must be done in such a way that the reader or audience can participate and understand the history (and its perspective) through narrative and how this is synthesized within the narrative. Academic history writing is often preferred over other representations of history because it makes an appeal to evidence to distinguish it from other more popular forms. Within *The Footnote* Grafton gives a sophisticated theory of this rigorous method. He makes it clear that the double story that arises within academic history, firstly of the actual history and, secondly, of the accompanying footnotes which detail how the writer arrived at these points, are both narratives within the text.

Grafton suggests that the reliability of the double story within history writing is about how the writer persuades the reader to believe in the rigour of their method. This double story also allows the reader to check for themselves within the references. Grafton says that 'no two anthropologists will describe the same description of a transaction in identical categories' (1997, 15) and it is through this double story that the reader is able to understand how the writer arrived at their particular interpretation (whether it is history, anthropology or screenwriting). 'In practice, moreover, every annotator rearranges materials to prove a point, interprets them in an individual way, and omits those that do not meet a necessarily personal standard of relevance' (1997, 16). Grafton suggests that truth is achieved through the conduct of the subject, shown within a history as the 'proofs' of the validity of the work—an argument which opens up the possibility that screenwriting can also utilize this double story within history writing.

Screenwriters do not simply consult Wikipedia before launching into a historical screenplay (one hopes). The archival research in a project such as *ANZAC Girls* is immense and it is the screenwriter's job to demonstrate this evidence within the texture of the screenplay, whether this be through the use of text cards and titles to establish context or the broader faithful rendering of events to assure the audience of the writer's knowledge. There are numerous commercial, ethical and structural concerns for the screenwriter writing history and, as such, it is a more challenging process for the screenwriter to demonstrate their archival research in a way which respects the flow of the drama.

Ethical Dramatic Construction

Marilyn Beker's *Screenwriting with a Conscience* details how, for both moral and commercial reasons, screenwriters need to be aware of ethics when constructing a screenplay (2004, 10). Beker highlights 'why' as the most important question a screenwriter needs to ask themselves when constructing a screenplay which deals with real events. While there are considerations for structure and shape, when dealing with the stories and histories of people and places, the understanding of the enduring legacy of the work and the lasting imprint it could leave should factor in the screen-writer's considerations. When dramatizing 'real' events it is important to ensure the subject and the writer retain dignity and legitimacy to ensure the impact and reputation of the work so that the integrity of the adapted history may remain long after the writing process is completed.

AN ETHICAL AUTO-ANALYSIS

In this section, we examine how the four-part framework of truthful representation, subjectivity, the double story and ethical dramatic construction operated in the writing of *ANZAC Girls*. While focused primarily on the perspective of the screenwriter Felicity Packard, television is, however, a collaborative medium. Packard's was not the only voice in the creative and ethical debate about how history was represented in *ANZAC Girls*. Also deeply engaged were the second writer, Niki Aken, series producer Lisa Scott, and executive producers from both Screentime and the ABC, Greg Haddrick and Des Monaghan, and David Ogilvy and Carole Sklan respectively. Hence the use of collective pronouns in the discussion that follows.

ANZAC Girls is based on the lived experiences of five young women (four Australians and one New Zealander) who served with the Australian Army Nursing Service (AANS) in World War I. The inspiration for the show came from the desire to make a drama for the centenary of World War I, but with a point of difference. The experiences of Australia's military nurses of World War I are somewhat neglected by both historians and popular culture (Rogers 2003; Hallett 2009; Harris 2011). Our primary source materials were the five nurses' war diaries and letters, and the book *The Other ANZACS—The Extraordinary Story of Our World War I Nurses* by Peter Rees. The competing concerns operating on our creative choices included the desire to accurately represent the nurses' representations of themselves; sensitivity towards the nurses' families and their concerns about how their deceased relatives would be represented; awareness that in making a drama based on real events we would be making substantial truth claims which would invite scrutiny; and, the need to create a work that met the episodic structural conventions and commercial expectations of a mainstream television drama.

Truth Claims and the Double Story

Before the commencement of the title sequence, every episode of *ANZAC Girls* is preceded by the following card of text:

This drama is based on the lives of real people. Certain characters, events and timelines have been created or changed for dramatic effect.

This card is the first statement about our approach to the dramatization of the past and is integral to our ethical construction of history. This disclaimer predated production and was negotiated through several drafts. The ABC has a substantial 'Factual Drama Policy' which addresses key editorial standards including the possible need for 'appropriate labels of other explanatory information' which seek to avoid presenting factual information in a way that 'will materially mislead the audience' (ABC, 2011). The disclaimer's first sentence makes a truth claim about the actuality of the events and people to be represented. The second sentence then disclaims absolute actuality, acknowledging the consciously fictive elements inherent in that representation. Both sentences commence the double story, which invites the audience to gauge the reliability of our representation. Though based on real events *ANZAC Girls* is not a documentary,[1] nor, as this card makes apparent, does it claim to be one. Indeed, this pre-title 'disclaimer' specifically foregrounds the combination of fact and fiction that informs our representation of history.

Following the title sequence but before the drama, every episode of *ANZAC Girls* is preceded by one, two or three 'cards' of text that place the events to follow in historical context.

Following the outbreak of World War I, the Australian Army Nursing Service was hastily deployed. (episode 1, pre-drama card #1)

Post-drama cards also appear at the conclusion of some episodes where the events that have been depicted in the preceding drama are supported and expanded upon:

In May 1916, Matron Grace Wilson was awarded the Royal Red Cross 1st Class for her management of No. 3 Australian General Hospital on Lemnos. (episode 3, post-drama card #2)

As with the truth (dis)claimer card, all pre- and post-drama cards were not post-production additions to the screen. All had been part of the screenwriters 'work' in the screenplay through the drafting process. Along with providing factual information and historical context, the pre- and post-drama cards also operate as part of the ethical framework around which our representation of history is built. The cards make explicit that the particular lens with which *ANZAC Girls* examines and dramatizes World War I is female- and nurse-focused. The (male) ANZAC soldiers' experiences at the Gallipoli campaign and the Western Front are part of an already well-known historical narrative in both Australia and New Zealand (De Vries 2013); these cards highlight that *ANZAC Girls* offers an alternative history about the war that privileges women's experiences.

At points in some episodes, text is also superimposed at the bottom of the screen, over the action. The following three 'supers' appear at the end of episode 5, as one of our primary characters, Sister Olive Haynes, leaves No. 1 Australian General Hospital (AGH) in Rouen, France for the last time:

Olive Haynes married Pat Dooley in England in December 1917.

Olive returned to Australia in February 1918, working on a hospital ship.

The Army did not pay her for this service.

These 'supers', and others like them used in the series, add to and expand on the main narrative, supporting the overall truth claims of the representation and activating Grafton's 'double story' (1997). They invite the viewer to check the facts for themselves, constructing a secondary narrative that moves with, but differs from, the primary story and signal a desire to avoid deceiving or misleading the audience. Along with the disclaimer and pre- and post-drama cards, these text-on-screen supers also produce, following Beker, an ethical dramatic construction of history, building on and enhancing the reliability of the *ANZAC Girls* version of World War I. They help the audience to trust that the version of history represented in *ANZAC Girls* is truthful. They offer the audience warranty that the storylines that seem like 'fictions' possess historical authenticity. The truth claim for *ANZAC Girls* was an essential element in how the series was promoted and marketed as well as for its legacy as a historical document. The double story embodied in the cards and supers reminds audiences accustomed to fictional narratives that the people and events they are seeing represented on screen are drawn from lived experiences.

The double story in *ANZAC Girls* also addresses any accusation that we were freely inventing material, and playing fast and loose with events and timelines for purely dramatic purposes. The cards and supers are not offered as exhaustive proof of every assertion made by, or implicit in, the screenplay. They are instead supporting evidence of the historical actuality of the events depicted, offered in a such way that does not 'break the fourth wall' or take a viewer 'out of the drama' with a documentary history lesson. Operating within the conditions outlined by the pre-title disclaimer, the pre- and post-drama cards and supers offer the audience reassurance that the representation of history *ANZAC Girls* offers is not misleading; that it is a valid representation of past events and people.

Ethical Dramatic Construction

One of the most serious deviations from historical fact is the changing of a player's name, the alteration of an identity. Yet in order to satisfy our ethical representation of the ANZAC nurse's stories we took the decision to change a character's name. While reading the journal of Sister Alice Ross King, another of our primary characters, we came across the following entry. Alice was working in Cairo at the time.

> 1st March,
> Claude was telling me of a nice clean boy of ours who was put in a tent with a venereal case and has caught gonoreal [sic] conjunctivitis. His eyes are running with pus and he is almost sure to lose the sight of them both. The sad part of it was that the nurse (Miss Samsing) objected to nurse him for fear her own eyes become infected. I'm really longing to nurse that man and perhaps save his eyesight. This wretched woman made a fuss and would not go in the boy's tent—I could slay her. (Ross King 1915)

This is a very appealing incident for a screenwriter. Firstly, it shows the nurses as multidimensional, flawed characters. Following on from this, it contests the prevailing 'ministering angel' image of World War I nurses of popular sentiment (Harris 2011). Moreover, it comes straight from the diary of one of our main historical figures and speaks of her strong attitude and character. It also gives a different perspective on the war and opens up an instance of nursing that does not involve war wounds, but raises instead the huge challenge to the army that was venereal disease.

The incident was, however, reportage and our central character was not directly involved. Our first decision was to put our character Alice working in the venereal disease ward in order for her to become a direct witness to, indeed, a participant in, the incident. This conflation and restructuring of an event and its participants is standard practice in adaptation (Portnoy 1998) where the adapting writer faces the challenge to ensure 'the original material work(s) within a tight dramatic structure' (Portnoy 1998, 5).

In the first draft of the screenplay, the incident and players were represented thus:

INT. NO. 1 AGH/VD CORRIDOR - DAY

                    ALICE

Why haven't you cleaned his eyes?

ALICE has cornered SISTER SAMSING in the corridor. SISTER

SAMSING is somewhat defensive.

                    ALICE (CONT'D)

Private Leigh's your patient. Why haven't you cleaned his

eyes in two days?

SISTER SAMSING says nothing. ALICE is livid. Calm, but livid.

                    ALICE (CONT'D)

Sister Samsing?

                    SISTER SAMSING

         (bursts out)

Do you know how infectious gonorrheal conjunctivitis is?!

The slightest transfer of matter and my own eyes could be

at risk...!

ALICE stares at her, appalled.

                    SISTER SAMSING (CONT'D)

The orderlies should work this ward. We shouldn't have to

risk our health with these filthy men, their filthy

habits...

                        ALICE

    Private Leigh isn't 'filthy', he's a nice clean boy who

    contracted VD from using his tent-mate's towel. As you

    could have discovered if you'd actually bothered to talk

    to him!

SISTER SAMSING reacts - but the best defense is attack.

                    SISTER SAMSING

    Yes, well, we're not all of us coquettes with the

    patients like you Sister Ross King.

                        ALICE
    I beg your pardon?

                    SISTER SAMSING
    Being familiar with the men, glad eyeing every
    officer...you'dthink we were at war just so you can play
    the field!

ALICE is furious but she's also taken aback because there could
be some truth. But she recovers. Leans in close, practically
nose to nose.

                        ALICE

    I could slay you. Keep your rotten eyes closed.

This sees the dialogue for both characters drawn to a large extent from the diary entry and as such operates within Berkhofer's standard of truthful representation in that we have documentary evidence for the event and motivations we ascribe. Sister Hilda Samsing nursed with the AANS in World War I, serving on hospital ships as well as in Cairo, and later in London. She was a person of clearly very strong views, describing (in her diary) the British High Command during the disastrous Gallipoli campaign as 'those inhuman monsters' and calling for them to be sacked (Samsing, quoted in De Vries 2013, 112). The Australian Army saw venereal disease as a moral issue rather than a medical one, and the tens of thousands of men who became infected were regarded by High Command as 'rotten' and 'swindlers' with their pay stopped for the duration of their absence from duty (Rees 2008, 48).

Representing this incident was complex. We took the decision to give Sister Samsing the fictional name 'Sister Halliwell' which is how the character appears in the finished episode. Beker says that in order to ensure their work is ethical 'screenwriters who want to include controversial material must first examine their motives for doing so' (2004, 10). Refusing to nurse a patient is clearly a controversial incident and my evidence for it is hearsay—it is Alice's representation of what someone else has told her about a third person. The real Sister Samsing was a decorated nurse, whose service in the AANS is discussed extensively by historians (De Vries 2013; Harris 2011). To represent the historical Sister Samsing in what amounts to dereliction of duty, would have been to move beyond allowable subjectivism. The decision to fictionalize the character is encompassed by the fourth element of the framework that informed our representation of history: 'ethical dramatic construction'. Beker says that 'everything that appears in a screenplay should be considered in context and by the seeming intent of the scriptwriter' (2004, 10). To have taken Sister Samsing out of context would have been, we felt, ethically unjustifiable.

Had *ANZAC Girls* been Sister Samsing's story we would have had the opportunity to explore and dramatize the deeper motivations for her attitude to the gonorrhoeal conjunctivitis sufferer and fear for her eyesight. But she was, at best, a supporting player. Thus, in order to retain the incident, but treat the players within it in an ethical manner, we decided to avoid any inference that the nurse depicted was Sister Samsing.

Another alternative was of course, to drop the gonorrhoeal conjunctivitis incident altogether. But leaving aside the practical implications of reduced content and subsequent storytelling problems, to have ignored the 'refusal to nurse' incident and its examination of differences in the nurses' professionalism and attitudes would have been to homogenize and sanitize our representation of what were in actuality, complex human beings operating in a complex world (Harris 2011). Fidelity to and concern for an ethical representation of the past can and should involve looking beyond the facts, and include a consciousness of the period's complexity of milieu. By changing and creating events and characters in the way we did in this sequence, we were able to represent a version of World War I nurses that told a larger truth than just that available to us had we adhered strictly to the primary evidence of Alice Ross King's diary.

Subjective Perspectives

A final example of how we sought to represent a version of history that was engaging and 'refractive' (Jenkins 2003, 55), while also treating the real events and people on which it was based in an ethical manner, played out in the final episode of the series. The following entries come from the diary of another of our primary sources and major characters, Sister Elsie Cook. Elsie had joined the AANS in 1914 under her maiden name, as nurses were not permitted to be married. After having been forced to resign from the AANS in 1916, Elsie returned to the war, nursing with the Red Cross in various hospitals across France. Her husband was Sydney Cook, son of the former Prime Minister of Australia, Sir Joseph Cook. Syd had been wounded twice at Gallipoli (once very seriously) but had continued to serve in frontline duties.

> 27th December
> A letter from Syd and such a miserable one too—that is, in between the lines, writing on his knee with a candle on his tin helmet, in a ruin of an old chateau freezing with cold—poor old chap and going into the line. (Cook 1917)
> 5th June
> A very important document from the High Commissioner's office to say that Mr Cook was expected to arrive in England any day after 13th June—three letters from Syd all dwelling on the all important subject of leave for Blighty. Very awkward and difficult to arrange just at this moment, with so much to be done. (Cook 1918)
> 11th June
> A letter from Syd which again speaks of leave when the Pater arrives but my chance of leave looks pretty poor. (Cook 1918)
> 14th June
> Mr Cook arrived in London today. Got a letter from Syd to say he expected to go on leave today—the letter was written a week ago. Although I shouldn't, I asked for leave to go to England tomorrow. (Cook 1918)

These entries and several others like them were appealing as drama for two reasons. Firstly, they give an indication of the stress that Sydney Cook was under after three or more years at war. Secondly, and more significantly, they indicate the tension Elsie felt at her divided loyalties between her role as a wife and daughter-in-law, and her job as a nurse. This is the scene dramatizing the 'leave' issue alluded to by the entries:

INT. OFFICERS' HOSPITAL/ELSIE & FRASER'S ROOM (AMIENS) - NIGHT

SYD strides into the room, excited, up-beat.

                          SYD

    Have you had your leave for London approved yet?

ELSIE follows, closing the door behind her.

                          ELSIE

                  (beat)

    Not yet.

                          SYD

    Well it won't be a problem...

He pulls out a LONDON GUIDEBOOK (circa 1917), starts flipping.

                          SYD (CONT'D)

    Father's going to have a word to the head of the Croix

    Rouge, pull a few strings. Now, I've circled the places

    we should visit. Thought we'd start with the galleries

    then go onto Covent Garden...

But ELSIE is stunned by his earlier information.

                          ELSIE

    Your father's writing on my behalf?

SYD nods, smiles, keeps flipping...

                    ELSIE (CONT'D)

I do wish he wouldn't.

                    SYD

                    (smiles)

Not feeling squeamish over a bit of queue jumping are

you...?

                    ELSIE (OVER)

No -

SYD hasn't picked up on her tension. Teasing:

                    SYD

...because you've certainly never scrupled to play the

'my father-in-law is Sir Joseph Cook' card before!

(Syd isn't being deliberately cruel; he's just excited - on top

of being a typical unreconstructed upper middle class early

20th century man.)

ELSIE says nothing, turns away to hide her anger.

                    SYD (CONT'D)

Something wrong?

                    ELSIE

              (turns back)

I told you - with the big push on, things are very busy

at the hospital right now. They'll be hard pressed

without me.

                    SYD

Hard pressed?

              (a smile)

Are you sure? You're only a nurse.

On ELSIE, stunned, as the unintended slap in the face hits. It

takes her a beat to find her voice. And when she does, though

calm, she's as angry as we've ever seen her.

                    ELSIE

Only a nurse or not, now's not the time for me to go

gallivanting off to London.

              (an edge)

Even though I am 'only a nurse'...

SYD's getting angrier too now.

                        SYD

For goodness sake, I'm not saying they don't value you,

but I can't believe there's no-one else who can fill your

shoes.

                        ELSIE

And I can't believe that you expect me just to come to

your beck and call -!

                    SYD (CUTS IN)

Alright, alright!...Just seems a bit off, putting

your...(work)... what you do, ahead of us.

                (sadder; quieter)

We don't get many chances to be together.

He's hurting. His excitement drops away revealing that he's

utterly weary, utterly worn. And now ELSIE's dudgeon evaporates

and she comes to stand beside him.

                        ELSIE

And I would love to take this one. But I can't.

                    (beat)

I know you need me. But I truly believe that right now

I'm needed more here.

```
SYD's not convinced, but he's got no energy to argue. He puts
his guidebook back in his pocket.
```

```
ELSIE is miserable, their evening spoiled. And she's troubled -
there's a gap between them that's never been there before.
```

As evidenced in her diary, Elsie did, in reality, apply for and take leave to visit her father-in-law in London as her husband urged. But in our version of history we had her refuse, a decision to depart from the documentary evidence whose ethics required careful reflection. Like all our five primary historical subjects, Elsie Cook has living descendants with whom we were in contact during our research. The Cook family, like the families of the other nurses, were delighted that their grandmother's war service was to be celebrated on screen; but were also clearly concerned that she (and their grandfather) be represented ethically in a medium which has a reputation for using 'history … [as] just another tool for selling tickets' (Rosenstone 2012, 2). Inventing a serious 'gap' between these real people had to measure up against a stronger ethical framework than simply providing a lovers' tiff for the sake of dramatic conflict. Beker stresses that in order to assert that their work is ethical, it is critical that a screenwriter reflect not only on what they are saying but also on why they are saying it and strive to ensure what they say is what they actually believe (Beker 2004). We felt it was, in this instance, ethically responsible and justifiable to deviate from a literal representation of the events in our primary source (Elsie's diary) in order to make two larger points, to access and represent other historical 'truths'. The first is that nursing was, in World War I, a marginalized and little understood profession (Hallett 2009; De Vries 2013). Moreover, nurses often experienced substantial prejudice from officers and the Army hierarchy and were paid less than half the rate of untrained male orderlies (Rees 2008, xv). Having Elsie resist, in some small but significant way, an attack on her profession and identity outside of that related to her marriage, represented a refraction from the source material that we believe is valid. Like creatively adapting the gonorrhoeal conjunctivitis incident, it allowed for a legitimate plurality of histories and also speaks to the broader theme of the series which is based on a larger and, in this context, more important 'truth'. Moreover, various others of Elsie's diary entries do hint at occasional tension with Syd.

5th November
A letter from Syd (didn't like it).
(Cook 1917)

This brief allusion is tantalizing for a screenwriter, and while Elsie does not disclose the precise source of her frustration, the entry and others like it suggest that she was not always in complete harmony with her husband. This informed our decision to adapt the 'leave' debate in the way we did. Communication with their relatives had indicated that Elsie and Syd's relationship was not always perfectly harmonious. Thus we did not misrepresent them, nor the family's memories of them. Throughout the previous episodes of *ANZAC Girls*, in keeping with the evidence from Elsie's diary, we had represented Elsie and Syd as multidimensional people, and dramatized their deep attachment to each other. Adapting this 'leave' incident was not to suggest anything ethically problematic about them or their relationship—we were not inventing an infidelity, or a pregnancy or even a missed birthday.

Deviating from the source material (i.e. seeing Elsie and Syd in conflict) allowed us to explore and expose a second generic, historical 'truth'. As discussed earlier, rethinking history writing allows for a realism achieved by 'mimetic illusion' (Ankersmit 2001, 61). The reality embodied in the mimetic illusion of this conflict between Elsie and Syd is that the real source of the conflict is their prolonged war service. It is their nearly five years of constant exposure to the horrors of war that is driving this wedge between them and taking the toll on their intimacy. The ongoing, cumulative psychological and emotional damage done by their years of protracted front-line service (Bassett 1992; Harris 2011) was another aspect of the nurses' lived experiences we felt it was ethically critical to represent. In order to do so, while writing an effective screenplay that remained focused on our chosen historical figures, we departed from our primary source and 'invented' an element of what the series makes a generalized truth claim for.

CONCLUSION

Michael Hirst, writer of the feature films *Elizabeth*, *Elizabeth: The Golden Age*, and creator and writer of the TV series *The Tudors* and *Vikings*, says in relation to challenges of representing history on screen: 'What you're looking for is not historical accuracy—in any case there is no such thing as historical accuracy because otherwise all historians would agree. What you're looking for is authenticity, is plausibility, is consistency and hopefully some truth' (Hirst, in Taylor 2015). Just how a screenwriter may make ethical claims of having achieved 'some truth', when working in a form renowned more for narrative expediency than historical veracity, has formed the subject of this chapter. Each screenwriter writing history needs to weigh the needs of story against the demands of historical facts— and there is no ready measure. The balance shifts from screenplay to screenplay, from incident to incident; indeed, as shown in our analysis of *ANZAC Girls*, even from scene to scene. And attendant on every decision the screenwriter writing the historical screenplay makes are ethical responsibilities. We have sought to explore some of those ethical responsibilities, investigating how, in the writing of *ANZAC Girls*, screenwriting as history can be a creative and narrative form which operates within ethical boundaries while also extending both the reach and possibilities for retelling history.

Each historical event presents the screenwriter with its own unique creative and research challenges arising from knowledge gaps, subjectivity and temporal distance. Similarly, each historical event presents the screenwriter with its own unique set of ethical challenges. Considerations of gender, race, class, sexuality and geography (to cite but a few) may all impact upon the screenwriter's creative and interpretative decisions. The field is wide open for further research into the ethical considerations concomitant with screenwriters dramatizing different histories and how those considerations influenced what actually ended up on the page. Via our auto-analysis of the writing of the World War I drama *ANZAC Girls* we have discussed the ethical framework that worked for us. This framework, comprised of four key elements—truthful representation, subjectivity, the double story and ethical dramatic construction—supported the creation of ethically sound historical screenplays. Our framework is not exhaustive; commercial constraints and differences in approaches to production may see future screenwriters adapting it or applying it in different ways. The auto-analysis of the screenplays for *ANZAC Girls* demonstrates the ways in which one screenwriter writing history sought to represent past events and people in an ethically rigorous way that permitted legitimate truth claims while also allowing for the production of dramatically appropriate screenplays. We believe that approaching writing history via this framework, resulting screenplays have the potential to enrich the discipline of history writing, particularly during its current era of rethinking (Jenkins 2003; Ankersmit et al. 2009). We also believe that future screenwriters writing history may find our framework useful as they consider the ethical challenges of dramatizing historical actualities within their own work.

Note

1. Such disclaimers are not unusual; indeed they have become a kind of trope, attached to many screen narratives to convey a sense of legitimacy and reality to content whose connection to historical events may be somewhat tenuous, such as *Wolf Creek*, *Fargo* and *The Blair Witch Project*.

References

Ankersmit, Frank. 2001. *Historical Representation*. Stanford: Stanford University Press.
Ankersmit, Frank, Domanska, Ewa, and Hans Kellner. eds. 2009. *Re-figuring Hayden White*. Stanford: Stanford University Press.
Australian Broadcasting Corporation (ABC). 2011. *ABC Editorial Policies Guidance Note: Factual Drama*.
Bassett, Jan. 1992. *Guns & Brooches—Australian Army Nursing from the Boer War to the Gulf War*. London: Oxford University Press.
Beker, Marilyn. 2004. *Screenwriting with a Conscience: Ethics for Screenwriters*. Mawhaw: Lawrence Erlbaum Associates.
Berkhofer, Robert. 1997. *Beyond the Great History: History as Text and Discourse*. Harvard: Harvard University Press.
Cook, Elsie. 1914–1918. *Diaries*, AWM 2DRL/1085, Canberra: Australian War Memorial.
De Vries, Susanna. 2013. *Australian Heroines of World War One—Gallipoli, Lemnos and the Western Front*. Brisbane: Pirgos Press.
Grafton, Anthony. 1997. *The Footnote*. New York: Faber & Faber.
Hallett, Christine. 2009. *Containing Trauma—Nursing Work in the First World War*. Manchester: Manchester University Press.
Harris, Kirsty. 2011. *More than Bombs and Bandages—Australian Army Nurses at Work in World War I*. Sydney: Big Sky.
Iggers, Georg, Wang, Edward and Suriya Mukherjee. 2008. *A Global History of Modern Historiography*. New York: Pearson Education.
Jenkins, Keith. 2003. *Rethinking History*. New York: Psychology Press.
McArthur, Colin. 1998. 'Braveheart and the Scottish Aesthetic Dementia'. In *Screening the Past: Film and the Representation of History*, edited by Tony Barta, 167–87. Westport: Praeger.
Packard, Felicity. 2013. *ANZAC Girls* [Screenplays]. Screentime Pty Ltd.
Portnoy, Kenneth. 1998. *Screen Adaptation—A Scriptwriting Handbook*. Boston: Focal Press.
Rees, Peter. 2008. *The Other ANZACs—The Extraordinary Story of our World War I Nurses*. Sydney: Allen & Unwin.

Rogers, Anna. 2003. *While You're Away—New Zealand Nurses at War 1899–1948*. Auckland: Auckland University Press.

Rosenstone, Robert. 1995a. 'The Historical Film as Real History'. In *Film-Historia*, Vol. V, No. 1, edited by R. Rosenstone, 5–23. Barcelona: Film History research Centre.

Rosenstone, Robert. 1995b. *Visions of the Past: The Challenges of Film to Our Idea of History*. Cambridge: Harvard University Press.

Rosenstone, Robert. 2012. *History on Film/Film on History*. New York: Longman/Pearson.

Ross King, Alice. 1914–1918. *Diaries*. AWM PR02082, Canberra: Australian War Memorial.

Taylor, Andrew. 2015. 'Why *Wolf Hall* gets it Right and *Mad Men* is Wrong: History on TV.' *The Age*, April 10, Accessed 10 April 2015. http://www.theage.com.au/entertainment/tv-and-radio/why-wolf-hall-gets-it-right-and-mad-men-is-wrong-history-on-tv-20150408-1m8biq.html

White, Hayden. 1973. *Metahistory: The Historical Imagination in Nineteenth-Century Europe*. Baltimore: Johns Hopkins University Press.

FILM AND TELEVISION REFERENCES

ANZAC Girls. 2014. Wr: Felicity Packard, Niki Aken; Dir: Ken Cameron, Ian Watson; Screentime Pty. Ltd., for Australian Broadcasting Corporation, Australia, 57 mins. x 6 eps.

Braveheart. 1995. Wr: Randall Wallace, Dir: Mel Gibson, US, 178 mins.

Gallipoli. 1981. Wr: Peter Weir, David Williamson; Dir: Peter Weir, Australia, 110 mins.

CHAPTER 6

The Ethics of Actuality in the Scripting of Enrique Rosas's *The Gray Automobile*

María Teresa DePaoli

This chapter tackles the problem of how to make ethical judgements regarding actuality in nonfiction film where the conditions of actuality are fluid and complex issues of power and genre traverse the line between fact and fiction. It also shows how historical and archival research can inform ethical analysis. Considered the most prominent and accomplished film of Mexico's silent period, Enrique Rosas's *The Gray Automobile* (1981 [1919])[1] reached global attention because of its blend of fact and fiction (reality and fabrication), including footage of a real firing squad execution. It combines popular characteristics in international cinema: Italian historical epics, the French crime serials, and the developing Hollywood model (Ramírez Berg 2000).[2] Although Rosas's work has been discussed in terms of norms of objectivity, it can also be seen as political propaganda

M.T. DePaoli (✉)
Department of Modern Languages, Kansas State University,
Manhattan, KS, USA
e-mail: mmtzotz@ksu.edu

© The Editor(s) (if applicable) and The Author(s) 2016
S. Maras (ed.), *Ethics in Screenwriting*, Palgrave Studies
in Screenwriting, DOI 10.1057/978-1-137-54493-3_6

intended to sway public opinion. While John Grierson coined the term 'documentary' in 1926, Rosas's work can also be characterized as an incipient form of journalistic documentary since early cameramen, such as Rosas, were often perceived as a type of film reporter. These pioneers initially focused on the Lumière-style actualities (brief documentaries, or *vistas* in Spanish) that, unlike later more developed documentaries, were 1–2 minutes long. The *Gray Automobile* follows, in great part, the techniques used in actualities.

The ethical implications associated with the nonfiction film elements in Rosas's prose-based treatment, and in the surviving film have not been explored until now. The shooting script of the film, written by Rosas with the help of poet Juan Manuel Ramos, is lost, but there are a few original intertitles of this text kept by Rosas's granddaughter, Lourdes Rosas Priego (see Islas 2004). All of the existing intertitles are almost identical to certain passages in Rosas's prose-based treatment of 57 pages, available in *El automóvil gris* (1919): *Guiones del cine mexicano* (1981). Therefore, it is plausible to assume that the entire shooting script might have respected Rosas's treatment.

Rosas's project oscillates between fact and fiction, journalism and film narrative and, as such, it actively blurs boundaries. In *Blurred Boundaries: Questions of Meaning in Contemporary Culture* (1994), Bill Nichols discusses the importance of context to the understanding of historical social realities. Although some film critics believe that representing reality is impossible, asserting that 'there is no such thing as documentary,' Nichols stresses that while borders and classifications exist, 'the categories and boundaries surrounding documentary and reality, fact and fiction, defy hard and fast definition' (Nichols 1994, xiii). I focus on the fluidity of *The Gray Automobile* and its resistance to categorization as fiction or nonfiction film by taking into account the historical period during which it was produced.

The promotional publications of *The Gray Automobile* in 1919 imply that it was the faithful recreation of the historical facts surrounding the case of a famous gang of thieves. Rosas's aim was arguably also to vindicate the powerful 'Carrancista'[3] General Pablo González,[4] who was allegedly implicated in the gang's criminal activities. Thus, Rosas's work can be categorized as a work of persuasion. From this perspective, I focus on analysing *The Gray Automobile* as an ethical case study in fabrication. I examine Rosas's treatment in connection to claims made during the advertising and exhibition of the movie that *The Gray Automobile* was created to unveil the truth about the 'Gray Automobile Gang'—the name attributed to a famous group of thieves that terrorized Mexico City in 1915. I emphasize the tensions that exist between objectivity and fiction in Rosas's work in light of corruption and political interests invested in the project. I argue that *The Gray Automobile* treatment is shaped by the tight control that the government had over Mexico's film industry at that time. Finally, I discuss the inclusion of the firing squad execution from an ethical perspective. While several critics have discussed the altered historical facts concerning the Gray Automobile Gang in Rosas's film, I focus on the axis of objectivity and fabrication in Rosas's prose-based treatment, as the project was originally conceived as a form of journalistic documentary. In order to establish the basis of my analysis, I will also discuss Rosas's probable motivations, the historical facts surrounding the 'Gray Automobile Gang', and General Pablo González's political ambitions.

DOCUMENTARY, PROPAGANDA AND NEWSREEL

Co-existing with the Mexican Revolution of 1910, the nascent film industry was awakening to a new form of popular entertainment. Moisés Viñas documented in *History of Mexican Cinema* (1987) that people in Mexico relied on travelling *vistas* for information on the war. Emilio García Riera explains in his *Brief History of Mexican Cinema* (1998) that in Mexican early cinema *vistas* used footage of real events, places and things, and generally were not edited or structured into a larger argument (García Riera 1998, 27). In *The Origins of Cinema in Mexico (1896–1900)*, Aurelio de los Reyes underscores that 'films had an itch for objectivity; filmmakers had a desire to rely on reality, making the editing a rigorous process concerning location and chronological order' (2013, 47). Rosas emerged from this local filmmaking tradition, characterized by a demand for realism and an appetite for Mexican images (Ramírez Berg 2000, 3–4).

Enrique Rosas (1875–1920)—along with Salvador Toscano and Carlos Mongrand—was among the most active pioneers of Mexican cinema, introducing the Pathé projector. Rosas and Mimí Derba founded the first Mexican Film Company, *Azteca Films*. One of the first filmmakers to document noticeable historical events since the final decade of Porfirio Díaz's dictatorship,[5] he filmed various activities of President Díaz. He soon realized that it was best to travel—with his portable camera—in the train with Díaz in order to film whole presidential journeys. As Carl Mora has pointed out, 'filmmaking was limited in the prerevolutionary period to what we would now call propaganda features, designed to enhance the glory of the dictatorship'. Rosas's short nonfiction films not only entertained, but also were expected to inform: 'the weekly bullfights and the eulogistic recording of the chief executive's official peregrinations' established a style that 'succeeding decades of Mexican newsreel would faithfully follow' (Mora 2005, 12). After the unstable period of the civil war that followed the assassination of President Francisco I. Madero[6] in 1913, the socio-cultural importance of actualities was accepted. *Vistas* of the Revolution were popular until the end of 1915, when the public began to show interest in fiction films.

During the government of President Venustiano Carranza (1914–1920), Rosas documented the activities of General Pablo González, who funded the *The Gray Automobile* to exonerate his name from broad suspicion that he was the mastermind behind the gang. Although Rosas probably had financial and professional motivations, General González entertained presidential ambitions, and coveted the propagandistic reaches that cinema could offer.

FACT/FABLE: THE GANG

Taking advantage of the volatility of state institutions during the last phase of the Mexican Revolution,[7] the so-called 'Gray Automobile Gang' disguised themselves in military uniforms, used official search warrants to look for unauthorized firearms, and forced themselves into wealthy houses, stealing gold and jewellery, finally escaping in a gray Fiat.[8] The instability of the Mexican peso generated crime. From 1913–1915 the lack of currency forced the appearance of banknotes (termed *bilimbiques*) that often lost complete value from one day to the next, depending upon which government regime was in power: 'Carrancistas', or 'Zapatistas'. For this reason, the wealthy in Mexico City opted to keep their assets in gold or jewellery in their homes. This situation, along with the collapsed judicial system, made them a vulnerable target for robbers. Eighteen of the alleged members of the gang were caught between September and October 1915: thirteen men and five women. They were hastily tried and found guilty. While all of the women were sentenced to ten years in prison, ten of the men were sentenced to death after some of the thieves threatened to expose high military and police officials allegedly involved in their criminal activities. Four members of the gang were pardoned—for reasons unclear—by Pablo González, when they were about to be shot:

Rafael Mercadante, Bernardo Quintero, Luis Lara and José Fernández. Only six members of 'the gang' were finally executed by a firing squad on 20 December 1915. Rosas was granted access to the execution, and subsequently included it in his *National Historic Documentation 1915–1916* (1916)—which recorded relevant episodes of the Revolutionary period. In 1919, he recycled the footage of the firing squad execution in the last segment of *The Gray Automobile*. While numerous robberies occurred during this period of the Revolution due to the prevailing insecurity, the 'Gray Automobile Gang' attained notoriety because of rising (reasonable) suspicion that high military and police officials had links with the thieves.

THE MOVIE AND ITS RECEPTION

The Gray Automobile was released on 11 December 1919—a box-office hit. The original film was a twelve-chapter serial that lasted between three and four hours. It was condensed into a conventional feature length of 111 minutes in 1933 when sound (dialogue and music) was added, thus significantly altering the original version. This was the first time a national film had attained this level of commercial achievement (Ramírez Berg 2000, 4). The clever blend of fact and fiction was the major ingredient in the popularity of the film. Spectators were curious to know all of the details concerning the story of the gang through Rosas's film. González announced his Presidential candidacy the day before *The Gray Automobile* premiered. He had a vested interest in the success of this film, which he perceived as a medium of personal vindication, and financed Rosas's film to put an end to rumours that he was the mastermind behind the gang. The project aimed to restore González's reputation and the good image of the constitutional army amid the popular speculations and ongoing general discontent since 1915.

Official records of the 'The Gray Automobile Gang' have disappeared, or were probably destroyed. In this context Aurelio de los Reyes conducted comprehensive archival research, tracing the historical facts about the gang through information released in newspapers from 1915–1923. Reconstructing history, starting with the 1915 death sentence and information in the newspaper *El Pueblo*, de los Reyes (1996, 184–185) confirmed that most newspapers, such as *El Mexicano, El Renovador, Le Courrier du Mexique, El Demócrata*, etc., supported the Carrancista regime and were inclined to sympathize with the notion of General González's innocence by distorting facts. However, he also found publications, such as *El Pueblo* and *El Universal,* that questioned the actions taken by the government (de los Reyes 1996, 242–243).

In 'Ethical Issues in Media Production', Sharon Bracci states that, historically in Europe and in the USA, 'the connection between mass mediated messages and political systems took shape with print media's ability, through mass printing technology, to provide a wide forum for public discussion' (2008, 119). The press was to be the 'faithful eyes and ears of the public, reporting government working to them and raising the alarm when it appeared government representatives were working against public interests' (2008, 120). Unfortunately for Mexico, during Díaz's dictatorship, journalists who opposed the dictator were incarcerated or murdered, and newspapers that opposed the government were closed. Even though the Mexican Constitution of 1917 confirmed freedom of speech, not all newspapers felt safe enough to speak against the new Constitutionalist regime of Carranza, thus practising self-censorship. Nevertheless, through careful examination of contradictory information and thanks to some daring journalism, de los Reyes was able to weed out historical facts from fabrication.

NEITHER FACT NOR MYTH BUT SOMETHING ELSE: ROSAS'S PROSE-BASED TREATMENT

The search for objectivity in Mexican journalism was meaningful during the nineteenth century—previous to the last phase of the *'porfiriato'*—when the press was crushed. After Díaz was booted out of power in 1911, there was a brief period that focused on reporting the truth but it was short-lived. Following this turbulent period tabloid journalism would prevail in Mexico for the next 20 years. Rosas wrote the treatment of *The Gray Automobile* based primarily on the distorted news that supported the Carrancista regime, and the alleged incorruptibility of General González. He was assisted by Miguel Necoechea—a reporter who covered the news of these crimes, and Juan Manuel Cabrera—the Assistant Chief of Police in charge of the investigation (who also plays himself in the movie). At the time, 'the newspaper, *El Pueblo*, denounced Cabrera's arbitrariness at searching or apprehending the suspects' (de los Reyes 1996, 243). Despite the questionable reputation of Cabrera, and Necoechea's overt bias towards the Carranza regime, Rosas's collaboration with these figures can perhaps be best understood as trying to inject tangible evidence into his story. In other words, he felt the need to include these participants in the actual, historical event in order to increase interest and credibility. When examining Rosas's treatment, it is possible to identify instances when unreliable judicial and journalistic narratives are employed with the intention of manipulating actuality. Consequently, it is important to focus on the disparities between treatment and film. Despite Rosas's intention to exonerate González and the Constitutional army in his treatment, there are significant discrepancies in the text that only stress the crumbling state of the executive and judicial state branches in 1915, such as parts in the treatment that explore the characters and their motives. These are not explained in the film. Paradoxically, given the ambitions for the project, the slippages and inconsistencies that the treatment reveals only reinforce the theory that González was involved with the gang. In addition, it could be argued that the treatment calls into question Rosas's ethical responsibilities—as a filmmaker of actualities or *vistas*—for reconstructing and fabricating information in order to conform to the official account. In the end, *The Gray Automobile* project aims not only to serve the purpose of positive propaganda for González's political agenda, financial gains and professional prestige for Rosas, but also to function as a medium of social control through a cautionary tale of fear and intimidation.[9] De los Reyes asserts that González established a state of terror in Mexico City in 1915. In September, González threatened the citizens by declaring in the newspaper, *La Revolución*, that those who elect to remain neutral would be perceived as enemies, and that everyone should ally with the Constitutional army—headed by Carranza (de los Reyes 1996, 182).

In *Rhetoric and Representation in Nonfiction Film* (1997), Carl Plantinga discusses the debate on objectivity in the nonfiction film. He emphasizes that for some critics, 'objectivity' has been regarded as a necessary feature of nonfiction film, especially in the documentary genre. This is in spite of the fact that arrangement and editing in the creative process of documentary creation makes it 'untenable' to think of the 'nonfiction film as primarily or merely a recording of the real' (Plantinga 1997, 34). As Grierson observed: 'nonfiction film is the *creative*, not the *imitative*, treatment of actuality' (in Plantinga 1997, 35). Certainly Rosas's project follows Grierson's directive in the sense of trying to insert social change, and creativity, through structuring and composition. However, Plantinga ultimately dismisses Grierson's definition as too broad. Drawing on Noel Carroll's theory of indexing, he states that 'Nonfictions are taken to assert or imply that the state of affairs they present actually occur[ed]' (1997,

18), also inferring that nonfictions are perceived to make truth claims. *The Gray Automobile* was advertised in newspapers as a reconstruction of historical events, even publicizing the insertion of the footage of the actual execution of the bandits. Thus, according to Plantinga, Rosas's film would be indexed as nonfiction based on the fact that the project did make specific truth claims and included an actuality or *vista* scene of the firing squad execution. For Plantinga the ethical issue would depend on how a film is indexed. However, Rosas's film is complex and resists clear classification—since Rosas fabricated several facts to sway public opinion in favour of his associate's political interests. In 'When is a Documentary?': Documentary as a Mode of Reception', Dirk Eitzen offers an alternative to what he considers Plantiga's categorical—yet incomplete—definition of a nonfiction film. Eitzen asserts that the fact that a film is classified as fiction or nonfiction:

> ...does not depend upon whether it makes assertions or arguments. It does not depend upon whether or not it actually "tells the truth". It depends on whether it is perceived in such a way that it may make sense to ask, "Might it be lying?" (1995, 89)

Considering Rosas's project in light of Eitzen's work, we can suggest that the question 'Might it be lying?' is what distinguishes documentaries, and nonfictions in general, from fiction. Eitzen explains that nonfictions are full of images and practices that are not intended as truth claims (e.g. acting, music and sound effects, editing, etc.). However, what distinguishes such moments as nonfiction is not that they claim to be totally truthful but that they are supposed to not lie (Eitzen 1995, 90). This is precisely the problem with *The Gray Automobile*. Through Rosas's fabrication of historical facts concerning the gang's *modus operandi*, the film lies about what actually occurred. Intricate details of this case were widely considered in newspapers, yet Rosas brings new elements into the story that were never discussed in the newsprint, and furthermore play in favour of Pablo González's exoneration. On one reading of Eitzen's work, Rosas's film should be classified as fiction, plain and simple. Yet, it is not that simple, since the film exhibits techniques such as the inclusion of the actual footage of an execution, as well as the participation of non-professional actors, such as Cabrera—the police officer in charge of the investigation and apprehending the bandits, and who also plays himself in the movie. Plantinga concedes that 'in specific films the distinction between fiction and nonfiction will sometimes be fuzzy at best' contending that factual indeterminacies and unclear indexing of a film as fiction or nonfiction can make a film impossible to classify. Nevertheless, he concludes that 'a distinction with fuzzy boundaries is no less a distinction' (Plantinga 1997, 184).

The ethical implications regarding indexing certainly deserve examination. If the film is indexed as nonfiction, the issue of public safety takes prominence, such as when the spectator is assured that General González and the police ought to be dependable when in fact they may not have been worthy of the people's trust. Furthermore, Ramírez Berg asserts that *The Gray Automobile's* 're-creation of actual events is impressive' (2000, 3).The two sources consulted and employed during the conception of the project (Necoechea and Cabrera), the fact that the prologue intertitle of the altered film announces that it was shot in the locations where the events occurred, as well as the insertion of the execution footage in the last part of the movie, convinces Ramírez Berg to categorize Rosas's movie as a docudrama[10] since he judges that Rosas's film is a faithful staged recreation of the historical facts; which it is not. The category of docudrama itself introduces a number of complex factors into the ethical analysis of *The Gray Automobile*. According to Plantinga, as for many contemporary critics and filmmakers, the docudrama is a less prestigious form of nonfiction film than the documentary. In 'Ethical Issues of Presenting Misinformation in Docudramas', CT Charlton, Dan Kronisch, Kyle Stewart and Ryan Wilt stress that 'while docudramas have existed for years, they have only recently become the topic of ethical debates with emphasis on how facts can be stretched in order to create a more dramatic effect.... The idea of a docudrama is to incorporate historical fact with literary and narrative techniques in order to create a story-like depiction of an actual event' (Charlton et al. 2006, 189). They continue, 'docudramas have been used irresponsibly...directors tend to distort many facts and occasionally inject events that never actually occurred...this practice is unethical' (2006, 191). Since *The Gray Automobile* was, in large part, politically motivated, it raises questions concerning the objectivity of specific details. In addition, de los Reyes explains that Rosas had to comply with censorship regulations and thus made some changes before his film was released, leading to several instances where historical facts don't match what is told in the story (de los Reyes 1996, 260–261). In October 1919 the Carranza administration passed a censorship decree against any film that showed criminals in any kind of superior or positive light that may inspire empathy (de los Reyes 1996, 261). This probably explains why the last episode in prison—present in the treatment and possibly in the shooting script—was edited out of the film, which simply ends with the firing squad execution and a preaching intertitle.

Close examination of the prose-based treatment provides deeper insight into the imbalance between the attempt to sell the film as nonfiction and what the film actually delivers. This can be observed in the case of characters such as Don Vicente González—one of the gang's victims. In the treatment, Don Vicente is an old man who resists being robbed at first, but after being tortured, he reveals where he hid his assets. After the robbery, Don Vicente asks the Zapatista inspector if he may join the police to help pursue the thieves. His offer is accepted and, while he is in the inspector's office, Don Vicente recognizes Granada[11]—in actual life, his name was Higinio Granda, allegedly the leader of the gang—who is put in jail. Granada eventually escapes, and General González takes control of the city. Don Vicente returns to speak with the new police inspector (Cabrera),[12] and begs to be accepted again within the police force to help in the investigation, and he is welcomed again without reservation. Introducing the character of Don Vicente as an elderly man with no training who is able to instantly join the police is problematic. Not only does Rosas's treatment reveal that Don Vicente had power and influence, but more importantly, Rosas underscores how fragile and porous the judicial institution was during this unstable period in Mexico City. It is interesting however, that in the treatment, several times Rosas refers to Don Vicente as a *Javert*—the name of the antagonist in Victor Hugo's romantic novel *Les Misérables* (1862)—a characterization that stands in stark contrast to that of an ethical policeman: 'That day, Don Vicente prepares for his first service, armed with a thick cane and a good gun, and dressed according to his new occupation, which is almost a custom, the old man turns from a peaceful bourgeois into a formidable *Javert*' (Rosas 1981, 24, my emphasis). In addition, in the treatment Don Vicente accidentally shoots and kills a police driver: 'Don Vicente's bullet, the bullet of the fearsome *Javert*...Daniel's death is the epilogue of Don Vicente's police career...' (1981, 43, my emphasis). Later in the treatment, Don Vicente dies of pneumonia. In the surviving film, however, Don Vicente just disappears from the story; he is never seen shooting the police driver or dying.

Through the use of the term '*Javert*', and Don Vicente's mishaps, the reader of the treatment can infer a certain degree of scepticism towards the sudden transformation of Don Vicente into a police officer. Moreover,

Rosas expresses empathy for the thieves through his treatment. This is probably one of various elements that raised the attention of censors of the day, and which explains the incoherence in the last third of the film. A critic described it as an 'atrocious mess in which some characters die twice, others who were fugitives appear escaping from jail, and inexplicable scenes that makes one think of a pair of scissors used by the judge who requested to watch the movie first...' (de los Reyes 1996, 256). In the last part of his treatment, Rosas explores the psychology of various characters, particularly when they are spending time in jail. For example, Rosas describes the romantic relationship between Carmen and Mercado—in real life Carmen Aréchiga and Rafael Mercadante, and sees Carmen as a victim of tragic circumstances. These instances in the treatment—and perhaps in the lost shooting script—never made it to the film, which abruptly ends with the firing squad execution scene and the moralizing intertitle:

USELESS AMBITION...DESTINY BECOMES A MORAL LESSON WHEN IT REACHES ALL GUILTY PEOPLE...WORK IS THE MOST NOBLE WAY OF LIFE. (Serrano and del Moral 1981, 117, emphasis in original)

It is important to notice that no intertitles exist in Rosas's treatment. They appear in the altered film but there is no way to know if these exact ones were also present in the original film of twelve episodes that is lost.

Continuing with the theme of fabrication, perhaps the weakest part of Rosas's story (both treatment and film) is the explanation of who was the real gang's Commander-in-Chief. In the treatment, the Zapatistas evacuate the city and open the jail to let the prisoners escape, Granada among them. For this action the Zapatistas are blamed, which was a generally accepted practice in the newspapers of that period, which had to support the regime. By the time Pablo González's troops take possession of Mexico City, Granada has reinitiated criminal activities in a new office in a downtown location. He assures his accomplices that the business is guaranteed, since the new boss is a powerful figure. However, he explains that no one can see him, not even Granada himself, unless he is called first. When one of the thieves is talking to Granada, a bell rings and Granada tells him to wait because 'the boss' is calling him. To appease the accomplice, Granada shows him—through frosted glass on the door—the back of a man who is apparently busy writing at his desk. Later, when the inspector and his men finally discover Granada's office and they are searching through his desk, they break into the adjacent private room after hearing the bell ringing. As the treatment describes it:

> In an instant the officers pounce on a man who remains still at his desk...the grotesque surprise fills them with indignation: that "man" is only a manne-quin...who, then, rang the bell? Searching the room again they can discover the clumsy trick...on the floor there is a hidden switch, that Granada skill-fully controlled, to make his accomplices believe that the gang's boss, the one who planned the felonies, the high commander, was calling him. (Rosas 1981, 34)

This episode is evidence (and possibly a metaphor) of Rosas's fabrication, and it cannot pass unnoticed that the other term for the mannequin is a 'dummy'. First, it is barely convincing that members of the gang were naive enough to believe in Granada's scheme. But most importantly, Rosas introduces an entire new device into the story out of nowhere. Neither in the treatment nor in the film does Rosas explain Granada's purpose of deploying this mannequin within his own organization. In the treatment it is mentioned several times that the members swore to keep a secret, yet this 'secret' is never revealed. This is especially confusing since at that time all of the surviving thieves, including Granada, were serv-ing sentences in jail. The narrator in Rosas's treatment suggests that José Fernández, one of the thieves, hates and distrusts Mercado (Mercadante). According to the narrator in the treatment, even Granada is able to notice the negative feelings that Fernández harbours against Mercado. Because of the likelihood that Mercado may speak of 'the secret', the narrator proposes that it was Fernández who poisoned Mercado three years after both were pardoned from their death penalty: 'Fernández... fears that one day Mercado breaks the oath of silence that everyone has kept until now' (Rosas 1981, 56). What stands out about these references to Granda, Mercadante, Fernández, and 'the secret', is not whether it was correct or dishonest for Rosas to introduce instances of fiction into his treatment, but rather that he integrated these pieces of speculation while claiming to present actual facts about this case. Elements such as these work against the Rosas's promised objectivity. Returning to Eitzen's proposed ques-tion, 'might it be lying?' (1995, 89), the mannequin device raises precisely this question for the reader. Despite the fact that the film was promoted as a movie made to clarify the mystery behind the gang's criminal activi-ties, Rosas probably didn't convince the reader that he was delivering a nonfiction film. *The Gray Automobile* succeeded as a commercial product but failed as a propaganda tool. General González lost the presidential elections in 1920. That year, Carranza was assassinated and—during the interim presidency of Adolfo de la Huerta (1 June 1920 to 30 November 1920)—González was arrested on charges of treason. He was originally sentenced to be executed, but was pardoned and instead went into exile in the USA. He returned to Mexico in 1940 and died impoverished in 1950 in Monterrey.

HISTORICAL FACTS AND THEIR CONNECTION WITH THE MEDIA

Having conducted extensive historical research on the subject, de los Reyes reconstructs the actual judicial process faced by the gang starting with the death sentence of ten of the thieves announced in newspapers. The most reliable was the research of a reporter for the newspaper *El Pueblo* that was published on 19 December 1915. Not surprising, he found out that the majority of papers supported (willingly or not) the Carranza government, and published distorted information of the actual events. This biased news 'has contributed in blurring history and to spread a legend that would be in large part, echoed in...Rosas's *The Gray Automobile* in 1919' (de los Reyes 1996, 185). Research on reporting of the period is significant considering that, during this first stage of Mexican cinema, cameramen such as Rosas 'were inspired by the press to create their movies' (de los Reyes 1996, 201). Rosas chose to base his treatment on information provided by newspapers sanctioned by his boss, General González.

Based on the historical facts concerning the gang's case, de los Reyes discerns several discrepancies in both the treatment and the film. He argues that perhaps Rosas, aware of those historical distortions, included the prologue intertitle in the altered film—unlike the treatment where there are no title cards. The prologue intertitle in the surviving film reads as follows:

> The story represented here unfolds in the same locations that were the stage of the feats on which the story was created. The scenes of the robberies, the houses in which the members of the sinister Gray Automobile Gang lived, and the sites where they were apprehended or paid for their crimes are rigorously authentic. The action takes place in 1915. (Rosas 2010)

A male voice-over in the film reads each title card, taking the role of controlling narrator. According to de los Reyes, with this prologue intertitle, Rosas sought to exercise a certain degree of poetic licence and fictionalize or modify historical facts, not the physical locations—which were genuine. However, despite de los Reyes's insightful reading, there is concrete evidence that the film was vigorously promoted as an authentic reconstruction of the historical events in the press. In their introductory note to Rosas's prose-based treatment and the cutting continuity document (created after the altered film)[13] of *The Gray Automobile* (1981), Federico Serrano and Antonio Noyola include a promotional piece published on 11 November 1919 in the newspaper *El Universal*:

> ...Traced over historical facts, *it is an exact transcription of the truth...* reconstructed on the crimes perpetrated by the "Gray Automobile Gang"... [the movie]... has dramatic and emotional details, terrible scenes, and poetic strokes that are like lightning, but also merciful beams of virtue that, from time to time, tear out the shadow of the dreadful cavern where evil, impiety, and crime seek refuge. (Serrano and Noyola 1981, 14, emphasis added)

Aside from the addition of the Assistant Chief of Police—Cabrera, as a character playing himself in the film—there is the noticeable inclusion of the actual firing squad execution of six members of the gang. It is difficult to accept that Rosas's editing was simply creating a fictional story inspired on a real event, as de los Reyes suggests.

ACTUALITY: EXECUTION BY FIRING SQUAD

The prominent *vista*, showing the firing squad execution, merits its own ethical analysis. In 'Spectacles of Violence and Politics: *El automóvil gris* (1919) and Revolutionary Mexico's Sensational Visual Culture', Rielle Navitski argues that Rosas's film 'exemplifies the visual culture of violence that flourished in early twentieth-century Mexico, at once intensely national in its preoccupations and influenced by foreign journalism and cinema, which marshalled the reality effects of mechanically reproduced images in the service of both popular entertainment and social control' (Navitski 2014, 134). The scene is not only violent and sensationalist, but it has a different feel to the rest of the film. As an actuality (*vista*), already included in Rosas's *National Historic Documentation 1915–1916* in 1916, the visual codes in this scene are consistent with the *vistas* of the period, displaying a long take shot of the firing squad execution of six men who appear very different—in terms of race and social class from the actors who play their roles. The scene is a chilling reminder of the tight control and intimidation that the regime exerted over the population of Mexico City in 1915. Rosas's prose-based treatment does not clarify that a *vista* was used in this part of the story. However, the text describes the elements observed in this particular scene only omitting the part in which the soldiers approach the fallen men on the ground to give each the coup de grace: 'Several bodies bend and fall like marionettes with broken strings...' (Rosas 1981, 54). While Rosas included this real scene in *The Gray Automobile* film, his editing is a fabrication of the historical facts that culminated with the execution of six men. In the treatment, General Pablo González is never a suspect but a high-ranking commander with integrity who—with the help of virtuous police officers—was actively engaged in pursuing and bringing to justice the robbers. In reality however, González rushed the execution of six men who never faced a proper trial, becoming in effect scapegoats for propaganda and political gain. It is interesting to note that in the sound version of the 1933 film (when General González had almost disappeared from Mexican history), González's name is never mentioned and his participation is condensed to one scene in which he is not identified. Since there are no surviving copies of the original film, Rosas's treatment is relevant in the sense that Pablo González does appear as a key, distinguishable character.

In addition, the ethical implications involved in filming and watching people die merit examination. In *Regarding the Pain of Others* (2004), Susan Sontag discusses the notion of spectators becoming insensitive to photographed human misfortunes through a proliferation of images. She favours the importance of the image to encourage critical thinking and inspire social action, and asserts that the moral problem of the 'educated class' lies within 'our failure of empathy' (Sontag 2004, 7). By 1915, people in Mexico were probably desensitized to watching individuals die as people died because of the war, disease and starvation every day. In addition, de los Reyes observes that under González 'there were two executions of thieves and banknotes counterfeiters per week'. If thousands of spectators went to watch Rosas's film, it was probably not for the execution scene, which has already been exhibited in Rosas's 1916 documentary film, but in hopes to find answers to the mystery and silence that the government kept with respect to the 'Gray Automobile Gang' historical case.

Rosas's treatment doesn't discuss differences such as the thieves' level of education, their social class, and/or their ethnicity. These are important omissions, though, especially considering that—as Francisco Ramírez Plancarte underscores in his book, *Mexico City During the Constitutionalist Revolution* (1941)—many people in Mexico City, particularly the poor, were dying of starvation in 1915, a fact that consequently had an impact in the increase in delinquency. In addition, a judge prevented Rosas from using the actual names of some of the surviving prisoners involved in the crime, as they were suing for defamation and intellectual property in 1919. Therefore, 'Higinio Granda turned into Granada, Rafael Mercadante into Mercado, Francisco Oviedo into Otero, and Ernestina, the kidnapped girl, was Enriqueta' (Serrano and del Moral 1981, 16). Rosas didn't assign new fictional names to everyone in his treatment, however, which is unfair when considered that the historical Granda (Granada in the treatment)—allegedly the bandits' leader—never faced the death penalty, which became illegal in Mexico by 1917. The changing of historical names in the treatment—which can also be observed in the shooting script's surviving intertitles (see Islas 2004)—are evidence of fabrication, as Rosas was intending to portray historical subjects, not historically-inspired (or fictional) characters, in his film. Given the history of social relations in Mexico, race and social class are elements that are worthy of discussion in Rosas's work. Historical photos of Granda reveal a white, blue-eyed person, and it is also known that Mercadante had an advanced education level as a student of law.[14] These indications emphasize the contrast between these two men and the six others who lost their lives. Although the execution scene is brief and darker than the rest of the film, it is still possible to notice the Indigenous features of the bandits that are closer to the camera. Paul A. Schroeder Rodríguez underlines that '...the film closes with documentary footage of the real bandits being shot by a firing squad. However, these real-life bandits do not look anything like the ones played by actors (in the film). Rather, they look like Indigenous-mestizo Zapatistas with their wide-rim hats and tight pants, but they are dehumanized by the way the event is shot and edited...' (Schroeder Rodríguez 2008, 50). The men—who never gave consent to be photographed by Rosas in 1915 and could not give consent when the scene was sold as entertainment and political propaganda in *The Gray Automobile* in 1919—don't look at the camera as if refusing to make eye contact with the spectator that will inevitably reduce them to spectacle (see Corbin 2012).

CONCLUSION

Grierson's traditional definition of documentary as 'the creative treatment of actuality' (Grierson 1933, 8) has endured for most of the last century, as it is comprehensive enough to comprise any cinematic text. Plantinga is correct in dismissing this definition as too broad because it does not address the essential question: how much actuality survives the creative treatment? Indexing offers a partial solution; however, it remains very problematic when the viewer does not perceive the film as nonfiction, despite truth claims made by the work (as in the case of Rosas's project). *The Gray Automobile* does not tell the truth entirely—it clearly contains many fictional elements. I addressed the problematic hermeneutics that arise when connecting Rosas's work with the documentary genre by centring on his prose-based treatment. It does contain elements that approach nonfiction, such as the inclusion of non-professional actors and the actual footage of a firing squad execution. Nevertheless, although Rosas had a good reputation as a filmmaker of *vistas*, not even the general spectator was persuaded that *The Gray Automobile* was nonfiction in 1919. Commercially, the movie was enormously popular, bringing big profits for its producers. However as a political tool, the film was disastrous for Pablo González, who lost the presidential election the following year, and perhaps for Rosas too, whose reputation may have been tainted by the fact that so many people connected with the gang's activity died in such mysterious circumstances during this period. Although there are numerous articles on *The Gray Automobile*, none have focused on the complex and contradictory gestures made towards objectivity—advertised in the press when the movie was promoted—and fabrication that can be traced from the prose-based treatment. The film did not deliver in its objectivity promise, as spectators in general felt that Rosas was deliberately trying to deceive them. Most scholars agree that there are ethical responsibilities within the creation of a nonfiction film. When historical facts are purposely altered to advance personal interests and political agendas, as such is the case in *The Gray Automobile*, it is important to remember that 'objectivity and its related concepts—fairness, impartiality, balance, etc.—are vital for a nonfiction pragmatics' (Plantinga 1997, 201). Aiming to absolve González from any type of involvement with the gang by showing that Granda acted alone, Rosas's creation of the mannequin artefact did not convince since this piece of fabricated evidence was exposed as new absurd information never mentioned or debated in the newspapers.

The firing squad execution scene, with special emphasis placed on the ethical consequences of shooting images of people dying without their consent, has also been discussed. Rosas clearly recycled these images to mislead public opinion in favour of González, fabricating facts at the expense of showing the execution of six men through the teaching of a 'moral' lesson. From a contemporary perspective, the execution is disturbing because it underscores the history of violence and injustice that has characterized the politics of control that the emergent group in power—later the PRI (Revolutionary Institutional Party)—imposed for decades. Although in general terms, the treatment explains that the thieves were given a proper hearing and thus were treated with impartiality, historical facts proved otherwise; they were quickly tried and never received a fair trial. Yet, there are also some instances in the treatment in which Rosas empathizes with the thieves by dimly showing his own convictions. These do not appear in the film—which was subjected to censorship right before it was ready to be exhibited.

Drawing on close analysis of the discrepancies between treatment and film, as well as the marketing of the movie, I have sought to present Rosas's work as a hybrid project that requires a flexible and diverse approach, relying on history, media, film and screenwriting studies. It would be ineffective trying to classify or 'index' Rosas's *The Gray Automobile* under a fixed category of fiction or nonfiction; it is neither one thing nor the other, and requires to be analysed within the unstable Mexican context within which it was produced. Rosas's treatment demonstrates the fluidity of *The Gray Automobile*, a film that continues to pose ethical challenges for scholars.

NOTES

1. All of the original quotations in Spanish from Rosas's prose-based treatment, Aurelio de los Reyes's text, Federico Serrano and Antonio Noyola's introductory note, as well as Serrano's cutting continuity text, are my translation.
2. See Charles Rodríguez Berg article, 'El automóvil gris and the Advent of Mexican Classicism'. Ramírez Berg explains the influences evident in Rosas's film.
3. The term 'Carrancistas' was used to designate the followers and supporters of President Venustiano Carranza (1859–1920).
4. Pablo González (Monterrey, Mexico 1879–Monterrey, Mexico 1950). Once Venustiano Carranza's strong man, González was a General during the Mexican Revolution. He lost the presidential elections in 1920 after his

image was discredited under general suspicion that he was the actual brain behind the Gray Automobile Gang. He is also widely known for planning the assassination of Emiliano Zapata, who over the years became one of the most popular and venerated heroes of the Mexican Revolution.

5. Porfirio Díaz Mori (Oaxaca, Mexico 1830–Paris, France 1915) was a prominent General who served seven terms as President of Mexico between 1876 and 1911. Díaz's long dictatorship is called the 'Porfiriato', which ended in 1910 with the Mexican Revolution.

6. Francisco I. Madero (Coahuila, Mexico 1873–Mexico City 1913). President Madero was democratically elected in 1911. Madero was essential in leading the Revolution that kicked Porfirio Díaz out of power in 1910.

7. See Francisco Ramírez Plancarte, *La ciudad de México durante la Revolución Constitucionalista* [*Mexico City During the Constitutionalist Revolution*]. The author was a witness of the population's instability and famine in 1915, when different factions were fighting.

8. In *Cine y sociedad en Mexico 1896–1930*, Aurelio de los Reyes underscores that it was never confirmed what exactly was the brand of the car or cars that the gang used to commit their crimes.

9. González used the death penalty resource to scare a decimated and starving population (de los Reyes 1996, 182–190).

10. The docudrama film genre features dramatized reenactments of real incidents. In principle, it should strive to closely follow history, allowing a moderate degree of dramatic license only in the marginal aspects where there might be historical gaps that require to be fulfilled, but without altering the essential historical aspects or events.

11. Some of the surviving thieves—Higinio Granda, Luis Lara and Bernardo Quintero (in jail)—sued Rosas in 1919 for defamation and robbery of intellectual property. Therefore, a judge prevented Rosas from using the real names of these people in the project (de los Reyes 1996, 247). However, the altered film shows the original names of the historical characters in the intertitles, which suggests that these were added later. The few original intertitles of the lost shooting script, kept by Rosas's granddaughter, show the changed names done by Rosas. See Islas's documentary.

12. Although he plays himself in the movie, Cabrera's name is never mentioned in the prose treatment or in the film.

13. Federico Serrano created a cutting continuity, an exact transcription of Rosas's altered sound film of 1933, and published it, along with Rosas's original treatment in 1981.

14. See de los Reyes text where he shows several photos of the thieves.

REFERENCES

de los Reyes, Aurelio. 1996. *Cine y sociedad en México, 1896–1930, vol. 1: Vivir de sueños (1896–1920)*. Mexico City: Universidad Nacional Autónoma de México/ Cineteca Nacional.

de los Reyes, Aurelio. 2013. *Los orígenes del cine en México*. Mexico City: Fondo de Cultura Económica.

Bracci, Sharon L. 2008. 'Ethical Issues in Media Production.' In *A Companion to Media Studies*, edited by Angharad N. Valdivia, 115–136. Hoboken, NJ: Wiley–Blackwell.

Charlton, CT, Dan Kronisch, Kyle Stewart, and Ryan Wilt. 2006. 'Ethical Issues of Presenting Misinformation in Docudramas.' Retrieved January 2, 2015 from http://www.ethicapublishing.com/ethics/4CH13.pdf

Corbin, Megan. 2012. 'Neutralizing Consent: The Maternal Look and the Returned Gaze in *El infarto del alma*.' *Lucero* 22 (1): 55–75.

Eitzen, Dirk. 1995. 'When Is a Documentary?: Documentary as a Mode of Reception.' *Cinema Journal* 35 (1): 81–102.

García Riera, Emilio. 1998. *Breve historia del cine mexicano*. Mexico City: CONACULTA/IMCINE/Canal 22, Universidad de Guadalajara, Ediciones MAPA.

Grierson, John. 1933. 'The Documentary Producer.' *Cinema Quarterly* 2 (1): 7–9.

Mora, Carl J. 2005. *Mexican Cinema: Reflections of Society, 1896–2004*. 3rd ed. Jefferson, NC: McFarland & Company, Incorporated Publishers.

Navitski, Rielle. 2014. 'Spectacles of Violence and Politics: El automóvil gris (1919) and Revolutionary Mexico's Sensational Visual Culture.' *Journal of Latin American Cultural Studies* 23 (2): 133–52.

Nichols, Bill. 1994. *Blurred Boundaries: Questions of Meaning in Contemporary Culture*. Bloomington: Indiana University Press.

Plantinga, Carl R. 1997. *Rhetoric and Representation in Nonficton Film*. Cambridge: Cambridge University Press.

Ramírez Berg, Charles. 2000. 'El automóvil gris and the Advent of Mexican Classicism.' In *Visible Nations: Latin American Film and Video*, edited by Chon Noriega, 3–32. Minneapolis: University of Minnesota Press.

Ramírez Plancarte, Francisco. 1941. *La ciudad de México durante la Revolución Constitucionalista*. 2nd Ed. Mexico City: Ediciones Botas.

Rosas, Enrique. 1981 [1919]. *El automóvil gris*. In *El automóvil gris* (1919). *Guiones del cine mexicano*, edited by Federico Serrano and Fernando del Moral, 19–57. Mexico City: Cuadernos de la Cineteca Nacional.

Serrano, Federico and Antonio Noyola. 1981. 'Nota a *El automóvil gris*.' In *El automóvil gris*. *Guiones del cine mexicano*, edited by Federico Serrano and Fernando del Moral, 11–17. Mexico City: Cuadernos de la Cineteca Nacional.

Serrano, Federico and Fernando del Moral. 1981. *El automóvil gris* (1919): *Guiones del cine mexicano*, Mexico City: Cuadernos de la Cineteca Nacional.

Schroeder Rodríguez, Paul A. 2008. 'Latin American Silent Cinema: Triangulation and the Politics of the Criollo Aesthetics.' *Latin American Research Review* 43 (3): 33–58.

Sontag, Susan. 2004. *Regarding the Pain of Others*. New York: Penguin.

Viñas, Moisés. 1987. *Historia del cine Mexicano*. Mexico City: Coordinación de Difusión Cultural/Direccion de Actividades Cinematograficas UNAM.

Film References

Islas, Alejandra. 2004. *La banda del Automóvil gris*. Mexico City: CINRAM Latinoamericana S.A. de C.V.

Rosas, Enrique. 1916. *Documentación histórica nacional 1915–1916*. Mexico City: Azteca Films.

Rosas, Enrique. 2010. *El automóvil gris*. Commemorative Edition. Mexico City: Filmoteca de la UNAM.

CHAPTER 7

Blurring Boundaries, Transmedia Storytelling and the Ethics of C. S. Peirce

Renira Rampazzo Gambarato and Alessandro Nanì

INTRODUCTION

Transmedia storytelling, a term coined by Henry Jenkins (2003, 2006), denotes a process in which instalments of a story are spread across multiple media platforms to create an integrated experience that promotes audience engagement. According to Jenkins (2011), 'integral elements of a fiction get dispersed systematically across multiple delivery channels for the purpose of creating a unified and coordinated entertainment experience. Ideally, each medium makes its own unique contribution to the unfolding of the story'. In recent years, numerous studies have focused on transmedia storytelling, its definition and praxis (Bernardo 2014a; Gambarato 2013; Jenkins 2003, 2006, 2011). However, the study of transmedia storytelling from an ethical perspective is still in its early stages. Screenwriters working in this area face significant challenges in creating

R.R. Gambarato (✉)
Faculty of Communications, Media and Design, Department of Media, National Research University Higher School of Economics, Moscow, Russia
e-mail: rgambarato@hse.ru

A. Nanì
Baltic Film, Media, Arts and Communication School, Tallinn University, Tallinn, Estonia
e-mail: alessandro.nani@tlu.ee

© The Editor(s) (if applicable) and The Author(s) 2016
S. Maras (ed.), *Ethics in Screenwriting*, Palgrave Studies in Screenwriting, DOI 10.1057/978-1-137-54493-3_7

spaces, scenarios and, especially, forms of play, that encourage audience participation and co-creation and the blurring of fact and fiction, whilst also respecting ethical norms.

In this chapter, specific ethical issues of transmedia storytelling are discussed through the conceptualization of ethics developed by Charles Sanders Peirce (1839–1914), the American philosopher, logician, mathematician and chemist. Across the humanities, scholars are drawing on 'Peirce's ideas to reach beyond him' (Fabbrichesi and Marietti 2006, xiv). The aim is to apply the philosophical tools learnt from Peirce to 'the treatment of new problems and the formulation of new themes' (Fabbrichesi and Marietti 2006, xiv). Scolari (2009) highlights the relevance of complementing useful old theoretical paradigms with new theoretical discourses to be able to broadly comprehend digital media phenomena. In our own work we draw on the *Collected Papers* of Peirce (1931–1935, 1958; hereafter referred to as CP, followed by volume and paragraph), together with the work of Gregory Bateson (1987), Kelly A. Parker (2003) and Arnold Shepperson (2009).

Our rationale for turning to Peirce's concepts today relies on several reasons. Transmedia storytellers should be interested in the work of Peirce because of his semiotics. His approach to 'the sign' is dynamic and not static, placing it at the centre of an interaction between interpreter and interpretant. His understanding of communication thus complements what happens in transmedia storytelling. Furthermore, Peirce proposes an immediate connection among aesthetics, ethics and logic, which enriches and enlarges the approach to ethical issues in the realm of transmediality. Moreover, Peircean ethical actions transcend the individual sphere in favour of collectivism and apply perfectly to transmedia storytelling; in the sense that one of the pillars of transmedia strategies are the communities created around transmedial storyworlds, as we will discuss later. Building on his semiotic theory, Peirce places interpretation at the heart of his ethics. This is especially useful in exploring what we term 'blurred boundaries' and the need for disclaimers/disclosures in each media platform involved in a certain transmedia project (or not) and the consequences for the audience and the transmedia authors that result from the blurring boundaries between fact and fiction. Finally, Peirce's concepts support a framework in which different forms of transmedia storytelling can be considered contextually, allowing for consideration of different ideas of the overall good (*summum bonum*) and reasonableness.

This chapter focuses on two case studies—the transmedia projects *Sanningen om Marika/The Truth About Marika* (Swedish Television (SVT), 2007) from Sweden and *Castigo Final/Final Punishment*

(Oi TV, 2009) from Brazil. These two projects operate differently in their respective contexts. The Brazilian project has the clear purpose to advertise the mobile service, digital TV and internet portal provided by the project's sponsor, while the Swedish project, produced by Company P and SVT, a public service broadcaster, focuses on exploring new production methods for participatory media landscape. Despite their differences, we argue that although the two case studies in principle comply with Peircean ethics (mainly because of the cases' emotional appeal to save the characters' lives), the concrete implementation of the projects is not aligned with the normative ideals that guide our actions, because the fictional stories do not necessarily clarify the audience's real role.

The chapter is organized in five parts. The first part addresses the definition of transmedia storytelling and the second part is a theoretical reflection on Peircean ethics. The third part discusses the direct implications of Peircean ethics on transmedia stories, which is followed by a literature review of particular ethical issues of transmedia storytelling. In the fifth part, the two case studies are presented to enhance the discussion about ethical issues within transmedial worlds.

TRANSMEDIA STORYTELLING

Transmedia storytelling is not a monolithic construct. Every project responds to different contexts, socio-economic situations, demographics and end goals, articulated into narrative form. Transmedia projects are complex phenomena that embrace multiple dimensions, such as narrative, cultural context, business models and technology. Terms such as 'multimedia', 'intermedia', 'cross-media', 'hybrid media', 'media mix', and 'deep media' are commonly considered, to a certain extent, synonyms for transmedia storytelling. However, these terms are not synonyms, and a core characteristic that differentiates transmedia storytelling is that it is not a matter of adapting the same content from one medium to another (as in the case of cross-media), and it is also not a simple matter of text, audio and visual representations used together (as in the case of multimedia). Instead, transmedia storytelling is about expanding the content and spreading it across multiple media platforms.

There are, furthermore, different kinds of transmedia stories. One of the first genuinely transmedial productions is *The Matrix* (1999) by the Wachowskis (Gambarato 2013, 85). This kind of transmedia story is a franchise, which includes a series of individual and independent media outlets, such as films, video games, comic books and so forth that cover different narrative spaces, such as prequels, sequels and spin-offs (Pratten 2015, 15). A transmedia franchise implies that the audience can choose which media outlets they want to follow, since they do not need to follow all the media platforms in order to understand the storyworld. Transmedia franchises are especially common in the American market, which is highly interested in the building of blockbuster storyworlds for commercial purposes. Although the franchise format does not necessarily involve audiences having to turn to other platforms within a certain storyworld, the challenge for screenwriters and transmedia producers is to develop a story compelling enough to motivate audiences to migrate from one media platform to another. Jeff Gomez, a pioneer transmedia producer with a portfolio that includes transmedia projects for Disney, Coca-Cola and Mattel, emphasizes that 'the result of successful transmedia storytelling ... yields intense loyalty from your audience: long term engagement fosters the consumer's desire to share the experience, encouraging the extension of a property's lifespan beyond normal retail windows, leading to substantially increased revenue' (Andersen 2010).

Another type of transmedia story is portmanteau transmedia, which can be described as a kind of puzzle in which multiple interdependent platforms contribute to a single experience (Pratten 2015, 16). This is the case of Alternate Reality Games (ARGs). An ARG is 'an interactive narrative that blends real life treasure hunting, interactive storytelling, and online community' (Gambarato 2013, 86). To participate in an ARG, and achieve a fulfilling experience, audience members should follow all the media outlets within the game. A well-known example of ARG is *Why So Serious?*, produced in 2007, which played out for 15 months before the release of Christopher Nolan's film *The Dark Knight* (2008), and involved phone calls, coded websites, printed posters, newspaper ads and live events, for instance. ARGs are often free to play and usually target a community of devoted fans of a storyworld. Apart from further engaging committed fans with the story/characters, the specific goal of ARGs can be to connect fans to each other, reinforcing the sense of belonging to the transmedia storyworld and, consequently, sharing the experience with others. The end goal is for the community of devoted fans to disseminate their experience within the story and attract new audiences. In case the ARG is involved in a broader transmedia universe, there is the potential for new audiences to increase revenue among other transmedia extensions within the same storyworld.

A third type of transmedia story, the complex transmedia experience (Pratten 2015, 16), combines franchise and portmanteau, offering the audience a broader experience. A prominent example of a complex transmedia experience is the TV series *Lost* (ABC, 2004–2010), which incorporates traces of franchise (TV series, mobisodes, books, and more) and an ARG called the *Lost Experience*, produced in 2006. The ARG contributed to the storyworld expansion, revealing the background story of the Hanso Foundation and the DHARMA (Department of Heuristics and Research on Material Applications) Initiative, which were at the heart of *Lost*. *Lost Experience* played a key role luring audiences to the *Lost* universe. Jenkins (2014) interviewed Denise Mann to discuss the struggle writers endure 'to define digital extensions as part of creative content and not simply as part of the promotion of a series'. Mann mentions that, in the case of *Lost*, all the creators had their work on derivative content recognized, but 'more and more studios formed their own in-house social media marketing groups to oversee these "content-promotion hybrids" going forward' (Jenkins 2014).

The complexity of transmedia narratives, which involve diverse media and user-generated content, represents a challenge for writers and story designers, and even a stronger challenge in terms of ethics, especially because the platform matters: 'We know that chunks of the same "story", when presented on different platforms can have different impacts' (Finch 2012). Before discussing the specificities of ethical issues in the realm of transmediality, we introduce Peirce's approach to ethics.

PEIRCE'S APPROACH TO ETHICS

The philosophical study of ethics refers to morality, moral beliefs and behaviour, often constructed through dualistic approaches that polarize social configurations into opposite poles such as true/false, right/wrong and good/bad. Peirce, by contrast, does not construct ethics through dichotomies and emphasizes a non-dualistic approach. Throughout his life, Peirce was interested in ethics. Until the 1880s, he believed ethics was not a theoretical science but an art or a practical science. From 1882 on, he recognized the importance of theoretical ethics and began to suspect a much more in-depth connection between ethics and logic existed than he had supposed (Santaella 2000, 119). Peirce differentiated morality from ethics: while morals are directly concerned with the announcement of our actions as right or wrong, ethics, as a normative science, deals with the norms and ideals that guide our actions (Santaella 2000, 22). In addition, 'Peirce sharply distinguishes the normative science of *philosophical ethics* directed by reason, from the practical matter of *moral conduct*, guided by instinct and sentiment' (Parker 2003, 29). Thus, Peircean ethics focuses on the reasons for what could be denominated right or wrong; ethics is the investigation into the nature of right and wrong actions.

Several aspects of Peirce's thought lend themselves to the ethical analysis of transmedia storytelling. Firstly, Peirce presented aesthetics as the foundation of ethics—his ethics embraces rather than disregards aesthetics. Secondly, Peirce based the development of his well-known theory of signs (semiotics) as well as other important concepts of his extensive philosophical production on triadic structures that embraced the role of the interpreter—an important element in transmedia storytelling. Thirdly, Peirce adopted a critical relationship to ethical norms. Peirce examined '*how one should act* and not with *what actions are acceptable*' (Shepperson 2009, 285, emphasis in original).

According to Peirce, the normative sciences aim at reaching norms and ideals, which refer in particular to the supreme ideal of human life: the *summum bonum* of aesthetics, that is, the ideal worth pursuing, 'which forms the subject of pure ethics' (CP 1.575). The *summum bonum* is a core Peircean concept applied in this chapter in order to examine ethical issues from an innovative viewpoint. The *summum bonum* determines what seems to be admirable (*kalos*). According to Peirce, the *summum bonum* 'must be an admirable ideal, having the only kind of goodness that such an ideal can have; namely, aesthetic goodness. From this point of view, the morally good appears as a particular species of the aesthetically good' (CP 5.130). However, there is no guarantee that this ideal can be attained. The only possible ethical rule is to incessantly pursue it. In 1903, Peirce stated, 'Ethics (...) must appeal to Aesthetics for aid in determining the *summum bonum*' (CP 1.191).

Taken together, these three aspects open ethics to what Santaella describes as an 'aesthetics of action' (1992, 128). The proposed ends of action are preceded by aesthetics or, in Shepperson's (2009, 286) words, by 'admirability'. For instance, 'if someone asserts that some thing or situation or story is "terrifying", then it is the quality of *being-terrifying* that aesthetics considers, and not whether this is right or wrong' (Shepperson 2009, 251).

Although, at first glance, Peirce's idea of the *summum bonum* may appear prescriptive, it in fact accommodates different understandings of the role of the transmedia storyteller and the rationale behind different projects. The significance and flexibility of the *summum bonum* relies on the identification of the person with the whole community of which he/she is only a part (Redondo 2012). For Peirce, the *summum bonum* entails that 'the achievement of the higher stages of reasonableness has to be grasped within the flexible boundaries' (Redondo 2012, 222) of the community. While changeable and dependent on cultural, temporal, historical and geographic factors, Peirce's aesthetic ideal is geared toward collective, not individual, purposes. The 'admirable' is what attracts collectively, what should be experienced regarding its own inherent value. Furthermore, the aesthetic *summum bonum* coincides with the growth of concrete reasonableness (CP 5.433):

> The destiny, the *summum bonum* of evolution, is concrete reasonableness or the development of generals or laws in the universe. Peirce linked this with the ethical ideal of human action, which is to cooperate with evolution in achieving concrete reasonableness. (Roth 1998, 79)

For Peirce, the task of aesthetics is to establish what we ought to admire, what it is possible to be admirable *per se*. Within transmedia storytelling, this idea of admirable *per se* can be found in different kinds of projects with purposes that resonate both artistically and/or commercially for audiences. Ethics proposes and analyses reasonable purposes of the ideals to be pursued. Peircean ethics is the 'study of what ends of action we are deliberately able to adopt' (CP 5.130). Peirce considers that 'the problem of ethics is to ascertain what end is possible' (CP 5.134). Concrete reasonableness is his response to the question what is possible.

PEIRCE AND TRANSMEDIA STORYTELLING

Peirce's ethical commitment to what is admirable, to performing the right action, combined with his semiotics, opens up a different prism through which to consider transmedia storytelling, where a dynamic relationship between the text and the reader/viewer is the norm. In the realm of Peircean logic or semiotics, the action of the sign results in interpretants that are neither ultimate nor static, but are continuously generated. By way of definition, 'the interpretant is the effect generated by the translation of signs, while the interpreter is the one who allows this translation' (Alzamora and Gambarato 2014, 5). The generation of dynamical interpretants are constantly updated; that is, the productive incompleteness of the interpretants can transform the overall experience offered within transmedial experiences. 'Each user/*prosumer* would produce different interpretants related to the same object according to his/her informational level and within his/her own repertoire. This variability of signification could be a desirable characteristic of transmedia productions' (Alzamora and Gambarato 2014, 10). For Peirce, the sign chain is continuously mediated by each interpretant. Through the variability of signification, connection and integration specific to transmedia stories, new articulations are made between the narrative instalments dispersed across diverse media outlets. These integrated articulations contribute to transforming the whole in something over and above the sum of the parts (Gambarato 2012, 70).

In Peirce's view, the supreme ideal should always evolve, promoting the continuous growth of ideas. In the realm of transmedia narrative, this growth can be achieved with the constant generation of interpretants. The fact that the generation of interpretants belongs to the transmedia designer/writer and the audience, the productive incompleteness of interpretants contribute to maintaining the wheel of the story rolling through expansion of content within the story universe. In the midst of participatory culture, this expansion can be developed by the authors and co-created by the audience, thus adding a new dimension to writing for transmedia narratives.

We must add two caveats, however. The first is that the constant generation of interpretants must occur within frames that facilitate an appropriate (or reasonable) experience of story or play, or both. We explore this point below. The second caveat has to do with the sense of community. For many transmedia producers, 'storytelling is a social experience' (Bernardo 2014c). Bernardo adds:

> As producers, we shouldn't forget how important this need to interact and participate is to telling and experiencing a story. The most effective stories therefore are inclusive, not exclusive. They create a community of viewers engaged in ongoing dialogue. Unlike the "choose your own adventure" style of storytelling, **transmedia enriches stories by activating our human affinity for shared experiences**. (Bernardo 2014c, emphasis in original)

Peirce's ethics, or right action, involve exerting individual effort in concert with the efforts of the extended community (Parker 2003, 33). In this sense, his ethics apply remarkably to transmedia storytelling because a core principle of transmedia experiences is creating communities around the story universe (Jenkins 2006).

As critics have noted, this co-option of audiences and communities into the story universe brings with it ethical considerations of its own, particularly related to unpaid fan labour. This is a subject extensively explored by critical media studies' scholars (Andrejevic 2009; Baym and Burnett 2009; Caldwell 2009; De Kosnik 2012; Fuchs 2010, 2012; Hesmondhalgh 2010; Sokolova 2012; Stanfill and Condis 2014; Terranova 2000), highlighting both the dark and brighter sides of free fan labour. On the one hand, there is the discourse that fan work generates surplus value that is extracted and exploited by industry (Stanfill and Condis 2014). On the other hand, there is the discourse that not all freely circulated cultural production constitutes exploitation (De Kosnik 2012). Stanfill and Condis (2014) discuss 'the proliferation of value generated by fans for fans. Fandom runs on fan labor, and this work produces enjoyment, collectivity, and various material and immaterial goods that give fandom shape as a practice, community, or culture'.

ETHICAL CHALLENGES IN TRANSMEDIA STORYTELLING

The newness and complexity of the multiplatform writing realm, and the ethical issues involved in transmedia scripting, demands further research. The main current reference regarding ethical challenges in transmedia storytelling is the work of Andrea Phillips (2011, 2012a), who elaborates on her own experiences as a writer and game designer. In addition, Carter (2012), Finch (2012) and Picard (2013) identify different layers or dimensions of key transmedia cases affected by ethical concerns.

Phillips (2012b) describes herself as 'a *writer*. A content creator. A builder of imaginary cities and conspiracies and lives, either out of nothing at all or built on the foundation of someone else's work'. Transmedia storytelling is all about storyworlds unfolding across media platforms (Dena 2009, 18). Readers, users and players use 'the blueprint of a finished text to construct a mental image of this world' (Ryan and Thon 2014, 3). In Peircean terms, the reader's imagination is inserted in the productive incompleteness of the interpretants, enabling the generation of new interpretants *ad infinitum*.

A key aspect of the design and scripting of transmedia texts is to establish parameters for interpretation, which can have ethical implications on the way the work is received, as well as the terms for participation in that work. Two particular dimensions are important: (1) blurring, disclaimers and disclosures and (2) author and audience ethical involvement. The first dimension, *blurring, disclaimers and disclosures*, refers to the audience's ability to discern the blurred lines between fact and fiction and the need for disclaimers or disclosures in each media platform involved in a certain transmedia project. A disclaimer is a sort of statement that normally denies something, that repudiates a claim, a disavowal. A disclosure is an act of exposure, a sort of revelation, of transparency. However, within the variability of signification of transmedia storytelling, the audience may accept or disregard such attempts at responsibility and transparency. The second dimension, *author and audience ethical involvement*, deals with potential deception, disappointment, endangering and actual consequences for the audience and the transmedia authors and producers resulting from the blurring boundaries between factual and fictional aspects.

Both of these dimensions have an impact on the way user-participation with the story is framed. Especially in the terrain of ARGs, the idea of boundary leads us to the concept of cognitive frame, which 'is (or delimits) a class or set of messages (or meaningful actions)' (Bateson 1987, 192). According to Bateson (1987), frames organize the viewer's perception and our experience of signs. Cognitive frames generate contexts for interpretation, which interfere in the perception of reality and fantasy.

> As a player steps in and out of a game, he or she is crossing that boundary, or frame, which defines the game in time and space. The cognitive frame is a concept connected to the question of the "reality" of a game, of the relationship between the artificial world of the game and the "real life" contexts that it intersects. (Salen and Zimmerman 2003, 370)

Salen and Zimmerman (2003, 370) emphasize that 'the frame of a game communicates that those contained within it are "playing" and that the space of play is separate in some way from that of the real world'. The boundaries, or frames, are inherent parts of play. Moreover, the transmedia storyworld functions as a cognitive frame that can shape audience response.

The blurring of boundaries that arise from unclear or ambiguous frames is central to the ethical consideration of author and audience ethical involvement. A useful example is *The Agony and Ecstasy of Steve Jobs*, a retroactive kind of transmedia story created by American author and actor Mike Daisey as a monologue presented at the Public Theatre in New York. Retroactive 'transmedia stories are the ones that start to be planned after the fact normally based on a successful preexistent project' (Gambarato 2013, 87). While originally a performance piece it became an object of discussion for writers interested in transmedia storytelling (Carter 2012). The play explored Jobs' life, foregrounding the poor working conditions of Chinese labourers in FoxConn factories in Shenzhen, China, which produce most of Apple's devices. In January 2012, the monologue received extensive attention after the episode *Mr. Daisey Goes to the Apple Factory* was aired on the radio programme *This American Life*. Two months later, the producers of the programme discovered that the facts exposed by Daisey were partially fabricated, and the airing of a *Retraction* episode on the same radio programme received significant international media attention, with Daisey confronted with the real facts. From Carter's perspective,

> Going to the theater, whether for a live performance or film, we suspend our disbelief. We do this with books, games, and even campfire stories. We know there's not really a boogieman coming to slash us in our tent in the night, but we still might lose sleep as our imaginations run wild. Even with true stories, we all know there's a little embellishment tossed in for flavor. (Carter 2012)

However, *This American Life* holds itself to different (journalistic) standards, and the expectations are diverse. Carter's solution to this divergence in expectations or standards is a clear disclaimer, which would perfectly match the Peircean ethical ideal to increase order, harmony and connectedness within a community. Notwithstanding, in the case of *The Agony and Ecstasy of Steve Jobs*, the two-line disclaimer emphasized the nonfictional nature of the story by stating in capital letters: 'THIS IS A WORK OF NONFICTION. SOME NAMES AND IDENTITIES HAVE BEEN CHANGED TO PROTECT THE SOURCES' (Carter 2012). Overall, Carter (2012) insists, 'whether it's a stage play, film or ARG, letting the audience know a story isn't 100% factual protects artists from a world of scrutiny and offers the audience an opportunity to go along for the ride with abandon'. It is not that simple. From an opposing viewpoint, Finch (2012) discusses whether the audience should assume that, for instance, live theatre is fictional because it is staged and assume that a radio programme tells the truth unless the programme's creators state the programme is fictional. He stresses that instalments of the story can actually have different impacts, depending on the platform (Finch 2012) and we add, depending on the frame as well. Within transmedia stories, it is possible to create and recognize different layers of frames. For instance, the story universe functions itself as a cognitive frame; inside the storyworld, an ARG serves as a frame; inside an ARG, disclosures/disclaimers work as frames, and so forth. However, it is not merely a matter of 'frames within frames' (Bateson 1987, 194). For Bateson (1987, 193–194), 'a frame is metacommunicative. Any message, which either explicitly or implicitly defines a frame, *ipso facto* gives the receiver instructions or aids in his attempt to understand the messages included within the frame'. His concept of a metacommunicative level of abstraction was formulated while he observed monkeys 'play' fighting in a zoo. '[T]his phenomenon, play, could only occur if the participant organisms were capable of some degree of meta-communication, i.e., of exchanging signals which would carry the message "this is play"' (Bateson 1987, 185).

Finch (2012) challenges Carter's arguments about stories being 100 % factual and the need for a disclaimer and/or a disclosure on every platform and ponders if there are any 100 % factual stories, if every story should have a disclaimer on each platform, and if a simple disclosure like 'this is a work of fiction' would be enough to avoid ethical issues.

Disclosures do not always solve the issue of an appropriate or reasonable frame. At least it did not in the case of the transmedia promotion of the Sony Pictures movie *2012* (2009). This transmedia marketing campaign developed by Andrea Phillips was condemned by the National Aeronautics and Space Administration (NASA), despite the 'references to Sony Pictures and the film in both text and logos' (Minchew 2011). The movie is about the end of the world in 2012 based on predictions in the Mayan calendar, and the too realistic website The Institute for Human Continuity (http://archive.bigspaceship.com/ihc/) spread the message, which eventually reached scientists. Consequently, Dr. David Morrison of NASA's Astrobiology Institute, who received more than 1,000 inquiries from the public worried about the end of the world, declared the website was 'ethically wrong' (Allen 2009). Phillips (2011), in her talk about The Ethics of Pervasive Fiction, described pervasive fiction as fiction that uses the real world as a platform, fiction that could be indistinguishable from real things that are happening in the world, and admitted that they changed some details and deleted others after NASA's comments. She states that 'the world is not optimized to distinguish what it is true from what is fictional' (Phillips 2011), and points as an example to the confusion created by Orson Welles' 1938 legendary radio adaptation of H.G. Wells' *War of the Worlds*, which was presented in part as news bulletins, with reports from the novel read on the air as if a real alien invasion was taking place (Minchew 2011).

Finch (2012) suggests that best practice should focus on the potential harm, instead of indiscriminately fulfilling each platform with disclaimers or disclosures. He emphasizes that the audience should be alerted in situations 'when the platform might cause them to accept a fictional story as true, or where the circumstances create a greater risk of harm'. The collective purpose of Peirce's *summum bonum* would be favoured in this case, which would encompass the goals of the producers as well as the welfare of co-creators.

A technical alternative for helping the audience with the issue of distinguishing truth from fiction could be a 'fictional tag' (Minchew 2011) that would display an icon on the browser to mark the page as fictional in the same way the lock icon appears on secure websites. However, the disadvantage in this case is that the audience does not always pay attention to such details. A transmedia label, stamp or tag, which describes to users up-front what to expect, could cause the loss of the sense of discovery, the mystery or aura of such projects (Minchew 2011).

Phillips (2011) warns that 'the more realistic something is, the more you should worry about legal and ethical implications'. Even with all the precautions and implications considered, things can unpredictably go wrong. Under the scope of the second dimension (author and audience ethical involvement) is the case of *I Love Bees*. In 2004, part of the campaign to promote the video game *Halo 2* was *I Love Bees*, an ARG produced by the pioneering company 42 Entertainment. Players could answer a payphone as an offline task included in the ARG, and one player had the extremely dangerous idea of answering the phone in the middle of Hurricane Frances in Florida (Minchew 2011; Phillips 2011). This example illustrates that the risk of harm (which could be involved in transmedia stories) should be controlled by the authors but also observed by the audience.

Phillips (2011) proposes four considerations to minimize ethical issues and guide the design and writing process of transmedia stories: (1) consider if the story is so realistic that people would be fooled by it, (2) ponder the situation in which the audience would see just a little part of the transmedia story, (3) take into account what potential harm the transmedia project could cause, and (4) consider if there is the possibility for the creators to be sued or arrested. We add the following propositions: (5) consider if there is a reasonable purpose (connected to Peirce's concrete reasonableness) behind the story or experience, and (6) reflect upon what could be done to clarify the fictional essence of the project without 'killing' the experience but avoiding harm.

Terms such as hoax, mock, fake and fraud can be used to describe different situations related to transmedia projects that cross the line between fact and fiction. This situation does not imply, however, that make-believe projects and 'fiction-masquerading-as-reality-TV genre' (Williams 2014) are necessarily unethical or not admirable, in Peirce's sense. Mentioning authentic experiences such as *The Blair Witch Project* (1999) and *Cloverfield* (2008), Woerner (2011) concludes that the reason the audience did not feel duped by them is 'instead of demanding that people believe their lie, they dreamt up a world people were desperate to be a part of'. This argument goes along with the logic of world building behind transmedia scriptwriting and recognizes the audience's capability of making their own choices.

The blurring of boundaries, in terms of cognition and communication, is taken further in ARGs. The popular motto 'this is not a game' (McGonigal 2003, 112), introduced by the producers of the ARG connected to the feature film *A.I.* (2001), and transformed into a general motto for the genre (Waern and Denward 2009, 1), is an indicator of the blurring of fiction and reality that certain experiences might induce in an attempt to craft engaging experiences.

Bateson's approach to games and play is important here. It recognizes 'a more complex form of play. The paradox here is that even when we have the message "this is not a game", it denotes "this is a game"' (Bateson 1987, 198). For Bateson (1987, 198), paradoxes of abstraction should be part of all complex communication, otherwise 'life would then be an endless interchange of stylized messages, a game with rigid rules, unrelieved by change or humor'.

Although ARGs might resemble role-playing games, when playing an ARG, participants usually do not take on another identity (a fictional one) but take on a role or task within the given narrative, accepting its frame. In ARGs, the participant has a shared goal that should be accomplished with other players. As Szulborski (2005, 1–3) remarks, one of the main goals of ARG authors and participants is to create an immersive experience that blurs the line between fiction and reality and complies with the motto 'this is not a game'. Therefore, the two dimensions of ethical issues within transmedia cases (blurring, disclaimers and disclosures, and author and audience ethical involvement) are potentially involved in ARGs. Ideally, ARGs draw participants into a second reality that is a surrogate of the daily actual reality. The adjective *alternate* refers to something happening in turns in the sense of a recurring shift between the real and fictional realities offered by the experience, or a shift in framing, in Bateson's (1987) terms. Despite the 'this is not a game' formula, the playful nature of such experiences is intrinsic to ARGs. Furthermore, play does not deny the possibility of full immersion. In contrast, play supports full immersion and strives for it.

ETHICAL ISSUES IN *THE TRUTH ABOUT MARIKA*

To delve more deeply into ethical questions, we wish to consider two case studies: *The Truth About Marika* deals with the fictional disappearance of a young woman in Sweden, and *Final Punishment* explores the lives of eight women imprisoned in a fictitious high-security facility in Rio de Janeiro, Brazil, who are suddenly being killed one by one. Both projects adopt ARGs among the other narrative components that characterize complex transmedia experiences. In relation to the layers of ethical matters, both projects involve the two dimensions previously presented: blurring, disclaimers and disclosures, and author and audience ethical involvement. *The Truth About Marika* intends to blur real and fictional lines, employs a disclaimer and arguably deceives the audience. *Final Punishment* also blurs boundaries, uses disclosures and allegedly disappoints the audience. Thus, both projects form case studies in the investigation of ethical challenges within the context of transmedia storytelling. This is not to say that the projects are identical. Indeed, the contexts and purposes of each work are different: in the Swedish project, the motivation is to develop a participatory format erasing borders between drama and entertainment and, in the Brazilian project, the commercial context is evident.

The Truth About Marika is a transmedia drama produced by The Company P and Swedish Television (SVT) and broadcast in autumn 2007. The full broadcast of each of the five episodes was composed of two different parts. The first part was a traditional 45-minute drama episode featuring the disappearance of Marika several days before her wedding. The second part was a television (fake) debate. The pretext for the make-believe debate was the accusation made by a blogger named Adrijanna who claimed that SVT had taken the real story of her friend Maria's disappearance from her blog http://www.conspirare.se and made it into a TV series by only changing her name from Maria to Marika. Adrijanna claimed that every year 20,000 people disappear in Sweden and that an organization named Ordo Serpentis could be behind it. SVT first denied the accusation but then decided to admit that part of Adrijanna's claims were true. During the fake debates, the audience was invited to participate in the search for Maria by visiting the SVT website and, consequently, Adrijanna's website.

The search took place on different platforms, such as internet forums and real-life events. *The Truth About Marika* was a fictional experience. The story was fictional. Adrijanna was part of the production, and Maria was an imaginary character. The TV series was recorded a year earlier, but the fake debates were recorded only a day before each episode aired to blur the line between fiction and reality as much as possible and to engage the audience.

In July 2007, Adrijanna began touring Sweden spreading the message that the upcoming TV series was based on her life story, and that Maria really had disappeared. The initial participant recruitment took place through one-to-one promotion and did not hide the real nature of the search: a game and a media stunt. Early participants, however, quickly adhered to the metacommunicative rule of ARGs: know it is fiction, but pretend it is real.

When a new participant entered one of the websites crafted for the game, he or she was warned about the fictional nature of the experience. A disclaimer appeared the first two times the participant logged in:

> Warning: Conspirare is part of a fictional creation. Opinions expressed here do not always reflect opinions of [The Company] P or SVT. Random similarities with real people are sometimes purely coincidental. Participation is at your own risk and under your own responsibility. Conspirare has only one rule–pretend that it is real. You participate through following the blog, watching the movie clips, and discussing in the forum. The search will lead you out on the Internet and out on the streets of your own city. Click on OK to show that you have understood this. (Waern and Denward 2009, 4)

Thus far, *The Truth About Marika* seems to follow the Peircean ethical ideal by designing an emotionally attractive story that has the admirable (collective) goal of saving the protagonist's life. The blurred boundaries *per se* are not contrary to Peircean ethics in the sense that blurred lines can be an important factor in building a compelling storyworld, which complies with the *summum bonum*, has a reasonable purpose, and, therefore, contributes to achieving concrete reasonableness. However, in this case, other details should be observed.

Martin Ericsson (2010), a former producer and art director at The Company P, emphasizes that seeking immersion means designing and writing an experience that can take over reality. He sees immersion as 'the quest for the perfect manifestation of a dream' (Ericsson 2010) where, in a well-crafted experience, and contrary perhaps to critics of unpaid fan labour, participants are so engaged with the storyworld that they start dreaming in character. The immersion in the fictional world was a primary element implicitly agreed upon by the participant and the ARG, but, at the same time, television viewers were not alerted about the fictional nature of the show. Instead, viewers were told that the debate was a live event, making the line between reality and fiction almost impossible to see. This difference in the message delivered to the public created two distinct groups of participants/viewers: those who knew about the fictional nature of the show but pretended it was real, and those who were unaware and believed they were following a real search for one of thousands of people missing in Sweden.

According to Waern and Denward's (2009) research findings published in the article 'On the Edge of Reality: Reality Fiction in "*Sanningen om Marika*,"' the fictional reality took over reality so much that even internet users started finding it difficult to separate reality from fiction. The results of Waern and Denward's (2009, 4) survey concerning audience awareness of the fictional nature of *The Truth About Marika*, conducted among online users immediately after the last episode aired, demonstrate the following: (1) 30 % thought it was real, (2) 29 % did not think it was real, (3) 24 % pretended it was real, and (4) 17 % made no distinction between reality and fiction. Since the survey was carried out among people who had previously entered one of the internet gates with the pop-up warning, it can be inferred that the awareness among viewers who did not immerse themselves in the internet experience was lower than the data showed. We argue that, under the second dimension of ethical issues, the audience could have experienced disappointment. Waern and Denward (2009) stress that the illusion among TV viewers was further achieved by the make-believe debate publicized as a live broadcast in TV guides.

A key question to highlight here is whether the blurring between fiction and reality was ethical, especially when it was carried out by Swedish Public Service Broadcasting. In light of Peircean ethics, the project invested in an emotional appeal to find a missing person, which could be considered something collectively admirable in itself and, therefore, consistent with Peirce's approach. However, the project benefited from the reasonable purpose of the ideals that guide our actions, without making the fictional nature of the story necessarily clear to all audiences. *The Truth About Marika* received sharp criticism because of that. Britta Svensson (2007), a columnist for the Swedish newspaper *Expressen*, referring to the fake debate of the first TV episode, wrote:

This "scandal" seems to be part of the drama in which SVT, in a way that has never happened before, tries to trick viewers by relaxing the boundary between fiction and reality. It is completely idiotic. [The fact] that people disappear without a trace is a reality that news programmes sometimes need to report on. To then pretend that it is true that SAPO [Swedish security service] silences the truth about the 20,000 missing Swedes is purely irresponsible. (Our translation)

Christopher Sandberg argued otherwise:

The project was clearly communicated as fiction to all audiences and participants. We used the SVT fiction logo on television and a disclaimer online. Our approach was to tell people it was a drama, and then base it on real global issues, eventually blurring the lines between fiction and reality, to make the audience challenge what they experienced. ... Our goal was specifically to give the younger audience tools to get agency in their life, to feel and be free to search for individual happiness and collective sense of belonging. (Christopher Sandberg, CEO/creative director of The Company P, who produced *The Truth About Marika*; interview by Alessandro Nanì, 17 March 2014)

Sandberg's remarks seem to contradict Waern and Denward's research and Svensson's criticisms; notwithstanding, the remarks are aligned with Peirce's ethical approach, especially regarding the collective sense of belonging. Sandberg adds:

We found it extra important to discuss the role of media, when shaping the world- view of a younger audience. All news, art and entertainment is produced with an agenda, and *The Truth About Marika* aimed at making you aware and equipped to deal with sorting truth from propaganda. (Christopher Sandberg, interview by Alessandro Nanì, 17 March 2014)

However, the desire to promote media literacy did not necessarily match the concrete results of the experience, as Waern and Denward's (2009) research demonstrates. Therefore, *The Truth About Marika* apparently failed to fully embrace Peirce's ethical ideal because the project did not necessarily clarify to the audience, or at least to some of the audience, that the admirable task of helping to find a missing person was completely fictional. The frames offered within the ARG (online disclaimer) and on television (SVT fiction logo) were not enough: 47 % of the public were not aware that it was fiction (Waern and Denward 2009, 4). The interpretants generated by almost half of the audience strongly differed from the ones imaged by the authors.

ETHICAL ISSUES IN *FINAL PUNISHMENT*

In 2009, the pioneering Portuguese transmedia production company beActive launched a multiplatform thriller series in Brazil commissioned by Oi Telecom, a major Brazilian telecommunication company (Machado and Guerreiro 2010). The corporation was expanding beyond its mobile operation, adding internet services and a digital TV channel. Entitled *Castigo Final/Final Punishment*, the transmedia project focused on eight women imprisoned in a fictitious high-security facility in Rio de Janeiro. The detention centre was controlled by a computer system, and after the surveillance connection was lost, someone started killing the inmates in the same way they had committed their crimes. The production invited the audience to search for clues that would enable them to figure out a password that could open the prison's doors and save the inmates (Gambarato and Alzamora 2012, 58). Oi Telecom's purpose was to showcase and advertise its own services: mobile, digital TV and internet portal. The transmedia experience incorporated these three media platforms, among others, according to the interests of the sponsor. 'The company wanted something edgy that would cause a buzz and potentially attract the demographic they were interested in: 18–35 year-olds' (Gambarato 2014, 98).

beActive had tried to produce this violent script in Europe, but no European sponsors were willing to be associated with it (Bernardo 2010). The opportunity offered by Oi Telecom seemed appropriate, since the story would involve multiple platforms and the narrative about inmates being killed in a prison would not (theoretically) be problematic in Brazil. According to Bernardo (2010), the strategy for engaging the Brazilian audience was to make it personal by promoting a bond between the public and the inmates and giving the audience the task of saving the inmates via an intricate ARG. Within the Peircean ethical approach, this premise would apparently fulfil the ideal of the *summum bonum*. However, the fact that the project's story was not previously accepted in Europe but was in Brazil could raise ethical concerns. In fact, Brazil is used to a higher level of criminality than Europe, and unfortunately, the script was not necessarily impressive or touching in the South American country. The strategic focus was then to make the story more intimate and touching; otherwise, the Brazilian audience, commonly known as an emotional one, would not be particularly interested. Nevertheless, the astonishing amounts of violence toward women involved in this project represents an ethical problem *per se*, perpetuating the culture of denigration and violence against women— and our acceptance of that violence. In a recent study concerning violence in modern Brazil, Larkins (2015) argues that there is a growing market and a substantial audience interested in consuming representations of violence through media and other leisure-based practices and products. In this context, Larkins (2015) states that disenfranchised people can be eager for images of themselves, unconsciously embracing stereotypes and building an overlay of hyper-reality that actually detaches them from the depicted reality. 'Clearly, these processes are not unique to Brazil but are implicit in the production and consumption of images of structural and physical violence in a variety of settings' (Larkins 2015, 108).

Final Punishment was a mockumentary that blurred the line between fact and fiction. The complex transmedia experience had as its tent pole a four-part series aired on Oi TV and was accompanied by an ARG, which integrated different media platforms, such as mobile, internet and print media. The narrative began with fake news published in Brazilian newspapers and on websites ('Inaugurado Novo Presídio', 2009) reporting the opening of a new prison called 'Ivo de Kermartin' in Rio de Janeiro. Shortly afterwards, other fabricated news items informed readers about a group that had hacked the prison's computerized security system, and surveillance camera footage was unveiled. The images featured eight women trapped in one corridor inside the prison. One by one, they were being killed the same way they had committed their crimes. When the audience started searching online for more information about 'Ivo de Kermartin' prison (a clear reference to the French saint Yves de Kermartin, referred as an 'advocate of the poor'), they were directed to the penitentiary's 'official' website: http://www.ivokermartin.com/. When audience members accessed it, they saw a hacked page displaying the content of nine surveillance cameras. This was the entry point to the ARG, and the public could see specific disclosures about the fictional nature of the story. In the top-right hand corner of the screen, it was possible to read (in small letters) the following disclosure: 'Enter the five-digit code necessary to free the inmates. This code can only be found if you participate in the game final punishment'. Final punishment was an underlined link that directed the player to the rules of the game. Side by side, there was another clickable link to access the rules called *8 steps to play Final Punishment*. In addition, at the very bottom of the page, in tiny letters, were the names beActive and Oi channel.

Bernardo highlights that 'since day one all the communication around the ARG included a reference that it was a game in order to avoid misunderstandings and problems for' both the game and Oi' (Nuno Bernardo, CEO of beActive and producer of *Final Punishment*, interview by Renira R. Gambarato, 14 March 2014). Recalling 'this is not a game' (ARG's motto), an emerging concern is if the information in the corner of the screen would be sufficient to grab people's attention or trigger the right metacommunicative frame. After all, this declaration could be read as a lure into the 'game'.

The logic behind the *Final Punishment* engagement strategy was to sell the idea that the audience could save the inmates, which a priori complies with the *summum bonum*. Although not everybody would necessarily consider saving inmates as socially desirable, in Brazil, a country without death penalty and with the largest Catholic population in the world (Toro 2013), this idea sounds favourable. To do that, the ARG players searched for clues scattered throughout social media outlets, blogs, websites and mobile phone messages, for instance, to decipher the code that could open the prison's doors and save the women. The game was played right before the TV series was aired. The four-part TV mockumentary revealed what happened to the characters and who was responsible for the murders. The process of screenwriting intertwined the different media platforms involved in the transmedia project. Bernardo claimed that 'the players had a direct influence on the story. We shot various endings and the result displayed is directly related to the outcome of the game' (Nuno Bernardo, interview by Renira R. Gambarato, 14 March 2014). However, this was not clear to the public, and even if it was the case, the ending options had been pre-determined. The script was well crafted in the sense of connecting the dots and concluding the puzzle, and developing 'various endings' would not have been easy for the scriptwriters (Gambarato 2014, 103). Bernardo added:

> Our goal—and we've implemented it in other projects—is to ensure that the audience won't leave disappointed. Meaning that, if we want them to get involved with the story, we have to ensure that the actions of the players really have an impact on the game and on the interactive series. The worst thing you can do is simulate the interactivity and not give voice to the player. (Nuno Bernardo, interview by Renira R. Gambarato, 14 March 2014)

In *Final Punishment*, although the audience can interact within the ARG, the experience did not necessarily foster full participation, in the sense of expressing 'their creativity in a unique, and surprising manner, allowing them to influence the final result' (Gambarato 2012, 74). Participation involves co-creation. Bernardo reinforces that most ARG players know that it is a fictional story, and argued that 'the player does what the Americans call "suspension of disbelief". The game becomes more interesting if you really believe it is really happening and that our actions can even save people' (Nuno Bernardo, interview by Renira R. Gambarato, 14 March 2014). Suspension of disbelief, a term coined by the poet Samuel Taylor Coleridge in 1817, refers to accepting events or characters as believable when they are seen as incredible, a semblance of truth sufficient to instigate the suspension of disbelief for the moment (Coleridge 1985; Brown 2012). This convention implies first that the audience consciously knows that it is fiction and then comes the decision of whether the audience willingly suspends its disbelief or not. For instance, in the Orkut community especially dedicated to the ARG, an anonymous member posted:

> Final Punishment
>   Guys, apparently this community is a little slow, but there are 6 women isolated in a women's prison in risk of death. There is a crowd already helping: anyone else willing to help? ... Otherwise, there won't be anyone to tell the story. Except for the videos that have been (and are being) captured by closed circuit TV. In a country without law, we can't let people do justice with their bare hands! Otherwise, we go back to the middle ages! Help!!! (Anonymous 2009)

It is not clear if this post is the perfect example of the suspension of disbelief because we cannot assure whether it is a genuine audience post, or it was posted by the authors, since this was a moderated community and the author was anonymous. While it is possible for a post to support dual frames, in the context of current debates around the ethics of transmedia storytelling, it seems that the main objective is to clarify that it is a fictional story before believing it is real. Bernardo concludes:

> Personally, I think any ARG must be assumed as a work of fiction and never lie to the spectator. Everything must be done to make it look as real as possible, but always have a tag saying that it is a game, a work of fiction. I usually say it is like Santa Claus: who[ever] wants to play and participate in the ARG will "believe" that the game is real, because the whole experience is much more interesting. Imagine Christmas without Santa? (Nuno Bernardo, interview by Renira R. Gambarato, 14 March 2014)

Final Punishment focuses on the emotional appeal to save people's lives, a collectively admirable action consistent with Peirce's approach to ethics, albeit embedded in a context of gendered violence. Ethics, for Peirce, should take the aesthetic ideal of the unconditionally admirable to ask what kind of action or conduct guides us towards the growth of reason or rationality, which Peirce called the growth of concrete reasonableness. The right action is the one that is self-controlled (not simply for isolated individuals) and attempts to achieve the ultimate aesthetic ideal, which is always collective. Nevertheless, both *The Truth About Marika* and *Final Punishment* manipulate concrete reasonableness, and do not clarify how the audience's actions in the ARG lead to audience members' genuine participation in the story. This could then allegedly imply that the audience experienced disappointment, which denotes ethical issues. Overall, *Final Punishment* had a million viewers per episode and 115,000 registered ARG players (Bernardo 2010). In 2009, when the project was launched, notwithstanding any ethical concerns, it represented a great advancement in transmedia developments in Brazil with well-articulated multiplatform scriptwriting.

CONCLUSION

Independently of commercial interests or corporations' strategic purposes, as Woerner (2011) suggests, the main goal for transmedia writers and designers should be to build a storyworld that people would love to be involved with. This would then pave the way for potential profit, or would inspire meaningful engagement, in the case of non-profit projects. Audience engagement, a pillar of transmedia storytelling, implies to attract, to inspire, to motivate, and to allow people to (somehow) be part of the story. 'The age of multiplatform media is defined by audience behaviour' and 'audiences [have] become increasingly sophisticated' (Bernardo 2014b).

Within the terms of critical theory, profit implies exploitation. Within this essay we do not provide solutions beyond noting the ethical tension highlighted by Sokolova (2012, 1581): namely, the tension between the enthusiastic opportunity for the audience to creatively participate in transmedia projects and the commodification of their creativity in favour of commercial interests. According to Bateson (1987), paradoxes, contradictions and tensions should be part of all complex communication. In this context, both the celebratory and critical approaches to fan labour are not mutually exclusive. Baym and Burnett (2009, 446) remind us that to claim audiences are necessarily exploited is to ignore how much they enjoy generating content and sharing their experiences and, foremost, to deny the capacity they have to simply stop doing what they do.

Peirce's ethics provides an additional layer of consideration. His core concepts '*summum bonum*' and 'concrete reasonableness' invite the transmedia storyteller to reflect on what it means to offer audiences meaningful and enriching experiences, including participatory opportunities, and to ponder why multiple media stories are relevant. Beyond the true/false, right/wrong and good/bad dichotomies, Peirce's ethics involves a commitment to increase order, harmony and connectedness. What these values mean will be dependent on the communities in which they circulate. According to the Peircean prism, action that disregards this premise is harmful and should be overall avoided.

The Truth About Marika and *Final Punishment* play with an emotional appeal to save people's lives, which could be considered collectively admirable in itself and therefore consistent with the Peircean approach to ethics. However, the poignant violence toward women in both cases could already represent a doubtable choice in the ethical sphere. Furthermore, as mock stories, the projects take advantage of the reasonable purpose of the ideals that guide our actions, not necessarily making it clear how the audience, especially within an ARG, genuinely participates in the story. Participation implies that the audience can co-create and influence on the story's result. Although the two cases in principle comply with the Peircean supreme ideal of human life, the practical implementation of the stories across different platforms, which depended on the screenwriting process, is not aligned with the concrete reasonableness because they do not necessarily clarify the audience's real role. Screenwriters could achieve Peirce's concrete reasonableness by developing a reasonable purpose behind the story or experience to be designed and ensuring that it is communicated appropriately to the audience. Peirce's concept of *summum bonum* serves as a reminder to multiplatform screenwriters to offer audiences meaningful, relevant and enriching experiences. ARGs are designed to disguise the facts to 'make believe' the game is real. Nevertheless, this does not imply that the audience should not be aware that this is an ARG indeed. The audience choose to be part of the ARG and pretend that it is real. For Bateson (1987, 190): 'Within the dream the dreamer is usually unaware that he is dreaming, and within "play" he must often be reminded that "This is play"'.

References

Allen, Nick. 2009. 'Nasa: World Will Not End in 2012.' *The Telegraph*, October 17. http://www.telegraph.co.uk/culture/film/film-news/6356140/Nasa-world-will-not-end-in-2012.html

Alzamora, Geane, and Renira R. Gambarato. 2014. 'Peircean Semiotics and Transmedia Dynamics: Communicational Potentiality of the Model of Semiosis.' *Ocula—Semiotic Eye on Media* 15: 1–13.

Andersen, Michael. 2010. 'Jeff Gomez Reveals Secrets to Transmedia Franchise Development at Cinekid.' *Wired*, November 18. http://www.wired.com/2010/11/jeff-gomez-reveals-secrets-to-transmedia-franchise-development-at-cinekid

Andrejevic, Mark. 2009. 'Exploiting YouTube: Contradictions of User-Generated Labor.' In *The YouTube Reader*, edited by Pelle Snickars and Patrick Vonderau, 406–23. Stockholm: National Library of Sweden.

Anonymous. 2009. Final Punishment Orkut Page, October 30. http://www.orkut.com.br/Main#CommMsgs?cmm=7709883&tid=5387913323458118628&na=3&npn=2&nid=7709883-5387913323458118628-5390564164516823677

Bateson, Gregory. 1987. *Steps to an Ecology of Mind: Collected Essays in Anthropology, Psychiatry, Evolution, and Epistemology*. Northvale: Jason Aronson Inc.

Baym, Nancy K., and Robert Burnett. 2009. 'Amateur Experts: International Fan Labour in Swedish Independent Music.' *International Journal of Cultural Studies* 12 (5): 433–449.

Bernardo, Nuno. 2010. 'Case Study: *Final Punishment*.' Online video. Accessed 16April2014.http://blip.tv/power-to-the-pixel/case-study-final-punishment-4356116

Bernardo, Nuno. 2014a. *Transmedia 2.0: How to Create an Entertainment Brand Using a Transmedia Approach to Storytelling*. Lisbon: BeActive Books.

Bernardo, Nuno. 2014b. 'Nuno Bernardo: Audience Behaviour Is Defining Multiplatform Media.' *Mipworld Blog*, March 18. http://mipblog.com/2014/03/nuno-bernardo-audience-behaviour-is-defining-multiplatform-media/

Bernardo, Nuno. 2014c. 'Nuno Bernardo: Storytelling Is a Social Experience.' *Mipworld Blog*, May 28. http://blog.mipworld.com/2014/05/storytelling-social-experience/#.U4WxxvmSySq

Brown, Douglas W. 2012. 'The Suspension of Disbelief in Videogames.' PhD diss., Brunel University.

Caldwell, John T. 2009. 'Hive-Sourcing is the New Out-Sourcing: Studying Old (Industrial) Labor Habits in New (Consumer) Labor Clothes.' *Cinema Journal* 49 (1): 160–167.

Carter, James. 2012. 'The Transmedia and Transgressions of Mike Daisey.' *James Carter Blog*, March 17. http://onemuse.com/2012/03/17/the-transmedia-and-transgressions-of-mike-daisey/

Coleridge, Samuel T. 1985. *Biographia Literaria* (1817). Princeton: Princeton University Press.

De Kosnik, Abigail. 2012. 'Fandom as Free Labor.' In *Digital Labor: The Internet as Playground and Factory*, edited by Trebor Scholz, 98–111. New York: Routledge.

Dena, Christy. 2009. 'Theorizing the Practice of Expressing a Fictional World across Distinct Media and Environments.' PhD diss., University of Sydney.

Ericsson, Martin. 2010. 'The Question for the Manifestation of a Dream.' Online video. Accessed 12 June 2014. http://youtu.be/HkM-ix2G24w

Fabbrichesi, Rossella, and Susanna Marietti, eds. 2006. *Semiotics and Philosophy in Charles Sanders Peirce*. Newcastle: Cambridge Scholars Press.

Finch, Randy. 2012. 'Ethics of Storytelling: Must You Tell Your Audience It Isn't Real?' *Randy Finch's Film Blog*, March 18. http://finchclasses.blogspot.fr/2012/03/ethics-of-storytelling-do-you-met-your.html

Fuchs, Christian. 2010. 'Labor in Informational Capitalism and on the Internet.' *The Information Society* 26: 179–196.

Fuchs, Christian. 2012. 'Class and Exploitation on the Internet.' In *Digital Labor: The Internet as Playground and Factory*, edited by Trebor Scholz, 211–24. New York: Routledge.

Gambarato, Renira R. 2012. 'Sign, Systems, and Complexity of Transmedia Storytelling.' *Communication Studies/Estudos em Comunicação* 12: 69–83.

Gambarato, Renira R. 2013. 'Transmedia Project Design: Theoretical and Analytical Considerations.' *Baltic Screen Media Review* 1: 80–100.

Gambarato, Renira R. 2014.'Transmedia Storytelling in Analysis: The Case of *Final Punishment*.' *Journal of Print and Media Technology Research* 3(2): 95–106.

Gambarato, Renira R., and Geane Alzamora. 2012. 'Transmedia Storytelling Initiatives in Brazilian Media.' *Medien Journal—Zeitschrift für Kommunikationskultur: Kommunikationsraum BRIC* 36 (4): 51–62.

Hesmondhalgh, David. 2010. 'User-Generated Content, Free Labour, and the Cultural Industries.' *Ephemera: Theory and Politics in Organization* 10 (3/4): 267–84.

Inaugurado Novo Presídio Feminino no Rio de Janeiro. 2009. *Baixaki Jogos,* October 1. http://www.baixakijogos.com.br/noticias/inaugurado-novo-presidio-feminino-no-rio-de-janeiro_167668.htm

Jenkins, Henry. 2003. 'Transmedia Storytelling.' *Technology Review.* http://www.technologyreview.com/news/401760/transmedia-storytelling/

Jenkins, Henry. 2006. *Convergence Culture—Where Old and New Media Collide.* New York: New York University Press.

Jenkins, Henry. 2011. 'Transmedia Storytelling 202.' *Confessions of an Aca-Fan Blog,* August 1. http://henryjenkins.org/2011/08/defining_transmedia_further_re.html

Jenkins, Henry. 2014. 'Transforming Television: An Interview with Denise Mann (Part Three).' *Confessions of an Aca-Fan Blog,* June 3. http://henryjenkins.org/2014/06/transforming-television-an-interview-with-denise-mann-part-three.html

Larkins, Erika M. R. 2015. *The Spectacular Favela: Violence in Modern Brazil.* Berkeley: University of California Press.

Machado, Alexandra, and Pedro S. Guerreiro. 2010. 'Tchau Vivo, oi Oi.' *Negócios Online,* July 28. http://www.jornaldenegocios.pt/empresas/detalhe/tchau_vivo_oi_oi.html

McGonigal, Jane. 2003. '"This Is Not a Game": Immersive Aesthetics and Collective Play.' Paper presented at the 5th International Digital Arts and Culture Conference, Royal Melbourne Institute of Technology, Melbourne, Australia, May 19–23, 110–18. http://hypertext.rmit.edu.au/dac/papers/McGonigal.pdf

Minchew, Brandie. 2011. 'SXSW 2011: Andrea Phillips on Blurring the Lines.' *ARGNet,* March 24. http://www.argn.com/2011/03/sxsw_2011_andrea_phillips_on_blurring_the_lines/

Parker, Kelly A. 2003. 'Reconstructing the Normative Sciences.' *Cognitio* 4 (1): 27–45.

Peirce, Charles S. 1931–1935, 1958. *Collected Papers of Charles Sanders Peirce.* Vols. 1–6, edited by Charles Hartshorne and Paul Weiss, vols. 7–8, Arthur W. Burks, ed. Cambridge: Harvard University Press. Cited in this chapter as CP (volume).(paragraph).

Phillips, Andrea. 2011. 'Hoax or Transmedia? The Ethics of Pervasive Fiction.' Audio File. Accessed 8 February 2014. http://schedule.sxsw.com/2011/events/event_IAP5713

Phillips, Andrea. 2012a. *A Creator's Guide to Transmedia Storytelling: How to Captivate and Engage Audiences across Multiple Platforms*. New York: McGraw-Hill.

Phillips, Andrea. 2012b. 'I am not a Transmedia Producer.' *Deus Ex Machinatio Blog*,January25.http://www.deusexmachinatio.com/blog/2012/1/25/i-am-not-a-transmedia-producer.html

Picard, Melanie. 2013. 'Jury Q&A: Questioning Transmedia and Ethics.' *Story 2023 Blog*, June 26. http://story2023.nextrends.swissnexsanfrancisco.org/jury-qa-questioning-transmedia-ethics/

Pratten, Robert. 2015. *Getting Started in Transmedia Storytelling: A Practical Guide for Beginners*. 2nd ed. London: CreateSpace.

Redondo, Ignacio. 2012. 'The Normativity of Communication: Norms and Ideals in Peirce's Speculative Rhetoric.' In *The Normative Thought of Charles S. Peirce*, edited by Cornelis de Waal and Krysztof Piotr Skowroński, 214–30. New York: Fordham University Press.

Roth, Robert J. 1998. *Radical Pragmatism: An Alternative*. New York: Fordham University Press.

Ryan, Marie-Laure, and Jan-Noël Thon, eds. 2014. *Storyworlds Across Media: Toward a Media-Conscious Narratology*. Lincoln and London: University of Nebraska Press.

Salen, Katie, and Eric Zimmerman. 2003. *Rules of Play: Game Design Fundamentals*. Cambridge: The MIT Press.

Santaella, Lucia. 1992. *A Assinatura das Coisas*. Rio de Janeiro: Imago.

Santaella, Lucia. 2000. *Estética—de Platão a Peirce*. São Paulo: Experimento.

Scolari, Carlos. 2009. 'Mapping Conversations about New Media: The Theoretical Field of Digital Communication.' *New Media & Society* 11 (6): 943–964.

Shepperson, Arnold. 2009. 'Realism, Logic and Social Communication—C.S. Peirce's Classification of Science in Communication Studies and Journalism.' *Critical Arts: South-North Cultural and Media Studies* 22 (2): 242–94.

Sokolova, Natalia. 2012. 'Co-opting Transmedia Consumers: User Content as Entertainment or 'Free Labour'? The Cases of S.T.A.L.K.E.R. and Metro 2033.' *Europe-Asia Studies* 64(8): 1565–583.

Stanfill, Mel, and Megan Condis. 2014. 'Fandom and/as Labor.' *Transformative Works and Cultures* 15. Accessed 7 March 2016. doi:10.3983/twc.2014.0593

Svensson, Britta. 2007. 'That Is Absolutely Ridiculous.' *Expressen*, October 29. http://www.expressen.se/noje/kronikorer/brittasvensson/1.902196/britta-svensson-det-ar-ju-fullstandigt-absurt

Szulborski, Dave. 2005. *This Is Not a Game: A Guide to Alternate Reality Gaming*. Macungie: New-Fiction.

Terranova, Tiziana. 2000. 'Free Labor: Producing Culture for the Digital Economy.' *Social Text* 18(2): 33–58. Accessed 7 March 2016. doi:10.1215/01642472-18-2_63-33

Toro, Ross. 2013. 'The World's Catholic Population.' *Live Science*, February 19. http://www.livescience.com/27244-the-world-s-catholic-population-info-graphic.html

Waern, Annika, and Marie Denward. 2009. 'On the Edge of Reality: Reality Fiction in "Sanningen om Marika".' In proceedings of *Breaking New Ground: Innovation in Games, Play, Practice and Theory—Digital Games Research Association (DiGRA) 2009*. London, UK, September, 2009. Brunel University. Accessed 15 February 2015. http://www.digra.org/wp-content/uploads/digital-library/09287.50584.pdf

Williams, Mary E. 2014. 'Horror's First Viral Hit: How "The Blair Witch Project" Revolutionized Movies.' *Salon*, June 13. http://www.salon.com/2014/06/13/horrors_first_viral_hit_how_the_blair_witch_project_revolutionized_movies/

Woerner, Meredith. 2011. 'Are Audiences Sick of Being Lied to?' *Io9*, March 4. http://io9.com/5774422/are-audiences-sick-of-being-lied-to

FILM AND TELEVISION REFERENCES

2012. 2009, Wr: Harald Kloser and Roland Emmerich, Dir: Roland Emmerich, USA, 158 mins.

A.I. 2001, Wr: Steven Spielberg and Ian Watson, Dir: Steven Spielberg, USA, 146 mins.

Castigo Final/Final Punishment. 2009, Cr: Nuno Bernardo, Brazil, beActive for Oi TV.

Cloverfield. 2008, Wr: Drew Goddard, Dir: Matt Reeves, USA, 84 mins.

Lost. 2004–2010, Cr: Jeffrey Bieber, Jeffrey Jacob Abrams, and Damon Lindelof; USA, Bad Robot Productions and ABC Studios; tx. ABC 22/09/2004–23/05/2010, 40 mins x 121 eps.

Sanningen om Marika/The Truth About Marika. 2007, Cr: Christopher Sandberg, Sweden, The Company P for SVT.

The Blair Witch Project. 1999, Wr: Daniel Myrick and Eduardo Sánchez, Dir: Daniel Myrick and Eduardo Sánchez, USA, 81 mins.

The Dark Knight. 2008, Wr: Jonathan Nolan and Christopher Nolan, Dir: Christopher Nolan, USA and UK, 152 mins.

The Matrix. 1999, Wr: The Wachowskis, Dir: The Wachowskis, USA and Australia, 136 mins.

PART III

Character and Narrative

Doubled Ethics and Narrative Progression in *The Wire*

Jeff Rush

Traditional approaches to feature film screenwriting claim that ethics are expressed through the line or spine of the main character's personal growth. The spine poses the script's moral question which is ultimately answered by the character's final resolution. For instance, Kate Wright's *Screenwriting is Storytelling: Creating an A-List Screenplay that Sells!* argues that, 'Spine emerges from the main character's moral dilemma ... the moral of the story is the final synthesis of the spine of the story .... [Resolution of the] spine reveals the moral of the story' (Wright 2004, 137). Ron Suppa in *Real Screenwriting: Strategies and Stories from the Trenches* says, 'this internal conflict is the true heart of drama—the main character's struggle within himself to resolve a difficult moral dilemma ...' (2005, 113).

J. Rush (✉)
Department of Film and Media Arts, Temple University, Philadelphia, PA, USA
e-mail: jrush@temple.edu

© The Editor(s) (if applicable) and The Author(s) 2016
S. Maras (ed.), *Ethics in Screenwriting*, Palgrave Studies
in Screenwriting, DOI 10.1057/978-1-137-54493-3_8

179

This can be clearly seen, for instance, in the feature film *Rushmore* (1998) where fifteen-year-old Max Fischer (Jason Schwartzman), the son of a barber, obsessively organizes extra-curricular clubs as a way to deny his isolation as a poor townie attending the rich private boarding school, Rushmore Academy. He responds to self-made Rushmore donor Herman Blume's (Bill Murray) appeal to: 'Take dead aim on the rich boys. Get them in the crosshairs. And take them down' (*Rushmore* 1998). After falling for a teacher and living Blume's advice, Max is suspended from Rushmore and must attend a public high school where he forgoes his clubs to begin a personal self-examination. At the film's climax, however, Max demonstrates the resolution of his personal conflict, returning to his extra-curricular activities by staging a successful play, which brings together both the world of Rushmore and his public high school, the rich boys and the barber's son. Using Wright's/Suppa's approach to moral conflict and character growth, the thesis of *Rushmore* might be stated as 'through acknowledging and accepting his status, Max discovers his own identity and bridges the conflict in his town'.

This approach, however, uses public conflict as merely a vehicle for expressing and then resolving personal conflict. Rhetorically, it suggests that once Max overcomes his own problems, the deeper tension between the privileged who casually attend Rushmore and the children of barbers who are normally denied such opportunity, is easily solved; that the ethical implications of the more public elements pale in comparison to the personal issues driving the spine. As I have written elsewhere, this approach 'privileges the individual over any social, historical, economic and familial limitations' (Dancyger and Rush 2013, 39).

This privileging of character is not as frequently employed in contemporary long-form television serials. Because they are viewed and organized differently than feature films, television serials give their writing teams greater freedom to explore not only the character's conflict, but also the ongoing social and political ethics of the storyworld surrounding it, allowing the possibility of creating a more complex ethical universe. The viewing and organization of television serials differ from features because of a number of factors including (1) their length, and the fact that (2) their viewers may not watch the whole serial, (3) serials may be structured as a multithreaded story with several arcing and competing spines freeing the writer to alternate focus and modulate narrative distance, and (4) long-form television audiences, interacting with other viewers, may be open to varied and evolving interpretations. These differences tend to 'open up' long-form television stories, and give television writers more flexibility in locating ethics in serial forms. They offer a complexity[1] which allow some serials to suggest a 'doubled' set of ethics: one that turns on character growth and another set that focuses on the larger, social world of the story.

In this chapter, I will explore this doubled[2] ethics in the context of the HBO (US cable network) serial, *The Wire* (2002–2008), which poses two sets of interlocking ethical questions: one asks how characters, consumed by living and working within failing urban institutions, come to terms with their own moral compromises; while the other focuses on the urban environment itself, and asks more generally, how society can address the deterioration in Baltimore as well as other American cities. Unlike in *Rushmore* and the personal character-driven approach to storytelling discussed above, the public world in *The Wire* is not used as a vehicle for character development, nor does character overwhelm the urgency of the storyworld. Instead, both co-exist, and invite the audience to consider the tension between them as part of the meaning of the serial. I illustrate this point by looking at the presentation of two characters, Major 'Bunny' Colvin (Robert Wisdom) and Detective Jimmy McNulty (Dominic West). I will argue that Bunny engages the more public ethical questions raised by *The Wire*, while McNulty engages the conflict between the personal and the public. Drawing on ideas from moral philosophy I will link character conflict to the ethics of care, and the more public or institutional-based conflict to the ethics of justice.

FROM CHARACTER SPINES TO NARRATIVE ALIGNMENT

A different approach is needed if screenwriters are to give as much ethical weight to the public world as to the personal one. Concepts of character spine and internal conflict alone offer limited resources. In order to revalue the public world in ethical terms, I will introduce the concept of narrative alignment with which to examine the treatment of narrative progression and conflict. The work of narrative theorist James Phelan is useful here, especially his reading of the narrative judgements that the storyteller brings to the characters' actions, and how they evolve over time. As Phelan notes, 'as key elements of narrative experience, narrative judgments and narrative progressions are responsible for the various components of that experience, especially the significant interrelation of form, ethics, and aesthetics' (2007, 3).

In order to discuss narrative judgements, the viewer must situate them in a relevant context. In literature, many narrative theorists posit an implied author, an agent constructed from within the text, which organizes all the story resources to convey some perspective that goes beyond the story. Since my focus will be specifically on television serials rather than other forms of stories, instead of the more general term 'storyteller', I will use 'inferred showrunner', which I will abbreviate as IS.

While a contested concept in literary narrative theory (for a few contrasting views, see Booth (1961, 71–76), Bronzwaer (1978, 1–18), Chatman (1978, 148–151), Diengott (1993, 181–193) and Lanser (2011, 153–160)), the implied author is constructed for at least two reasons: (1) to separate the 'author' or guiding intelligence that the reader infers from the text from the historical author, and (2) to suggest an ethical centre which allows the reader to evaluate the story's diverse narrative strategies. The second of these will be my focus here.

As the ethical centre of the literary story, the implied author serves as the guiding intelligence, the reason for telling the story the way that it is told. Drawing on Phelan's definition of narrative as 'somebody telling somebody else on some occasion and for some purpose that something happened' (Phelan 2007, 7), the implied author is the agent of that purpose. Because the concept of authorship is more slippery in television where the number of people and commercial forces involved in 'authorship' cannot easily be reduced to an individual, there is no exact equivalent to the literary author, who is understood to be the sole biographical author of a single-authored book. The closest equivalent in television is the 'showrunner', who combines the role of the executive producer and head writer; or as the Writer's Guild, speaking to the newly named showrunner, puts it, 'You are now in charge of pre-production, production, and post-production. In other words, everything' (Writers Guild of America, West 2016). In this paper, I will use the concept of the showrunner in place of author (or more abstract critical terms such as 'narrative agent'). However, I will modify the term with the adjective 'inferred' to recognize that I am not basing my analysis on interviews or other direct knowledge of a particular, historic showrunner, but rather upon what I can take from the text. In fact, the modifier 'inferred' is designed to recognize a number of television realities, as well as my act of drawing conclusions. It is difficult to know or even infer the thinking of the actual showrunner from a finished television text, given the many contributions of the other writers, directors, actors, designers, cinematographers and the rest of the creative personnel involved in the production process. Further, the nature of television authorship, the vagaries of the writing teams, and the collective and private nature of the serial's writers room makes individual attribution suspect. Part of my interpretative project, the concept of the IS is not an attempt to ferret out the historic showrunner, but to construct something akin to a collective implied author, a guiding intelligence that reflects what I can infer from the finished television text.

A final reason to use the term 'implied' is to attempt to account for the intellectual and provocative work that showrunners do through their programmes as 'cultural *bricoleurs*' (Newcomb and Hirsch 1994, 563). Since the mid-1980s, Horace Newcomb's and Paul M. Hirsch's concept of television as a cultural forum has played a large role in television scholarship. Their paper, originally published in 1983, makes the argument that 'television does not present firm ideological conclusions—despite its formal conclusions—so much as it comments on ideological problems' (1994, 565–566). Further they add that, 'for the most part the rhetoric of television drama is a rhetoric of discussion' (566). Newcomb and Hirsch wrote in the twilight of the network era,[3] a time of weekly, mass-media television which drew large numbers of viewers. Although television has since moved beyond the network era of weekly, mass-audience shows, I will argue that the concept of cultural forum provides a useful way of thinking about doubled ethics.

Storytellers use a number of devices to signal how an audience is to interpret character actions and what ethical values to ascribe to them. These may include intertextual references, symbolism, tone, presentational order and story shape among others. Here, I will concentrate on the device of alignment, particularly on the narrative judgements that the storyteller brings to the characters' actions, and how they evolve over time.

'Narrative alignment' is a broad term that refers to the relative ethical and emotional closeness between the IS, the characters and the viewer. One technique for modulating distance is the alignment or relationship between the IS's values and the values implicit in character's actions. Alignment is a relative term. Because storytelling involves the tension between conflicting perspectives which evolve over time, the IS never fully aligns with any single character; rather over the course of the serial the IS's relative alignment constantly shifts depending on the behaviour of the characters and the rhetorical argument made by the IS, which is expressed through the characters. Further the IS uses alignment to establish the story's tone. In a drama such as *The Wire*, the IS may at times be more closely aligned to a character's values than in an ironic show such as *All in the Family*, where the IS is rarely if ever aligned with Archie Bunker. This modulation is a particularly powerful tool in serials because both their length and multithreaded story structure offer the screenwriter many opportunities to vary distance. For instance, the serial may move the focus away from a character whose behaviour at one point in the story is problematic, only to bring that character back later when her previously problematic behaviour may be seen in another light.

Alignment may relate to the character's public and personal behaviour, or both, which is usually expressed through conflict. Public conflict refers to that between the character and other characters, institutions, circumstances or physical obstacles that represent some aspect of the world in which the character is engaged. It specifically identifies a character's behaviour when she is, at least implicitly, responsible to a larger whole or public. The larger whole may be institutions as formal as the city government, or as informal as a drug gang. It may even be comprised of guiding principles or abstract ideas. Public behaviour may be detached rather than immediate, intellectualized rather than emotional. By contrast, personal conflict represents the interior, psychological struggle that initially causes the character to question, fight against or even sabotage herself, until she finally comes to understand and commit to her own values which guide her actions. The character responds immediately to her own needs and to those attached most closely to her; her reactions are emotional rather than abstracted, connected and intimate rather than analytic. Most stories contain both forms of conflict, although their emphases may vary.

Alignment is closely linked to narrative progression, the evolving ethical meaning of the story over time. In the course of any narrative the relationship between the IS and a character may change, leading to shifts in alignment. Introducing a lack of alignment with an otherwise sympathetic character may introduce a form of dissonance that the viewer wishes to see resolved. If the IS distances itself from the values implicit in the character's actions, this may signal that the character is meant to be viewed on a spectrum that runs from a permanently ethically flawed character (i.e. an antagonist throughout the script) to one who has momentarily taken a wrong turn (i.e. a protagonist who is learning a lesson). In addition to creating a tension to drive the story, the IS may manipulate alignment in order to explore the evolution of an ethical view, by dramatizing the movement from a questionable position to one that the IS regards more favourably.

In some cases, the IS may not wish to present the character as aligned. Many of the characters in *The Wire* who are misaligned with the IS are presented ironically. These characters, such as Mayor Carcetti, Deputy Rawls and reporter Scott Templeton succeed in their career paths, while their personal ethics and character are questioned by the IS. Templeton, for instance, wins a Pulitzer Prize for an invented series of newspaper stories. The sympathetic characters, Colvin and McNulty, which will be discussed in this chapter are not, however, treated ironically by the IS.

Finally, alignment can also refer to the IS's relationship to the public world, which may also evolve over the course of the script. This is particularly important in *The Wire* given its focus on urban institutions. The viewer is not only directed to consider the character of Acting Police Commissioner Ervin Burrell, but the institution of the police department which allows him to rise through its ranks to a leadership position. The IS's attitude toward the institution may change when a more aligned character takes power. For instance, the serial suggests greater alignment between the IS and the police department when Cedric Daniels takes over as Commissioner and promises to end the falsification of crime statistics, only to fall again when the institutional resistance to change reasserts itself and Daniels is forced to resign. Having introduced an alternative framework for the treatment of narrative progression that goes beyond character spines, I now want to examine how *The Wire* develops and sustains its doubled ethics.

COLVIN: THE TREATMENT OF PUBLIC CONFLICT

The third season (2004) of *The Wire* features Major Colvin's creation of three arrest-free, drug zones, which will come to be known as Hamsterdam. Hamsterdam raises the public ethical question of whether removing drug dealers from residential neighbourhoods is worth the cost of tolerating their illegal activity in deserted and designated areas where they are isolated and confined.

At the end of the second episode of the third season, after his undercover officer Dozerman is shot, Colvin delivers the following speech (transcribed from the film) to his officers, justifying and prefiguring Hamsterdam's creation.

Colvin (puts a paper bag on the podium): Somewheres back in the dawn of time, this district had itself a civic dilemma of epic proportion. The City

Council had just passed a law that forbid alcoholic consumption in public places, on the streets, on the corners. But the corner is, was and always will be the poor man's lounge. It's where a man wants to be on a hot summer's night. It's cheaper than a bar, you catch a nice breeze, you watch the girls go by. But the law is the law, and cops rolling by, what were they going to do? They arrested every dude out there for tipping back a Hi-Life they wouldn't have time for any other kind of police work. And if they looked the other way, they opened themselves to all kind of flaunting, all kinds of disrespect.

Colvin (taking a bottle out of the bag): Now this was before my time when it happened but somewhere back in the fifties or sixties, there was a small moment of goddamn genius by some nameless smokehound who comes out of the cut-rate one day and on his way to the corner, he slips that just-bought pint of elderberry into a paper bag.

Colvin (puts the bottle back into the bag): A great moment of civic compromise. A small, wrinkly-ass paper bag allowed the corner boys to have their drink in peace and gave us permission to go and do police work. The kind of police work that's actually worth it, that's worth actually taking a bullet for.

Colvin (after a beat): Dozerman, he got shot last night trying to buy three vials (he holds up three drug vials). Three.

Colvin (taking the bottle out of the bag): There's never been a paper bag for drugs.

Colvin (dropping the vials into the bag): Until now. (*The Wire*, 26 September 2004)

Based on its syntax, language and commitment to persuasion, Colvin's speech is presented as closely aligned with the IS. The speech is thought-out and well constructed. It effectively uses staging and rhythm to build a sustained line which culminates in 'until now' when Colvin drops the vials into the bag. Within the logical argument, Colvin's folksy language, using phrases like 'somewheres', 'you watch the girls go by' or 'tipping back', connects with both his represented audience of police officers and the serial's viewers. It gains rhetorical strength from the use of adjectives in place of nouns, such as 'Hi-Life', 'elderberry' or 'cut-rate'. In sum, unlike the other senior police brass who seek only to command, Colvin tries to engage and convince his officers. This speech demonstrates his deep commitment to an ethics of justice couched in institutional terms.

To further the case for alignment, while the IS is not the same as the biographical author, Colvin's paper bag metaphor comes from *The Corner*, a precursor book by *The Wire*'s showrunner David Simon and producer/

writer Edward Burns. Unlike much of *The Corner* in which the IS is closely aligned with individual characters, the section on the paper bag is presented in an assertive, heightened authorial voice which is not dissimilar to that of Colvin's, as, for instance, 'The paper bag does not exist for drugs. For want of that shining example of constabulary pragmatism, the disaster is compounded' (Simon and Burns 1997, 158). Comparing the first sentence above with Colvin's line, 'There's never been a paper bag for drugs', makes clear the similarity between *The Corner* and Colvin's speech.

To some extent, of course, Colvin's language is heightened because he is making a formal speech, but even in casual conversation, Colvin's everyday diction is stately and precise, with just a touch of darker irony. For instance sitting with The Deacon after Dozerman is shot, Colvin says, 'You know what I was thinking. Tonight's a good night. Why? Because my shot cop didn't die. And it hit me. This is what makes a good night on my watch, absence of a negative' (*The Wire*, 26 September 2004). Robert Wisdom, the actor who plays Colvin, accentuates this ability to find dark humour in the absurdities he faces, while still letting the viewer feel his openness to all he is experiencing.

Even with a sympathetic public character, alignment does not remain constant. As season three progresses, the IS starts to raise doubts about Colvin's creation of Hamsterdam. First The Deacon questions the social conditions in the zones. Then a user is murdered in Hamsterdam, and two officers make an unsuccessful attempt to restage the scene outside of the zone. Finally, some of his officers start to rebel when they realize that Colvin is not going to arrest the dealers he has lured to Hamsterdam despite his initial promise to do so. The viewer is invited to consider some of the deeper implications of the zone. Still, although the alignment between Colvin and the IS decreases as the season progresses, the serial's largely sympathetic tracking of Colvin's character (in contrast to the treatment of those who oppose Hamsterdam such as Acting Commissioner Burrell or Deputy Rawls) suggests that Hamsterdam represents the kind of rethinking that is worth considering.

Yet, while the IS's presentation of Colvin as a public character is aligned, the presentation of him as a personal character is distant and unexplored. The viewer sees nothing of Colvin's personal life nor the subtext or unspoken motives that drive him. Except for his impatience with the police brass, his attempt to reform the policing policies of Baltimore represents nothing other than a desire to bring a better life to citizens who are suffering from current practices.[4]

Therefore, it makes narrative sense that Colvin is brought down by outside public forces rather than personal conflict. Hamsterdam as well as Colvin's police career is destroyed because they have to be; this is developed not only in the rhetorical frame of the serial, but in the historic reality to which it is pointing: in mid-2000's America, once discovered, Hamsterdam would not be allowed to survive. To draw this correlation between the viewer's assumed knowledge and the represented world of the film, I accept in *The Wire* a definition of realism that supports such an assumption. If *The Wire* proposed Hamsterdam as an acceptable solution to the Baltimore drug situation in 2004, if it did not maintain sufficient narrative distance to both celebrate it and recognize its eventual fate, viewers would have to adjust their sense of the conventions of the serial they had been watching.

Returning to the case of Colvin, media scholar Jason Mittel argues that a form of impersonal treatment is true of many characters in *The Wire*.

> While all of these characters have depth and complexity, we rarely see much of their existence beyond how they fit into their institutional roles. Even romantic relationships seem to foreground interinstitutional links between police, lawyers, and politicians more than interpersonal bonds that deepen characters' inner life and motivations. (Mittel 2011, 3)

Film scholar Linda Williams goes further, believing that the serial does not even focus on 'depth and complexity', but presents the characters as the representation of institutions and power, '…they are symptoms of the institutions they inhabit and this, I argue, is what makes *The Wire* a great melodrama of dysfunctional systems and not just a Manichean study of personal villains and victims …' (Williams 2014, 83).

To present Colvin in this way, the IS must construct a character capable of creating Hamsterdam, while minimizing his personal conflict so as to not distract the viewer from his public role. Colvin's actions, rather than his psychology, drive his character. As a result, his world, Baltimore, is presented not as a reflection of a psychological character state, but as an impersonal site of dysfunction. Since he is presented without personal conflict, Colvin in season three remains confined by his public role; someone who both challenges an institution, but who is still defined by it. Without any counter-indication, any subtext that would redirect the viewer's focus, Colvin is presented as a policeman at heart, one who wants to do the kind of police work that is worth taking a bullet for.

McNulty: Public and Personal Conflict

By contrast, Detective McNulty is presented as a character with both public and personal conflict. There is little question about his public commitment to challenging the institutional dysfunction of Baltimore, but his reasons are much more personal than are Colvin's. While Colvin is shown as consistently advancing public aims without regard for personal motivation, McNulty is presented as a character whose motivations swing wildly between self-serving and advancing justice. Early in the first season, he goes over his bosses' heads and convinces Judge Phelan to order an investigation that initiates the story that propels *The Wire*. At the same time, he undercuts this public motivation by telling his partner that he is doing this to make police work more meaningful for him. Nowhere is this contradiction more apparent than in season three, when he serves justice by aggressively pursuing drug dealer Stringer Bell, while at the same time perverts it by requesting that one of his officers illegally search for the address of a lover who refuses to tell him where she lives.

The IS's presentation of McNulty is quite complex. He both opens the serial and triggers its ending montage, suggesting a close alignment with the IS. While this public alignment gives McNulty more agency than any other character, the disconnect between the IS's values and those implied by McNulty's personal life calls into question his behaviour and motivations. This swing in alignment distinguishes McNulty from *The Wire*'s other characters who are not judged on the contrast between their public and personal ethics. Colvin acts outside of the system, but his personal values are not called into question. The schoolboy turned enforcer, Michael Lee (Tristan Wilds) has his mother's live-in boyfriend killed to satisfy his own personal conflict, but his public ethics are never celebrated. Only McNulty is presented with such overt contradictions, both personally flawed and publically fearless in challenging injustice.

This climaxes in season five, when McNulty, partnering with Lester Freamon, invents a false serial killer, whose imagined crimes succeed in creating a city-wide panic. This forces the mayor to pay for police overtime which McNulty diverts to capturing the drug lord Marlo Stanfield. At the same time, McNulty drifts away from Beadie Russell, his one stable and potentially sustainable relationship. Pretending to be the serial killer, McNulty calls the *Baltimore Sun* reporter, Scott Templeton, who at the same time is using this case to fabricate a story that will lead to his Pulitzer Prize. McNulty allows the tape of their conversation to be analysed by an FBI profiler.

The profiler's comments accurately describe the fictional killer, actually McNulty, as 'a white male in his late twenties to late thirties, who is not a college graduate, but feels superior to those with advanced education, and is likely employed in a bureaucratic entity, possibly civil or public service. He has a problem with authority and a deep-seated resentment for those that have impeded his progress professionally. ... He may be struggling with lasting relationships ...' (*The Wire*, 24 February 2008). McNulty reacts as if he finally hears the personal criticism that he has previously ignored and begins a transformation which will eventually bring him back to Beadie.

McNulty does change. In the last line of the entire serial, he says, 'Let's go home', implying his return to Beadie (*The Wire*, 9 March 2008). This description of McNulty's developmental 'arc' evokes the concept of character spine I critiqued in *Rushmore* in the beginning of the chapter, but it also highlights the difference between the two approaches to screenwriting. *The Wire* allows character development, however, it does not pretend that McNulty's personal resolution can overcome the public problems of Baltimore. The serial is very careful to make sure the viewer understands his ultimate lack of success. McNulty resolves his personal conflict, while the larger public conflict remains unsolved and maybe unresolvable. The drug dealer and killer, Marlo Stanfield, is freed due to Lester's illegal wiretap. Before he leaves prison, Marlo sells his drug connection to others. By the end of *The Wire*, the drug trade is in full swing; only the gang that controls it is different. McNulty's fake serial killing, his mission for the entire season, has solved nothing. Detective Sydnor, acting as McNulty did at the beginning of the serial, asks Judge Phelan to intervene over the police department's incompetency.

WHY DOUBLED ETHICS?

Implicit in this chapter is the assumption that if viewers approach the ethical meaning of a script purely through character or personal ethics, they will only see one part of the story. Personal ethics affect and are affected by a broader, social landscape; serials like *The Wire* explicitly engage the tension between the individuals and society, focusing not on either, but on the co-existence of both. To explore this further, I will engage a distinction made by feminist scholars, led by Carol Gilligan and Virginia Held, between the ethics of justice and of care. Here I will relate the ethics of justice with public ethics, and the ethics of care with personal ethics. I will consider this distinction in light of dramatic structure and doubled ethics.

According to Held, care ethics has little concern with objectivity and focuses instead on relationships. Care ethics deals with 'meeting the needs of the particular others for whom we are responsible' (Held 2006, 10). Valuing emotion and attachment, it rejects disinterested abstraction in favour of connection. 'The ethics of care respects rather than removes itself from the claims of particular others with whom we share actual relationships' (Held 2006, 11). By contrast, justice ethics celebrate the abstract, the generalizable, the independent relationship between the judge and the judged. It seeks to stand outside the system which it is evaluating. Based on this, I suggest that the more immediate and connected, personal ethics echo the emotional values of care ethics, while the detached and analytic public ethics reflect the abstract values of justice ethics.

In her defining article on the ethics of care, 'Moral Orientation and Development', Carol Gilligan celebrates the short story, 'A Jury of Her Peers', written by Susan Glaspell in 1917. In this story, two women choose to hide evidence related to the murder committed by a third woman of her emotionally distant and cruel husband. The wife's motivation is that her husband killed her canary, her only companion, a motivation that, given the circumstances, the women find justified (Glaspell 1917). According to Gilligan, the women are acting out of *attached* care rather than *detached* justice. As she puts it, 'detachment is considered the hall mark of mature thinking within a justice perspective, signifying the ability to judge dispassionately .... From a care perspective, detachment is *the* moral problem' (Gilligan 1995, 43).

Given the historical significance of the story and the time of its writing, Gilligan's celebration of 'A Jury of Her Peers' is reasonable. However, by highlighting personal attachment rather than objective detachment, the care ethic over that of justice, the story seems to reiterate the way that many subsequent popular narrative scripts are constructed—the viewer is invited to identify with the characters' personal reactions which drive the story, rather than the abstract ideas of social power that underlie it. In these works, rather than being overwhelmed by detachment as feared by Gilligan, the attachment of care frequently transcends justice. *The Wire*, however, redresses this imbalance. Personal ethics or the ethics of care is balanced against the broader and more abstract public injustices of Baltimore institutions. While the character stories involve the viewer, detachment is also reintroduced to critique and sustain the serial's focus on social injustice. The script privileges neither of these perspectives alone, but explores the essential tension between them, which constitutes the doubled ethics of *The Wire*.

THE CULTURAL FORUM: DOUBLED ETHICS
AND PROGRESSION IN *THE WIRE*

Long-form television's capacity to deal with complexity and doubled ethics suggests that it may have found a new ethical role in contributing to cultural debates around contemporary problems. This suggests a need to reconsider ideas of the cultural forum from the perspective of ethics. This is in line with Amanda Lotz's argument, that while its critical dominance has weakened in the post-network era, there remains 'continued utility of the cultural forum model in examining a topic or theme present across a variety of programmes or episodes' (2004, 424).

The concept of the cultural forum was developed in the network era, when television in the United States was limited to one public and three commercial networks. Now, it is rarely possibly to assume a large proportion of the television audience will watch a given show at any particular time and that subsequent conversations will take place around it. Rather the range of choices means that audiences self-select and are more closely aligned with the show's perspective. And certainly, despite its critical acclaim, *The Wire* has never been seen by a large audience.

Despite this, for the past 15 years, *The Wire* has endured as an ethical touchstone against which the United States views urban change. When Freddie Gray died at the hands of the Baltimore police in April 2015, journalists, cast members and scholars immediately related it to *The Wire*. David Simon gave a number of interviews discussing whether there were parallels between the serial and the riots following Gray's death. Sixteen members of the original cast reunited in an event called 'Wired Up' to recreate the unheard voices of the Baltimore community (Charlton 2015). A subsequent academic conference brought together television scholars, historians, and former cast members (The Wire—The Conference).

Yet the significance of all these reactions can be hard to pin down. Felicia Pearson, the actress who played Snoop in *The Wire*, takes a personal position, telling CNN that she knew Freddie Gray and he was a 'wonderful person who liked to laugh and crack jokes' (Pearson 2015). Lanre Bakare, in the *The Guardian*, stresses the opposite, arguing that, 'No riot in the human history has ever been about just one person' (Bakare 2015). Bakare's article challenges David Simon's condemnation of the Baltimore violence, while Ta-Nehisi Coates, writing between nights of rioting, says that 'Wisdom isn't the point tonight. Disrespect is' (Coates 2015). This range of interpretative positions is also celebrated, rather than reduced, by *The Wire*. The progression of the serial emphasizes the ultimate complexity of multiple perspectives, more reflective of the chaos of this reality, than character redemption as a source of closure found in a more traditional feature script. What actually happened, and continues to happen, in Baltimore takes place in the actual world; this makes it much more urgent than one television serial which is only a representation of a fictional construction that reminds viewers of what could happen there. David Simon highlights this when he states in an interview, 'Why don't you attend to what's actually happening right now in Baltimore. You don't need McNulty or whoever to access it' (Chotiner 2015). But, of course, it is not so simple. The act of representation that is *The Wire* is also in itself a part of the real world, its belief systems. This is something that Newcomb and Hirsch acknowledge when they tie television to 'not the act of imparting information but the representation of shared beliefs' (Newcomb and Hirsch 1994, 562).

Given the current range of television options, shared beliefs are more fragmented in the post-network era. The personal and the public are more difficult to tease apart and story progressions, whether in fiction or in the reporting of real events, resolve little. The cited discussion is only shared by the small percentage of the population which is both aware of the serial and seeking a progressive response to the Baltimore riots after Gray's death; many others do not consider *The Wire* or are not willing engage in this conversation. Yet to those who engage it, the parallels to the serial have great effect. This suggests a modification of the cultural forum model to allow it to speak to a more fragmented audience than was originally envisioned, drawing on narrative complex forms of narrative alignment and judgement. While the cultural forum model as originally written may no longer broadly apply in the contemporary media climate, it suggests the impact of some long-form television serials such as *The Wire* to provoke more ethically complex conversation over a longer period of time than did shows in the network era. Almost 15 years after its first episode, *The Wire*'s doubled ethics still address unresolved and fundamental questions over the meaning of individual lives and the pervasion of public urban dysfunction.

CONCLUSION

Not all long-form television serials seek to achieve the ethical complexity of *The Wire*, just as not all feature films employ ethical spines in the manner of *Rushmore*. There are, of course, many other strategies to be used and a range of pleasures to be enjoyed in all kinds of films and serials.

But those serials that seek to deal with the larger world and its effect on individuals need to find means to balance personal and public ethics, and to invite their viewers to engage in the tension between them. Drawing on theories of narrative progression, incorporating ideas of alignment and judgement, I have proposed a new framework for examining the dual ethics of television serials, thus avoiding a limited focus on character ethics.

The personal and the public mark two contrasting ways for characters to be in the world. The distinction expands the traditional division of internal and external conflict to include personal ethics, questions that arise when the character is acting for herself and immediate relationships, and public ethics, those that arise when she is acting for abstractions beyond herself. This distinction also refers to ways in which the IS presents characters. Some storytelling strategies privilege the characters' own resolution. In these cases, the public world and its concomitant justice ethics are designed to be an expression, an outward signpost of personal development, which signal character resolution, but ultimately have little autonomous importance on their own. Other cases, such as *The Wire*, seek to sustain the public issues beyond character's resolution and present the world as distinct from, rather than a reflection of, the character's personal growth and individual ethics. The tension between care and justice ethics becomes important to the way the IS modulates the viewing experience. No matter viewers' commitment to the public conflict explored in *The Wire*, they sometimes need the intimate respite of care ethics to balance out the unrelenting justice ethics depicted by the serial.[5] Both strands however contribute to narrative progression, and contribute to the operation of serials such as *The Wire* as a cultural forum for ethical debate and deliberation.

NOTES

1. This is not limited to television serials. Many feature screenplays, of course, have found ways to evoke this ethical complexity.
2. My notion of doubled ethics is distinct from 'double storytelling' as understood in the Danish public service broadcasting context, which is analyzed in Eva Novrup Redvall's chapter in this collection.
3. The network era in the United States begins to fragment with the popularization of the VCR in the mid-1980s and the launch of the Fox Broadcasting Company in October 1986.
4. In season four, Colvin's personal needs, particularly his desire to nurture, are explored more deeply, ending with his adoption of the boy Namond at the end of the season.

5. *The Wire* occasionally gives the viewer this respite, through Colvin's adoption of Namond and McNulty's reuniting with Beadie, which is balanced against, but does not replace, the remorseless public ethics represented in Baltimore.

REFERENCES

Bakare, Lanre. 2015. 'Go home, David Simon. Without justice in Baltimore, there can be no peace.' *The Guardian*, April 28. http://www.theguardian.com/commentisfree/2015/apr/28/go-home-david-simon-no-justice-no-peace-baltimore.

Booth, Wayne C. 1983 [1961]. *The Rhetoric of Fiction*. 2nd ed. Chicago: Chicago University Press.

Bronzwaer, W. 1978. 'Implied Author, Extradiegetic Narrator and Public Reader: Gérard Genette's Narratological Model and the Reading Version of *Great Expectations*.' *Neophilologus* 62 (1): 1–18.

Charlton, Meg. 2015. 'The Cast of "The Wire" Recreated Scenes from the Baltimore Community in the Wake of Freddie Gray's Death.' *Vice*. July 20. http://www.vice.com/read/the-cast-of-the-wire-recreated-scenes-from-the-baltimore-community-in-the-wake-of-freddie-grays-death-111.

Chatman, Seymour. 1978. *Story and Discourse. Narrative Structure in Fiction and Film*. Ithaca: Cornell University Press.

Chotiner, Isaac. 2015. 'Everything Is Not *The Wire*.' *Slate*, August 12. http://www.slate.com/articles/arts/culturebox/2015/08/david_simon_interview_the_wire_creator_on_his_new_series_freddie_gray_ta.html.

Coates, Ta-Nehisi. 2015. 'Nonviolence as Compliance.' *The Atlantic*, April 27. http://www.theatlantic.com/politics/archive/2015/04/nonviolence-as-compliance/391640/.

Dancyger, Ken and Rush, Jeff. 2013. *Alternative Scriptwriting Beyond the Hollywood Formula*. 5th Ed. Burlington, MA: Focal Press.

Diengott, Nilli. 1993. 'Implied Author, Motivation and Theme and Their Problematic Status.' *Orbis Litterarum* 48 (2): 181–193.

Gilligan, Carol. 1995. 'Moral Orientation and Moral Development.' In *Justice and Care: Essential Readings in Feminist Ethics*, edited by Virginia Held, 31–46. Boulder: Westview Press.

Glaspell, Susan. 1917. 'A Jury of Her Peers.' Accessed 29 April 2016. http://www.learner.org/interactives/literature/story/fulltext.html.

Held, Virginia. 2006. *The Ethics of Care: Personal, Political, and Global*. Oxford: Oxford University Press.

Lanser, Susan. 2011. 'The Implied Author: An Agnostic's Manifesto.' *Style* 45 (1): 153–160.

Lotz, Amanda D. 2004. 'Using "Network" Theory in the Post-Network Era: Fictional 9/11 US Television Discourse as a "Cultural Forum."' *Screen* 45 (4): 423–39.

Mittel, Jason. 2011. 'All in the Game: The Wire, Serial Storytelling, and Procedural Logic.' Accessed 19 May 2015. http://www.electronicbookreview.com/thread/firstperson/serial.

Newcomb, Horace and Paul M. Hirsch. 1994. 'Television as a Cultural Forum.' In *Television: The Critical View*, edited by Horace Newcomb, 561–573. 5th ed. New York: Oxford University Press.

Pearson, Felicia, interviewed by Brooke Baldwin. 24 April 2015. CNN. Accessed 29 April 2016. http://www.cnn.com/videos/justice/2015/04/24/nr-intv-pearson-freddie-gray-arrest-death.cnn.

Phelan, James. 2007. *Experiencing Fiction: Judgments, Progressions, and the Rhetorical Theory of Narrative*. Columbus: Ohio State University Press.

Simon, David, and Edward Burns. 1997. *The Corner: A Year in the Life of an Inner-City Neighborhood*. New York: Broadway Books.

Suppa, Ron. 2005. *Real Screenwriting: Strategies and Stories from the Trenches*. Boston, MA: Thomson Course Technology.

Williams, Linda. 2014. *On The Wire*. Durham: Duke University Press.

Wright, Kate. 2004. *Screenwriting is Storytelling: Creating an A-list Screenplay that Sells!* New York: A Perigee Book.

Writers Guild of America, West. 2016. *Writing for Episodic TV: From Freelance to Showrunner*. Accessed 19 May 2016. http://www.wga.org/subpage_writersresources.aspx?id=156#4.

FILM AND TELEVISION REFERENCES

Rushmore. 1998. Wr: Wes Anderson and Owen Wilson. Dir: Wes Anderson. American Empirical Pictures and Touchstone Pictures, USA, 93 mins.

The Wire. 2004, September 26. 'All Due Respect.' Wr: Richard Price. Dir: Steve Shill. Home Box Office, USA, 59 mins.

The Wire. 2008, February 24. 'Clarifications.' Wr: Dennis Lehane. Dir: Anthony Hemingway. Home Box Office, USA, 59 mins.

The Wire. 2008, March 9. '–30–.' Wr: David Simon. Dir: Clark Johnson. Home Box Office, USA, 59 mins.

The Wire—The Conference. 2016. 8 April–9 April 2016. Accessed 29 April 2016. http://heymancenter.org/events/the-wire-conference/.

CHAPTER 9

Writing from the Mouth of Shadows: Creativity as Ethics in the Screenwriting of Jean-Claude Carrière

Felipe Pruneda Sentíes

In the essay 'The Vanishing Screenplay', from his book *The Secret Language of Film* (1994), eminent screenwriter Jean-Claude Carrière observes the following regarding the origin of ideas: 'A true author never knows exactly what he meant. He scarcely knows what he said. He is what Victor Hugo called "the mouth of shadows".[1] Words are transmitted through him, often quite beyond his control. They come from obscure regions; the richer and deeper his genius, the vaster those regions will be' (1994, 178). Carrière thus gives his version of a frequent response to which artists turn when asked about their creative process—a question writers like Neil Gaiman (1997) refer to as 'a pitfall' of their profession—where they emphasize the ultimate obscurity of the inception of their work. In Carrière's case, his view comes from both a reluctance to rationalize his talent, and a stated

F. Pruneda Sentíes (✉)
English Department, Hendrix College, Conway, AR, USA
e-mail: pruneda@hendrix.edu

   197
S. Maras (ed.), *Ethics in Screenwriting*, Palgrave Studies in Screenwriting, DOI 10.1057/978-1-137-54493-3_9

belief in the unfathomability of its provenance. His text about it, then, is full of invocations of a symbolic darkness and of areas of low-to-zero visibility—ideas emerge from 'dark zones'; the writer delves into a 'life-generating mist' where 'true mystery dwells' (1994, 180–81); the original title of his book is *Le film qu'on ne voit pas*, or *The Film That We Do Not See*. While he describes his career in the introduction to his book as one 'that almost always favors action over reflection' (1994, 5), and his essays are filled with expressions of relief for what he perceives is a lack of study on matters of artistic creation, he is also willing to theorize the mouth of shadows as another, important tool available to the writer. He dedicates several passages to ways of preserving the mystery of creativity and how embracing it produces better writing. While often summoned, in a wide variety of ways, by writers, this enigmatic take on the creative process arguably remains an esoteric, underexplored approach in terms of screen-writing. My aim here is to show how a commitment to writing from the mouth of shadows is not only an aesthetic choice, but also a decision to enact a particular brand of ethics, one that is inextricably linked to a vision of creating as an act of groping in the dark in order to reach something beyond the visible. Carrière thus enacts an ethics of knowledge, one that refuses to be dictated to by the world of appearances and remains scepti-cal of false notions of expertise and familiarity. In that conception, growth and exploration must not cease.

Drawing on Carrière's writings in *The Secret Language of Film* and on readings of the film *That Obscure Object of Desire* (*Cet obscur objet du désir*, 1977),which Carrière adapted with Luis Buñuel from Pierre Louÿs's novel *La femme et le pantin* ([1898] 1999), this chapter elaborates on the ethi-cal implications of Carrière's methods and reflections on screenwriting. I borrow from the philosophy of Emmanuel Levinas, as well as Chloé Taylor's discussion of the 'ethics of blindness' (2006, sec. 2), to elaborate on the way screenwriting, in Carrière's conception of it, can contribute powerfully and positively to our sense of ethics for how its reliance on mystery—an element that remains unknown because of a metaphorical blindness to it—can foster an attitude of respect for the privacy and dif-ference of others.

The first section of the chapter delineates the contours of Carrière's thoughts on screenwriting in *The Secret Language of Film*, which defines writing from the mouth of shadows as a process of 'positive othering'. The second section investigates how a metaphorical blindness presents an ethical way to engage with what has been rendered other by keeping it productively unknown, and how *That Obscure Object of Desire* encourages such 'blind' engagement through certain scripted audio-visual features. Finally, the third section continues a reading of *Obscure Object* as a text where Carrière and Buñuel dramatize the problem of the encounter with the mystery of another person's interiority, and the dangers of the failure to embrace that mystery.

THE MOUTH OF SHADOWS

By its very nature, the mouth of shadows resists definition and location. Faced with something so difficult to define I will describe the strategies by which Carrière listens to the shadows and becomes aware of their presence. It is crucial to note, before going forward, that the very epistemic inaccessibility of the shadows calls forth, in Carrière's text, many declarations that appear to disparage 'intelligence', 'cleverness' and 'understanding'—all positive qualities that clarify, reveal and enhance learning. However, these declarations are more accurately attempts to describe different sorts of those same qualities, versions not dependent on conscious control, but on instinctive trust and judicious, willing abandon. Carrière also highlights the importance of humility, arising out of his experience of 'the obligatory passage [of the feature film script] through the hands of actors and technicians'. Given the transition, the writer 'must possess a particular quality that is difficult both to achieve and maintain: a certain humility. Not only because the film will most often belong to the director, and his name alone will be glorified (or vilified), but also because the thumbed and dog-eared written work will finally be tossed aside like the caterpillar's skin' (1994, 152). Whether his assessment of the screenwriter's position among filmmakers holds true or not, humility is central to the three approaches Carrière offers to get in touch with the mouth of shadows. These are: unselfconsciousness, improvisation and self-effacement.

For Carrière, the writer (and everyone else) is, to an extent, inevitably unselfconscious because of the mind's own condition as an enigma to itself. What the writer needs, then, is the ability to determine when to run with that enigma. Thought, Carrière argues, 'imagines it can distinguish itself from itself. It thinks it can examine itself from the outside as a discrete, static object, whereas it is exactly the opposite: indistinct, shifting, vague' (1994, 180). Because words 'flow through [the writer], often beyond his control' (1994, 178), Carrière proposes that a writer should work with a level of powerlessness over her craft or, to put it differently, the writer should hone the skill to know when control becomes counter-productive. 'At a certain stage', Carrière elaborates, 'understanding ceases. It has to. Beneath it ... we must let things go' (1994, 181). Alongside the abilities of 'a calm approach and thoughtful reading' (1994, 179), screen-writing benefits from moments of unprepared exploration, of the 'zones... which analysis can neither penetrate nor define' (1994, 180). Unable to absolutely comprehend the source of her creativity (and thus, herself), the author must often submit to its ineffable darkness and the ideas that flow from it.

This mindset enables improvisation. Throughout 'The Vanishing Screenplay', Carrière likens the screenwriter's work to the actor's. While fully acknowledging the practicalities of executing a script, and the value of analysis and discussion in reaching an agreement among filmmakers on what the film at hand is about, Carrière warns against 'the most serious, the most pernicious illusion' of convincing ourselves

> that the intellectual approach is enough, that intelligent analysis will cover every contingency. All that is needed... is for the author to know what he means, draw up a precise plan, define his structures—and the rest will follow. In which case the actor's performance, too, would simply be a translation into words and gestures of an idea the mind has already chewed over. (1994, 179)

Improvising starts when the chewing-over stops. For Carrière, improvisa-tion means 'abandon[ing] intelligence and its tricks' (1994, 180).[2] When analysis stops, the writer and the actor let life happen: 'we must let things go, we must not try to probe those life-generating mists. For real life, whole life, is there, in that constant back-and-forth movement between light and darkness, from light to the little-known jungle we can explore only through action and play' (1994, 181). Action and play (improvisa-tion) enable the writer to inject a pulsating vitality into her work. Imbued with life's energy, a mixture of mystery and revelation, the work acquires a life of its own.

Which brings us to self-effacement. Not only can action and play help writers find ways out of creative conundrums, but they can also change the screenplay's relationship to the writer's authorship. That change is neces-sary, Carrière tells us, because of the position of the screenplay in the pro-duction of feature films. Right from the essay's title, Carrière characterizes a script's strange fate as vital yet ephemeral; of great initial importance but of expendable value once the production commences. By the end of the essay, he celebrates that impermanence. Although he acknowledges the injustice inherent in granting authorship of a film to the director, he also believes that the disappearance of the screenplay in fact points towards a desirable state in all artistic endeavours and practices: the final disappearance of the artist herself. If the writing evolves from something larger than the writer herself—those 'dark zones' that she 'shares with others and even, in the case of the greatest authors, with all humankind'—then it is appropriate for the writer to think of the film as not belonging to her alone. Carrière sees this humble recognition as the end result of contemplating the fate of the greatest masterpieces:

> Flaubert admired without reservation the objective existence of Shakespeare's work, in which neither the heart nor the hand of the artist appear to be present. ... The peerless author hid behind his characters, to whom he gave the best of himself and who, in turn, became an expression of all human feelings .... Here's the true and most glorious "mouth of shadows". The triumph of the invisible. The peak of achievement—oh, surprise!—is anonymity. (Carrière 1997, 139)[3]

To speak of a vanishing screenplay, then, is to speak of a vanishing author. In Carrière's theory of the screenplay, the most generous aspect of his craft is its self-effacement, its gregarious desire to exert no authority, and its control of the 'appetite for glory, money, and power' (1994, 176). Carrière wishes this to be true of all the craftspeople involved in film production, which he announces by paraphrasing his colleague Buñuel's notion that 'films should be like cathedrals. The authors' names should be removed from the credits, leaving just a few anonymous reels, pure, free of any trace of their creator. Then we would watch them the way we enter a cathedral, not knowing the names of those who built it, or even the master builder' (1994, 176). Relinquishing credit, filmmakers take steps to make their films selfless gifts.

Unselfconsciousness, improvisation and self-effacement—all point to the mouth of shadows because they are procedures of what I term 'positive othering': as the writer practices her unselfconsciousness, she becomes an other to herself; improvisation estranges the writer from her own methods; finally, the screenplay itself, as a text, becomes an entity separated from the screenwriter when she makes her authorship inconspicuous. The screenwriter must hence contend with three mysteries, or shadows—herself, the act of screenwriting and the screenplay. To pledge her allegiance and her love to the film that is the end product of her efforts (which is Carrière's goal), the screenwriter can engage in a productive, harmonious interaction with these three others. It is here that an ethics of blindness can aid in accomplishing these multiple estrangements, because it is an ethics based on protecting and trusting a mysterious otherness that is reachable not through visible, but through visionary, means.

THE ETHICS OF BLINDNESS IN *THAT OBSCURE OBJECT OF DESIRE*

Carrière and Buñuel's script for *That Obscure Object of Desire* enacts the encounter with otherness typical of an ethics of blindness, and further brings Carrière's ethical creativity into sharper relief. *Obscure Object*, which would become Luis Buñuel's last film to see release, tells the story of middle-aged, affluent Frenchman Mathieu Fabert's growing obsession with young Spanish Flamenco dancer Conchita, who seems to both encourage and rebuff his advances with extreme volatility. Its most salient conceit—the choice of splitting the role of Conchita between two actresses, one 'a sort of Parisian, elegant, distinguished lady [Carole Bouquet]' the other 'a sort of Spanish, popular and easy-going girl [Ángela Molina]'— came up, according to Carrière, during one of his improvizations with Buñuel, then facing the problem of lending verisimilitude to a character that was 'psychologically unthinkable, capable of doing this and the opposite'. First dismissed by the director as 'the whim of a rainy day' (Carrière 2000), the notion returned only after Buñuel expressed his disappointment with the first and only actress he had hired. Filming resumed with Bouquet and Molina alternating their scenes as Conchita with Fernando Rey's Mathieu throughout the film, without any acknowledgement or explanation for the constant switching.

Buñuel and Carrière's accounts of the creative spark that led to the double casting highlight the importance of the scripting stage. It certainly bears the hallmarks of Carrière's commitment to exploration, a discovery of absurdity and wise irrationality. But while the choice is deliberately enigmatic, he does not speak of Conchita as the Freudian mysterious female. The alternating of two actresses does not mean to enhance her unknowability, but it is paradoxically tasked with adding plausibility to an implausible character. In other words, she is believable and unknowable at the same time, perhaps even more believable *because* she is unknowable. The doubling invites the viewer to communicate with her in concert with her unknowability, the way Carrière, as we saw above, approaches his writing process. That impetus extends to the whole film. The film is a drama about the characters' constant failures to 'see' one another. While the double casting, a deceptively simple device, has become the most infamous aspect of the film and the one with the strongest gravitational pull, it is only the first of a series of strategies that, when scrutinized through a Levinasian ethical blindness, sketch Carrière's version of creativity as a way to interact with others (characters, collaborators) without dissolving their intrinsic mysteries.

So let us start with that central stratagem, and consider the climax of the film. Mathieu's seething rage at Conchita's equivocations finally explodes, and he brutally beats her. Buñuel ends the harrowing scene with an image that creates great dissonance between the horror of physical abuse and its results. Bleeding, Conchita looks back at Mathieu from the ground. Rather than expressing pain, she smiles, ecstatically and charmingly. The contradictory signals Mathieu reads in Conchita's behaviour throughout the film have made it difficult for the viewer to understand her (see Rothman 2001).

Through the violence of that scene, Carrière and Buñuel show how much Mathieu has let his weakness erode his humanity and, in his attack of Conchita, also violated hers; they have also zoomed into Conchita's face as a mystery at the core of the film's ethical trajectory. In that moment, and several others throughout the film, Mathieu's frustration in his failure to understand Conchita comes largely from how her features are simultaneously expressive and impenetrable (is her smile coquettish, or amused?), which provokes him into causing her harm. Our inability to decipher the motivations behind a face are at the basis of Emmanuel Levinas's writings in *Ethics and Infinity* (1985) and *Totality and Infinity* (1991). It is the face that, in his philosophy, presents us with the difference of an Other— something that we will attempt to assimilate and understand because it affects us immediately in its expressivity and nakedness. We can begin to distinguish ourselves from, and relate to, others thanks to the face. Yet the face is also the first obstacle for ethics. In her reading of Levinas, Taylor observes that 'the way we look at (and also touch) faces is said to foreclose ethics' (2006, sec. 1), since 'seeing the other entails enveloping her into the same' (2006, sec. 3). The face's compelling power, in other words, accelerates our tendency to read it; the face thus becomes an efficient framework to begin surmising what others are feeling or thinking. This Levinasian insight appears in *Obscure Object*. Mathieu and the viewer might believe they know what Conchita is thinking and what motivates her from her face—to see, for instance, a masochistic bent in her reaction to Mathieu's beating—and yet the film refuses to verify those suppositions. Vision's imposing quality is the first limitation Levinas wishes to overcome, imagining a relationality where our knowledge of the other is not based on our ability to see the other's face and body and so 'reduce the other to myself, to my ideas of her, to my theories, categories, and knowledge' (Taylor 2006, sec. 1). This implies the capacity to allow the other's difference to remain intact and impervious to our sensory attempts to assimilate or inflict our understanding upon her—what Taylor has termed an 'ethics of blindness'. This approach disturbs the very idea of knowing someone and the role of mutual knowledge in our relationships with others. It leads us to wonder what would happen if, rather than react to the mystery of Conchita's face with assumptions, desperation and fury, Mathieu saw beyond it—if he was 'blind' to what he believes he knows about the powerful language of a face.

And then there is the fact that there are two faces. If the face is, for Levinas, a problem with which ethics must grapple, the double casting of Conchita seeks to actively undermine the face's interference. The fact that nobody in the diegesis seems to notice the shifts in Conchita's appearance gives the impression that the characters are victims of an outbreak of selective 'blindness'. Mathieu sees and interprets her face in a moment (she encourages him one instant, she mocks him the next) but cannot assimilate its totality, a kind of time-dependent short-sightedness. The dual casting underscores the difficulty of grasping a face's meaning and influence over human interactions. For critics, the doubling has also become the key to the film's ethos and its interrogation of knowledge of others as part of an ethics of relationships. Infatuated, Mathieu wants to possess Conchita, and for her desires to match his own. Her mercurial behaviour keeps her perpetually out of his reach, a condition that her ever-shifting look mirrors. Critics have wrestled with how the dual casting impedes fixing Conchita into Mathieu's (and the viewer's) expectations. William Rothman and Michael Wood explain that Conchita is unmasterable. Rothman (2001) says that 'Conchita can be viewed as a devil of a woman. But she can also be viewed as a modern heroine who refuses, on principle, to be reduced to an "object of desire"' (2001). Wood, by contrast, regards Conchita's twinning as an 'improvised joke' that obeys 'a careful avoidance of signifi-cance' (1981, 335).

As these passages indicate, the double casting has seismic effects on how viewers approach the character. The film induces in the viewers the characters' (and screenwriters') 'blindness'[4] to ignite in them a reflection on how to interact with others beyond vision. And blindness has a con-nection to ethics that filmmaking forcefully plays upon. Starting with the double casting, *Obscure Object* establishes how the viewer must be wary of trusting vision. Conchita's shifting visage makes us wonder what she looks like. The answer is that she looks both like Bouquet and Molina, but their alternating appearances make it impossible for our eyes to lock onto what, for Levinas, is the very start of ethical questions: the human face.

Conchita's doubling is the most immediate sabotage of vision in the film, but other details about it challenge us further. It is impossible to assign a face to Conchita and thus assimilate her through the eyes, but her character might be accessible through the ears: a third, uncredited actress provided Conchita's voice for both Molina and Bouquet. The dubbing, besides aiding the illusion of Conchita's singularity, makes her bodily iden-tity, like her self, simultaneously whole and discontinuous—she is both a single Conchita and the three women constituting her. Unlocatable through vision, she is sonically further prevented from attaining the sta-tus of a self-contained, graspable entity. As it happens, the same is true of Mathieu: French actor Michel Piccoli dubs Rey's voice. Mathieu/Rey is effectively doubled. The film's sound design highlights the conceptual face Levinas is after. As Taylor states:

> The "face" of ethics, according to Levinas, occurs in discourse rather than in visual form... language "slices" through [the] knowledge that vision imposes: "Speech cuts across vision" .... The slicing of language divides or differentiates the other from me. Discourse, like vision, may *try* to thematize the other, but while vision succeeds, the other can always evade the catego-rizations of language, slip behind the Said, remain a Saying, even in silence .... (2006, sec. 3, emphasis in original)

As creatures of voice, Mathieu and Conchita assert their non-identical selfhood and separation through their voices, and the impossibility to see the voice actors ensures the characters acquire the autonomy that Carrière and Buñuel designed into them. The film demands that the viewer listens to the characters, which is appropriate. 'Listening' is both the literal and figurative action of choice to exhort someone to acknowledge and strive to grasp what someone else is trying to convey in whatever form—the call for attention that is a sign of ethical respect for fellow humans. Film trains listening skills when the cinematic synchronization (and therefore separation) of sound and image make us pay attention to the voice as both discourse and noise.

This is not to suggest that the casting and dubbing take precedence over Buñuel's images. Rather, I have argued that the doubling and the mechanical ventriloquism both enhance and oppose the seduction of those images, stoking the viewer's desire to experience them while undermining her wish to somehow possess them. Carrière's ethical blindness is in fact a different kind of seeing, one that sees through images into their mystery rather than into their explanation. Hence characters, the others in the screenplay, are treated ethically, the enigma of their otherness and independence recognized and protected. The film does not render us literally blind, but when we see Conchita in every scene, it is as if we are seeing her for the first time. We are forced to find her over and over again, to listen carefully to what she says, and to let her surprise us. Her presence is a discovery, like she was for Carrière and Buñuel. She might not be the only road toward estrangement in the film, but she is an ideal embodiment of screenwriting from the mouth of shadows. The next section lingers on those who surround her, and how the film's plotting, which heavily departs from its source material, focuses on how the characters interact in the thrall of their mutual unknowability and furthers the film's, and Carrière's, discourse of otherness.

ETHICAL INTIMACY WITH OTHERS: ADAPTATION AND THE MYSTERIES OF CHARACTER AND COLLABORATION

On top of Carrière and Buñuel's decision to double Conchita, and thus distance her from their authorial dictates, the structure of the entire film revolves around failed identification—it is a story about people seeking to understand others (even achieve a level of closeness and intimacy with them) and encountering their unknowability. In their transformation of Louÿs's novel, which is primarily concerned with erotic desire, Carrière and Buñuel have also foregrounded the fallacy of what Nancy Yousef (2013) calls 'the ideal of mutuality'. Sharing Levinas's desire to preserve otherness, Yousef argues that for successful, ethical intimacy to occur, the parties must share knowledge of each other but also be able to keep something only to themselves. The word intimacy 'designates, and thus to a degree attests to, a confidence that individuals can and do disclose to one another thoughts, feelings, and experiences, but it also pertains to, and thus intimates the foreboding or wish for, an inward region of irreducible privacy, a fated or perhaps willed withholding' (Yousef 2013, 1). The assumption Yousef hopes to dismantle says that symmetry in relationships is necessary to connect with fellow humans—that what people know about one another should match. I have argued how *Obscure Object* asks viewers what would happen if they were willingly 'blind' to the face. But what if they were also 'blind' to the interiority of others? What if we could exercise asymmetrical relationships and partial mutual knowledge to construct an ethical intimacy, one that allows otherness to flourish?

Carrière's screenwriting from the mouth of shadows is shot through with this sort of fractured intimacy, all the way down to his approach to adaptation. All of Carrière and Buñuel's films based on previously published material—*Obscure Object, Diary of a Chambermaid* (1964) from Octave Mirbeau's novel, and *Belle de Jour* (1967) from Joseph Kessel's—are patently unfaithful adaptations, their objective inspired departure rather than slavish fidelity (again, asymmetry is favoured over symmetry). This is not surprising given the way they approach every source. In Carrière's words, his and Buñuel's primary raw materials were '[n]ewspapers, then dreams: our sum of the everyday' (1994, 165). These informed whatever project they were working on, and propelled their will to entertain ideas that fascinated them, even if they deviated from the text they were adapting. Fractured intimacy, furthermore, is an apposite description of their collaborations. To craft a script, they retreated somewhere where they could be reasonably isolated from distractions, where they engaged in discussions, read the newspaper, acted out scenes to tease out their rhythm and blocking, and shared anecdotes and impressions, all punctuated by 'silences in which each of us could, or almost could, like Edgar Allan Poe, gropingly follow the other's thoughts' (Carrière 1994, 166). Carrière further refers to this blind search for ideas as 'a strange activity, very hard to explain', and asks: 'What happens between two or more people who work together? Nobody is quite sure. We don't even know what goes on within ourselves at the moment of creation' (1994, 177). He places special importance on an exercise of estrangement that intensifies these unknowns:

> For a half-hour, at the end of every afternoon's work, I would stay alone in my room while Buñuel made his solitary way to the bar …. Thus separated, each of us committed himself to inventing, in half an hour, a story. It could be short or long, present or past, sad or slapstick, or even just a detail, a joke. Once this was done, I joined him in the bar and we traded discoveries. They could be related to the screenplay of the moment, or not—it didn't matter. (1994, 166–67)

Carrière's method does not rely on honest, intimate revelation. The writers don't so much tell each other what they are thinking or how they arrive at the thoughts they finally voice, as they are trying to figure each other out, groping in the dark that is their imagination. The half-hour separation actively estranges the writers as they come together.

The writers, who succeeded in composing their script through their partial knowledge of each other, write Mathieu as someone who fails in his relationships in large part because of his oversharing of his thoughts and his ill-advised attempts to be understood. In *Obscure Object*, he speaks his mind precisely to be clear about who he is and what he is thinking, only to be contradicted and mocked for what amounts to his campaign to portray himself as Conchita's victim and unfairly vilify her. The film begins with a sequence not present in Louÿs's text: Mathieu shares a cabin on a train from Seville to Paris with other passengers. Progressively, the travellers uncover coincidental linkages between them: they are all French, have been to the same places while in Spain, have read the same newspaper. One of them, a Magistrate (Jacques Debarey), recognizes Mathieu and claims to know the latter's cousin Edouard. A friendly atmosphere settles. Their bourgeois politeness (a favourite target of Buñuel's satire) even diffuses the awkwardness of a moment when a young girl, Isabelle (Valérie Blanco) attempts to help a little person, who will reveal himself to be a psychology professor (Pierre Pieral), onto his seat. Suddenly, Mathieu sees a bruised Conchita (Carol Bouquet in this section; her wounds, we later discover, are Mathieu's doing) looking for him, and proceeds to dump a bucket of water over her head. Nonchalantly, he returns to the cabin to the stunned, uncomfortable silence of his fellow passengers. Wishing to preserve their civilized courtesy, they say nothing until young Isabelle, the most likely to be unaware of social niceties, asks Mathieu:

ISABELLE: Mister, why did you throw water on the lady?
WOMAN: Hush, Isabelle. It's impolite to ask questions.

MATHIEU: No, Madam, she's right to ask. After all, it's not a very common act.[5]

Mathieu is more than eager to explain himself, so he takes the entire train journey to narrate his torrid affair with Conchita, whom he calls 'the worst woman in the world'. Mathieu's storytelling frames the tale of their relationship as a series of flashbacks.

With this scene, Carrière and Buñuel set a secondary plot: the passengers' attempt to make sense of Mathieu's actions. He has rather abruptly destroyed the pleasing familiarity they had developed with one another (through the comforts afforded by a shared destination, nationality and class) by performing an unexpected act. Alienating them further, Mathieu questions the harmfulness of the bucket stunt, and glibly implies that he would turn to murder, a most unethical alternative. The other passengers' curiosity ranges from scientific to unsettled and disciplinary, perhaps, in the Magistrate's case, who cannot comprehend a disruption of the order in which he believes, less so by one of his own. A deep anxiety about rationalizing Mathieu's behaviour courses through the dialogue, which is peppered with instances where mutuality is swiftly assumed, as in the exchange below:

PSYCHOLOGY PROFESSOR (to Mathieu): I don't mean to be indiscreet, but I'd give something to know why you did what you did.
MATHIEU: You're quite curious, sir.
PSYCHOLOGY PROFESSOR: I'm a psychology professor.
WOMAN: Do you teach at the Sorbonne?
PSYCHOLOGY PROFESSOR: No, I give private lessons.
WOMAN: I understand.
MAGISTRATE: Mr. Fabert... You seem like a normal person. Your cousin Edouard is a friend. So I think your act has an explanation, even if it is unusual.

It is as if the Magistrate, and perhaps the rest of the passengers, are ready to completely restore their faith in Mathieu's class-coded goodness (a moral judgement made largely on appearances) as soon as his behaviour is somehow explained away. Mathieu, already convinced of their empathy, is happy to fulfil that desire for symmetry between his listeners' impression of him and his own belief in the justice of his response to Conchita. He persists in thinking he knows himself transparently and that the others will assimilate him as he wishes. But when he begins his story, narrating what amounts to a character profile of both himself and Conchita, Mathieu takes the initial identification with his companions for granted. As Rothman notes,

> Mathieu is an obtuse narrator who patronizes the film's subjects without recognizing his affinity with them. Mathieu expects his story to vindicate him. Initially, his listeners seem to accept his view that the woman ... is a devil incarnate. By the time Conchita punctuates the climax of Mathieu's story by dumping a bucket of water on him, however, we have become fed up with his claims to authority.... (2001)

Ironically, while trying to make the passengers see Conchita the way he sees her, and see him as he sees himself—a good man manipulated by the woman he loves—he inadvertently exposes a truer side of himself—one that is selfish and vicious—and leaves the question of Conchita unanswered. An attempted, failed symmetry and totality give way to a more diaphanous asymmetry and fragmentation.

By scripting Mathieu's telling of how Conchita's capriciousness, in his eyes, justifiably drove him to violence, Carrière and Buñuel expand Louÿs's own framing to focalize their interest in misguided empathy. In the novel, a Frenchman called André Stevenol falls under Conchita's spell, but before meeting her in person, he meets Don Mateo, who regales him with a cautionary tale of Conchita's humiliating ways. The screenwriters multiply Don Mateo/Mathieu's interlocutors, spreading the hunger for identification among other characters and thus stressing precisely how pervasive the impulse for mutual knowledge can be. Rather than a warning of impending danger and a romantic and sexual desire for Conchita that André and Don Mateo definitively share (Don Mateo thinks he understands André, since he has been there), what binds Mathieu and his audience is a breaking down of epistemic reciprocity. When Conchita returns at the end of the train ride wielding a bucket (this time, as Ángela Molina) to mete on Mathieu his own wet punishment, she ridicules all of his past narration. Having listened to Mathieu's explanation of his own water-dumping, his listeners see him receive the same attack he perpetrated. The symmetry lends the events an air of justice, of a balance reestablished, and strengthens the feeling that Conchita holds another side of the story—a possibility Mathieu's fellow passengers are forced to allow. In the end, they might conclude that they know as little about this man to whom they have given their attention as they did before they ever met him. The ethical response, on their part, is to give Conchita the benefit of the doubt.

Carrière is not the only screenwriter to draw on ideas of creativity such as the mouth of shadows, but his commitment to the ethics of estrangement is unique. Compare Carrière's ethics of creativity with the approach to character creation outlined in Robert McKee's *Story*, where he invokes the medieval image of the 'Mind Worm' as a metaphor for the work of the screenwriter: 'Suppose a creature had the power to burrow into the brain and come to know an individual completely—dreams, fears, strength, weakness.' Armed with such knowledge, the Mind Worm/screenwriter can then weave a quest for that individual, and '[w]hether a tragedy or fulfillment, this quest would reveal his humanity absolutely' (McKee 1997, 374). McKee and fellow renowned screenwriting teacher Syd Field (2005) strongly suggest the writer put together detailed character biographies. Field's are particularly comprehensive: 'Break your character's life down into the first ten years, the second ten years, the third ten years, and beyond... When I write a character biography, I'll write more than twenty pages, starting with the character's parents and grandparents on both sides' (2005, 57). Field even admits to turning to 'past lives and astrology to get further insight' into his character before his final exhortation, printed in all capitals: 'KNOW YOUR CHARACTER' (2005, 58). By contrast, Carrière recalls an encounter between playwright Luigi Pirandello and an actress rehearsing a part from one of his plays. In that story, the actress came to Pirandello for answers on her character's motivations, feelings and reasons to behave the ways she does in the drama. Pirandello's response, which Carrière quotes with great admiration, was simply: 'But why are you asking me all this? I am the author' (1994, 178). The problem in Levinasian terms is that such concern with total character revelation 'abolishes difference and imposes the One and the Same on the other' (Taylor 2006, sec. 4). Carrière's own groping, adventurous, uninhibited creative process seeks to prevent that abolition.

This is not to say that a 'revelationist' approach to screenwriting automatically leads to unethical screenwriting or actions. Or that character biographies are futile. There are many geopolitical, economic, cultural and intellectual traditions behind each approach to screenwriting. Rather, I have argued that Carrière's focus on the mouth of shadows embodies an ethics of creativity more explicitly attuned to otherness, and the conditions of knowledge surrounding knowing that 'Other'. I have turned to Levinas, Taylor and a conceptual 'blindness' to locate the ethical import of Carrière's mouth of shadows, but this is distinct from a blindness that comes from sheer ignorance. Carrière himself warns against a 'willing blindness' to certain screenwriting issues. The trust and abandon he champions must not be confused with wide-eyed naïveté. Rationality must often prevail for the working screenwriter, and

> ... a last barrier of mistrust is essential—for both actor and author are widely considered to possess inspiration, passion, enthusiasm, even madness. In fact, these so-called poetic states usually proceed not from an expansion but a shrinking of the self. They are the product of a willing blindness. In everyday working reality, nothing justifies them. Instead of succumbing, of yielding to the flow, we should avoid them as we would a mood-enhancing drug, the kind that would have us adoring whatever we produced. (1994, 184)

This quotation points us to an extraordinary and complex interplay between blindness and insight at the heart of Carrière's ethics of creativity. This is embodied in another quote, this time from the screenplay of *Claire's Knee* (1970), used by Carrière and filmmaker and critic Pascal Bonitzer to close the chapter on character in their book *Exercice du scenario*. In the scene, novelist Aurora has invited Jerome to her chalet and is showing him a painting by a Spanish soldier of a blindfolded Don Quijote charging against the artificial wind of a bellows:

> AURORA: It's an allegory. The heroes of a story are always blindfolded. If they weren't, they'd do nothing, there would be no action. In the end, everybody is blindfolded, or at least, wearing blinkers.
> JEROME: Except for you, because you write.
> AURORA: Yes, when I write, I'm forced to have my eyes wide open.
> JEROME: And you operate the bellows?
> AURORA: Oh, no: it's not me who blows the wind: those are the hero's impulses. Or if you'd prefer it, his logic... I only observe. I never invent. I only discover.[6]

The penchant for mystery, and the impenetrability of creation, go hand in hand with a carefully calibrated watchfulness in 'The Vanishing Screenplay'. Carrière is ultimately on the side of lucidity. He might have populated his text with references to a metaphorical darkness, but it is equally charged with metaphors for a more intense vision—a visionary sense, as it were. Far from advocating for a certain thoughtlessness, Carrière calls for an ethics of abandon. For screenwriters, he wonders if an integral part of mastering the craft is finding and honing the skill of letting go.

EPILOGUE: A SIMPLE, KIND GESTURE

While acclaimed for his screenwriting, Carrière has also tried his hand at acting. For instance, he appears in Abbas Kiarostami's *Certified Copy* (*Copie Conforme*, 2010), the Iranian filmmaker's first film made outside of his native country. Co-written by Kiarostami and Caroline Eliacheff, the film follows British writer James (William Shimell) on a book tour and an unnamed French antiques dealer (Juliette Binoche) as they meet in Tuscany. Apparently a first encounter, their conversations during their seemingly aimless wanderings of the municipality of Lucignano hint at the possibility that the two have been romantically involved in the past. Their dialogue, glances and gestures are telling of both a deep intimacy and a profound estrangement—none of them ever verifies, for themselves or the audience, whether their recollections are true, even when they're charged with bruising, personal emotions. The lead actors beautifully sustain the ambiguity, but Kiarostami's casting masterstroke is Carrière. His scene appears designed to be a condensation of Carrière's philosophies and the meaning of his work for cinema history, brought to life by the screenwriter himself in the middle of a film about the dilemma of the unknown other. The scene starts when James and Binoche's dealer happen upon a busy public square, where they run into a man and a woman. The man, played by Carrière, takes James aside to dispense some unsolicited, but apparently pertinent, counsel about his situation with his companion:

MAN AT THE SQUARE: I forgot your last name. James...?
JAMES: James is fine.
MAN AT THE SQUARE: I'd like to tell you something. (*Pause*). Obviously, you're a knowledgeable man. But you could be my son. That's why I'd like to give you a piece of fatherly advice. May I?
JAMES: I'm listening.
MAN AT THE SQUARE: First, a question. I'd be curious to know... (*Pause*). Let's get straight to the point. I think [regards Binoche's character] all she wants from you is that you walk beside her and lay your hand on her shoulder. That's all she's longing for. But for her, it's vital. I don't know what happened between you and I don't want to. It's none of my business. But all your problems can be solved by a simple gesture. Do it, and set yourself free.[7]

Virtually all the hallmarks of Carrière's 'The Vanishing Screenplay' are present in the scene: the anonymity (his character, like Binoche's, remains nameless, called only '*L'homme de la place*'); the refusal to pry; and the exhortation to perform a kind gesture despite uncertainty over another person's thoughts. Fittingly, his character disappears after the exchange, having himself delivered a kind and simple gesture.

Carrière himself offered his own anonymous, kind gesture not in film but in life, when he received an Honorary Award from the American Academy of Motion Pictures Arts and Sciences in November 2014. In his acceptance speech, surprised at the fact that such honour was granted to a screenwriter, he said: 'very often, screenwriters are forgotten. They are like shadows passing through the history of cinema. Their names don't appear in reviews, very seldom. But still, they are filmmakers. That's why tonight I'd like to share this prize... with all my colleagues, the ones I know, the ones I don't know, from all over the world... so we all thank you' (Carrière 2014). It turns out that even when humility and self-effacement are, and in Carrière's own view, *should* be the way of the screenwriter, they appreciate being remembered and valued.

NOTES

1. Jeremy Leggatt's English version of Carrière's book *Le film qu'on ne voit pas*, titled *The Secret Language of Film*, translates this reference to Victor Hugo as 'mouth of darkness'. I have here made the more literal translation of '*la bouche d'ombre*', the 'mouth of shadows'.

2. An argument could also be cast from Buñuel's long-standing association with surrealism, which placed enormous importance on automatism in literature and art. Perhaps from Buñuel's perspective, his script work with Carrière could be termed a form of automatic writing. I have not brought surrealism explicitly into the chapter because Carrière's reflections seem to me to be more inclusive (or at least to be trying to be so) than couching the ideas in the admittedly robust surrealist discourse. Surrealism, however, haunts the above discussion.

3. I have chosen to use the Spanish translation for this excerpt because the English translation makes a stronger association of the mouth of shadows (which Leggatt translates as 'the voice of shadows' at this particular juncture) with Shakespeare, while the Spanish text more quickly connects the mouth of shadows with anonymity. Speaking of the latter, the word '*l'anonymat*' appears in the French text. Leggatt translates it as 'namelessness', which has implications beyond 'anonymity'.

4. Carrière even recalls moments when viewers completely missed the switches between Bouquet and Molina. He reports that a survey at an unnamed university showed 70 % of students who watched the film did not notice that two actresses played the part (1997, 75).
5. All dialogue from the film quoted in the chapter is transcribed from the English subtitles for the film in the Criterion edition.
6. Quoted in Pascal Bonitzer and Jean-Claude Carrière (1998, 137–38). The dialogue here is my translation to English from the Spanish translation of the original French text.
7. Dialogue transcribed from the English subtitles of the scene's French dialogue in the Criterion Collection edition of *Certified Copy* (2012).

REFERENCES

Bonitzer, Pascal, and Jean-Claude Carrière. 1998. *Práctica del guión cinematográfico*. Translated by Antonio López Ruiz. Barcelona: Paidós.
Carrière, Jean-Claude. 1994. *The Secret Language of Film*. Translated by Jeremy Leggatt. New York: Random House.
Carrière, Jean-Claude. 1997. *La película que no se ve*. Translated by Carlos Losilla Alcalde. Barcelona: Paidós.
Carrière, Jean-Claude. 2000. *Interview with Jean-Claude Carrière*. In *That Obscure Object of Desire*. New York: Criterion Collection. DVD.
Carrière, Jean-Claude. 2014. 'Jean-Claude Carrière receives an Honorary Award at the 2014 Governors Awards.' Accessed 20 November 2015. https://www.youtube.com/watch?v=3dOafuHB97U
Field, Syd. 2005. *Screenplay: The Foundations of Screenwriting*. New York: Delta.
Gaiman, Neil. 1997. 'Where do You Get Your Ideas?' in *NeilGaiman.com*. Accessed 20 November 2015. http://www.neilgaiman.com/Cool_Stuff/Essays/Essays_By_Neil/Where_do_you_get_your_ideas%3F
Levinas, Emmanuel. 1985. *Ethics and Infinity: Conversations with Philippe Nemo*. Translated by Richard A. Cohen. Pittsburgh: Duquesne University Press.
Levinas, Emmanuel. 1991. *Totality and Infinity: An Essay on Exteriority*. Translated by Alphonso Lingis. The Hague: Kluwer.
Louÿs, Pierre. 1999 [1898]. *The Woman and the Puppet*. Translated by Jeremy Moore. Sawtry, UK: Dedalus.
McKee, Robert. 1997. *Story: Substance, Structure, Style and the Principles of Screenwriting*. New York: Regan Books.
Rothman, William. 2001. 'That Obscure Object of Desire'. *The Criterion Collection*. Accessed 16 January 2015. http://www.criterion.com/current/posts/169-that-obscure-object-of-desire
Taylor, Chloé. 2006. 'Hard, Dry Eyes and Eyes That Weep: Vision and Ethics in Levinas and Derrida,' *Postmodern Culture* 16. Accessed 3 March 2014. http://pmc.iath.virginia.edu/issue.106/16.2taylor.html

Wood, Michael. 1981. 'The Corruption of Accidents: Buñuel's *That Obscure Object of Desire* (1977).' In *Modern European Filmmakers and the Art of Adaptation*, edited by Joan Magretta and Andrew Horton, 329–40. New York: Frederick Unger Publishing.

Yousef, Nancy. 2013. *Romantic Intimacy*. Stanford: Stanford University Press.

FILM REFERENCES

Claire's Knee [*Le genou de Claire*]. 1970. Wr: Eric Rohmer, Dir: Eric Rohmer, France, 105 min.

That Obscure Object of Desire [*Cet obscur objet du désir*]. 1977. Wr: Luis Buñuel, Jean-Claude Carrière, Dir: Luis Buñuel, France, 102 mins.

Certified Copy [*Copie conforme*]. 2010. Wr: Abbas Kiarostami, Caroline Eliacheff, Dir: Abbas Kiarostami, France, 106 mins.

CHAPTER 10

Screenwriting as Dialogic Ethics After *Animal Kingdom*

Steven Maras

At the heart of morality and ethics is interaction. The concept of doing good work, or of performing one's duty, implies a service to, or communication with, another. Even though morality can be imagined as a solitary decision, it is never fully carried out in isolation from some dialogue with others. This chapter explores dialogic ethics as a resource in thinking about ethics in screenwriting, specifically the important issue of the representation and mediation of relations. Wayne C. Booth suggests that one way of exploring ethics and fiction is by asking 'How can we describe the many relations we are asked to build?' (Booth 1988, 169). Following this line of thought, and drawing on the work of philosopher Martin Buber, I develop a dialogical ethical approach to screenwriting through a reading of the 2010 critically acclaimed Australian film *Animal Kingdom*, directed

S. Maras (✉)
Media and Communication, The University of Western Australia,
Perth, WA, Australia
e-mail: steven.maras@uwa.edu.au

© The Editor(s) (if applicable) and The Author(s) 2016
S. Maras (ed.), *Ethics in Screenwriting*, Palgrave Studies
in Screenwriting, DOI 10.1057/978-1-137-54493-3_10

and written by David Michôd, as well as an analysis of particular scenes from the screenplay. While Buber's approach encompasses our relation to the natural as well as to the spirit world, *Animal Kingdom* offers a sustained treatment of issues of family and social relations, and, as such, provides a useful example to focus in more carefully on the issues associated with depicting relations in a script. Rather than seek to create a final analysis of the film and script, my approach is better described as a dialogue with that work, focused on questions of relations and social existence.

DIALOGIC ETHICS

Viewed in terms of relations, screenwriting occupies a unique representational situation in which issues surrounding the representation and mediation of relations can be fluid. Much depends here on the idea of dialogue or relations being used. One area of ethics of particular relevance in terms of relations is what has been termed dialogic ethics. Here, I want to establish some of the core ideas of dialogic ethics as found in some of the work of Martin Buber (1878–1965), a renowned Jewish scholar and philosopher (http://plato.stanford.edu/entries/buber/), and translator of the Bible.

I and Thou, perhaps Buber's most famous work, was published in 1923 and first translated into English in 1937. Buber begins his work by distinguishing two word pairs: the I–It and the I–You. Both of these indicate different ways of inhabiting the world. The world is thus 'twofold' and so too is the 'I' of the human. The I is not transcendent or the same across both word pairs. For example, the I–You can only be spoken with one's whole being. The I–It can never be spoken with one's whole being (1970, 54). The word pair I–It defines a world of experience and our relations to things, objects, activities and goals. It also defines a world upon which the 'It' always has a border with other Its. For Buber, the I–It pair defines a particular approach to experience and gathering of information. 'Man [sic] goes over the surfaces of things and experiences them. He brings back from them some knowledge of their condition—an experience. He experiences what there is to things' (1970, 55). Regardless of whether the experience comes from inner or empirical experience, is mysterious or straightforward, it is limited by the I–It relation such that, for Buber, experience is not full participation in the world. Something is missing from this experience, a relation *in-between*. 'The world does not participate in experience. It allows itself to be experienced, but it is not concerned, for it contributes nothing, and nothing happens to it' (1970, 56). While a definite way of inhabiting the world, what is absent for Buber is the very issue of a relation with it, that is inaugurated by the I–You, and which 'establishes the world of relation' (1970, 56). And at the centre of the dialogic ethics is reciprocity: indeed, 'relation is reciprocity' (1970, 58).

The world of relation thus stands separate to the I–It. Further, it is a world made up of different spheres: the sphere of nature which resonates with us on the threshold of language; the sphere of our 'life with men', which is the space of language, in which 'we can give and receive the you'; and the sphere of spiritual beings. Important to grasp here is the unfamiliarity of Buber's treatment of experience. The example of nature helps clarify the difference between the world of relations of the I–You and that of experience in the I–It. While many would associate nature with experience and 'It-ness', for Buber, through the I–You, nature is more than an object. A tree can be an object, and fall under the I–It, but it also 'confronts me bodily' (1970, 58). Although he evades concepts such as whether the tree has consciousness, Buber is even willing to ascribe the tree reciprocity, since it can 'seize' us and we must deal with it in its entirety rather than abstractly or in parts in a 'reciprocity that has nothing except being' (1970, 173). There is a sense here of existence in duration, such as when Buber says that 'prayer is not in time but time in prayer, the sacrifice not in space but space in the sacrifice' (1970, 59; see also 81). Extending this to our lives together Buber draws out the gap between experience and relation in the following passage: 'The human being to whom I say You I do not experience. But I stand in relation to him, in the sacred basic word. Only when I step out of this do I experience him again. Experience is remoteness from You' (1970, 60). Not all I–You relations are always perfectly mutual and reciprocal—and Buber draws on the example of educators, psychotherapists and priests, as figures who in some ways must hold back from complete reciprocity and work through a more restrained interaction (1970, 178).

Buber's work, with its focus on perception, description and experience, offers rich possibilities for thinking about screenwriting. Reading and writing screenplays, for example, has been linked to performance in imagination: both in terms of acts of composition in the writing of scenes, and the image-building associated with reading the screenplay and hearing and seeing characters in particular settings, surrounded by things and sounds (see Maras 2009, 64). In a passage that could almost be applied verbatim to screenplay composition and reading, Buber writes:

> The form that confronts me I cannot experience, nor describe; I can only actualize it. And yet I see it, radiant in the splendor of the confrontation, far more clearly than all clarity of the experienced world. Not as a thing among the "internal" things, not as a figment of the "imagination" but as what is present. … It is an actual relation: it acts on me and I act on it. Such work is creation, inventing is finding. Forming is discovery. As I actualize, I uncover. I lead the form across—into the world of It. (Buber 1970, 61)

In the creation of screen works image-makers travel between the world of I–It and the I–You, the former being the world of narrative and technical details (of costumes, lighting and makeup, for example), and the latter encompassing the audience and at times the actors. In the case of orthodox feature film production, the screenplay frequently has a key role in this system as it provides one focal point for visualizing the moving image work to be. Interestingly, the screenplay has never been simply about describing things in an I–It way. Rather, it is the capacity of the screenplay to draw the reader into a relation, and a particular interplay between words and images in time, a lived moment, which makes it such a unique document in the creation of screen dramas. Buber captures this in the idea of forming and actualization, but also in the idea of leading the form across, into the practical world of It.

As well as providing a different frame through which to think about the script, Buber's ethics also holds potential as an audience principle (whereby the screenwriter imagines the audience as a You rather than an It), as well as a collaboration principle (encompassing how image-makers might treat the sources for their stories as well as their colleagues). This is because Buber's work provides a radical framework within which to imagine relations and experience. His work goes beyond a *love thy neighbour* position to explore 'complete mutuality' (1970, 178). Posing the question, 'What, then, does one experience of the You?', Buber responds, 'Nothing at all. For one does not experience it' (1970, 61). The You is not a thing. One does not merely experience the You (in which case the You would be reduced to a mere It). Rather, the You encounters the I. In this encounter we see the core aspects of a dialogic, reciprocal and direct relationship: 'The basic I–You can be spoken only with one's whole being. The concentration and fusion into a whole being can never be accomplished by me, can never be accomplished with me. I require a You to become; becoming I, I say You' (1970, 62). This, then, is a dialogic ethics that goes beyond how we conduct dialogue between two already constituted agents or parties. Rather, what we see is a mutually constitutive, plunging relationship between the I and You, which is in a sense what Buber means when he says the 'relation to the You is unmediated' (1970, 62), formed out of a presence that is 'waiting and enduring' (1970, 64). Central to this dialogic relationship are terms such as 'wholeness', 'unity', the 'lived relationship': at all points Buber is wary of a purely analytical dissection of the I–You relationship and its almost primal role in our culture's understanding of the appearance of being. 'In the beginning is the relation' (1970, 69). However, this relationship is also impermanent. Every You can easily be transformed into an It again. Many things can unexpectedly become a You. 'The It is the chrysalis, the You the butterfly. Only it is not always as if these states took turns so neatly; often it is an intricately entangled series of events that is tortuously dual' (1970, 69). How this ethical position might operate in the context of screenwriting, and function as a way to think about story and characters, is explored in the rest of this chapter.

THREE ORDERS OF SOCIAL RELATIONS IN *ANIMAL KINGDOM*

Animal Kingdom is the story of a young protagonist Joshua 'J' Cody (James Frecheville) who, following the death of his mother, reunites with his estranged extended family, who also happen to be career criminals.[1] The film is explicitly about how J attempts to survive a new set of relations. At the opening of the film we encounter what seems to be typical domestic scene, a son seated by his mother, watching television. Punctuated by the sound of ambulance sirens, gradually we become aware that the woman has overdosed. The absence of high emotion or grief suggests a situation in which the world of I–You is already dislocated and disoriented. Rather than infused with a sense of primal encounter, a 'longing for relation' (Buber 1970, 79), we encounter J as distant, unabsorbed and distracted by antics of a game show on the television. J, who is 16, has lied about his age to authorities to allow him to remain out of guardianship. Unprotected, unclear of what to do, he reaches out in a matter-of-fact phone call to his estranged grandmother.

Rather than detail each and every relation in the film, I want to argue that the narrative presents three orders of relations, and that the drama and ethical substance of the film arises out of the clash of these three orders which are: the Maternal order; the Papal order; and the Natural order.

The Maternal order is defined around the figure of Janine 'Smurf' Cody (Jacki Weaver), J's grandmother. This is an infantilized and sexualized world of I–You, exemplified in the over-passionate kisses she gives to her three sons. For Buber, the early development of a child is characterized by a drive towards the You. Commencing with glancing and touching, it is a 'motion' that will 'gain its sensuous form and definiteness in contact with a shaggy toy bear and eventually apprehend lovingly and unforgettably a complete body: in both cases not experience of an object but a coming to grips with a living, active, being that confronts us' (1970, 78). Within the maternal order in *Animal Kingdom* this process of definition and discovering the You is arrested. 'Smurf' (which is also the name of the blue creatures at the centre of a children's comic franchise) smothers the forming of relations of her children, monopolizing any craving for tenderness or reciprocity around the 'innate You'. Ultimately, within her matriarchy, Janine Cody is a controller of relations, maintaining a unit with a particular business in mind. The brothers have little sense of the 'You' of each other, or of others. There is little normal conversation between the siblings in the family, and Janine's success is in keeping the unit functional but immature.

Janine's eldest son, Andrew 'Pope' Cody (Ben Mendelsohn), embodies the Papal order in which symbolic power is used to dominate his subordinates. 'Pope' is no simple patriarch. He is a controller of relations, monopolizing and overwhelming those he comes into contact with. His order exists alongside, but also at times in competition with, the Maternal order. He is a sociopath that craves relations, with an idea of the You that is not grounded in any sense of equality with those around him. With religious undertones, he is an inquisitor, a self-ordained confessor—his catchphrase being 'you can tell me things', 'you can talk to me'—using the lure of listening and revelation to manipulate the You. He makes judgements and desires others to address him. His order is defined by debt and revenge. Also, while Pope is far from being a god or spirit figure, he has some god-like qualities as discussed by Buber, namely that he demands 'unconditional exclusiveness' from others (1970, 127). Pope is in hiding for much of the film, and is difficult to find (1970, 127), but his appearances are imposing like the '*mysterium* tremendum that appears and overwhelms' (1970, 127).

Together, the Maternal and Papal orders exist in what Buber would see as profound self-contradiction. 'When a man does not test the *a priori* of relation in the world, working out and actualizing the innate You in what he encounters—it turns inside' (1970, 119). Then it unfolds in an unnatural way 'it unfolds where there is no room for it to unfold'. This is a useful characterization of the domestic space in *Animal Kingdom*. The domestic cannot be realized and is never given its room. Dogs, domestic appliances are expunged from the family home in fits of rage. The family only socializes with itself, and cannot maintain relations or reciprocity with the outside world.

The final order of relations is the Natural order, defined by relations of the hunter and the hunted, prey and predator, and localized around the criminal world and justice system as a kind of animal kingdom. It is organized around the figure of the good cop Nathan Leckie (Guy Pearce), who is the antithesis of the 'bad cop' Randall Roache (Justin Rosniak). In a scene in a motel where Leckie has taken J in the hope of making J a witness for the state, Leckie explains the natural order:

> You know what the bush is about? It's about massive trees that've been standing for thousands of years and bugs that'll be dead before the minute's out. ... It's big trees and pissy little bugs. ... Everything sits in the order somewhere. Things survive coz [sic] they're strong and everything reaches an understanding. ... But not everything survives because it's strong. Some creatures are weak but they survive because they're protected by the strong. For one reason or other. ... You might think, because of the circles you've been moving in or whatever, that you're a strong creature. But you're not. You're one of the weak creatures. And that's nothing against you. You're weak because you're young. You've survived because you've been protected by the strong. But they aren't strong anymore and they certainly aren't protecting you. ... (Michôd 2010, 85–87)

This monologue from Leckie comes at a point in the film when both the Maternal and Papal orders are in crisis. Soon after, with Pope in custody and Smurf working with criminal elements of the police force to protect her sons, J will become an outcast. J's task in the rest of the film will be to work out where he fits (113), to establish his place in the relations that surround him.

SCREENWRITING, ETHICS AND RELATIONS

From the point of view of relations, the script for *Animal Kingdom*, and the film itself, forms a rich text, with the co-existence and competition between three distinct orders of relations forming a key part of the narrative. But my argument goes further, that as well as offering a sustained treatment of issues of family and social relations the film also allows us to focus in more closely on the issues associated with depicting relations in a script. If I am correct in arguing that central to screenwriting is the problem of relations, and how to mediate and represent them, then a particular focal point for discussion of ethics in screenwriting emerges: namely, the question of how the screenwriter and/or the script deals with relations.

To tease out this ethical issue I want to focus in on a particular scene from *Animal Kingdom*, to do with the murder of J's girlfriend, Nicky Henry (Laura Wheelwright). I want to continue to draw on Buber's work to look at this scene in terms of relations between characters, and the creation of I–You and I–It relations in the screenplay. The scene is written in the script as follows, with the sections in scene 111 with strike through omitted in the film:

```
110    INT. HALL / CODY HOUSE - NIGHT                    110

       An insistent BANGING at the front door. Pope walks the hall and
       opens it. Nicky is there, composed but upset.

                         NICKY
                    Is J here?

                         POPE
                    (pauses, thinks fast)
                    He's gone to the shops. He'll be back
                    in a tick. Come in.

       Pope steps aside, lets Nicky enter and closes the door.

111    INT. LOUNGE / CODY HOUSE - NIGHT                  111

       Darren is smoking a bong. He's surprised and discomfited by
       Nicky's arrival. She's drunk, ineptly flirtatious.

                         NICKY
                    Did he say how long he'd be?

                         POPE
                    Not long. Where you been tonight?

                         NICKY
                    Down at the Zanoni.

                         POPE
                    Yeah? What's going on down there?

                         NICKY
                    Nothing much really.

                         POPE
                    Was anyone you know down there? Who'd
                    you talk to?

                         NICKY
                    Nobody's there that I know.

       Pope studies her momentarily.

                         POPE
                    You want a drink?

                         NICKY
                    Thanks. Yeah.

       Nicky sits. Darren exhales bong smoke, wary. Pope exits to the
       kitchen, leaving Nicky with Darren. Awkward silence. Darren has
       a bad feeling about her being here.
```

CONTINUED:

~~NICKY~~
~~How's things?~~

~~DARREN~~
~~I don't know where J is. I dunno if~~
~~he's coming back anytime soon.~~

~~Pope enters with drinks and a syringe. He hands a drink to Nick.~~

~~POPE~~
~~I won't be long.~~

~~He opens his beer, sips. He holds up the syringe.~~

                    POPE
        I'm having a shot. You want a shot?

                    NICKY
        What is it?

                    POPE
        It's fun.

                    DARREN
        She just wants to go home.

                    POPE
        It's fun. Have some.

Pope crouches before her. ~~He smiles.~~ He rubs her arm gently and
slips the needle in. Nicky looks up at him. He pulls the needle
out and watches her. Seconds pass, her eyes droop.

                    POPE
        Have you been talking to the cops?

                    NICKY
        What? About what?

Nicky droops, scratches her nose. Pope is tender with her.

                    POPE
        About anything.

                    NICKY
        No. It's none of my business.

                    POPE
        Yeah it is. It's your business when
        you're in love, isn't it? When you
        whisper in each other's ears. I just
        got a call from someone says he saw
        you talking to the cops.

CONTINUED: (2)

              NICKY
     Cops.

              POPE
  Who were you talking to?

             DARREN
  What are you doing this for, Pope?

              POPE
     It's OK. You can tell me about the
     cops, honey.

Pope watches her. She can barely keep her eyes open.

             DARREN
     Pope.

Her eyes close. He watches her, then holds his hand over her
nose and mouth. She struggles weakly. An uncomfortably long time
passes before she goes limp. He takes his hand away, watches
her. He strokes her hair and stands.

             DARREN
     What the fuck?

              POPE
     You're doing it again, Darren. You've
     smoked yourself silly, thinking
     something's going on.

This is a confronting scene. Pope has earlier coveted J's girlfriend Nicky, who is significantly younger. Nicky is vulnerable having just had J break up with her—albeit to protect her, even though they both confess to loving each other before J is taken away for questioning by Leckie. Pope has become increasingly erratic and paranoid, especially over what Nicky and J might have said to one another. In an earlier scene, the overwhelming relationality of the events has been explained to J by Darren Cody (Luke Ford): 'Mate, everything has got to do with everyone'. In short, Nicky has walked into the Lion's den.

The scene is not performed exactly in accordance with the script. Despite the grotesque action, a murder by overdose and suffocation, this scene is written in a manner that suits the Papal order. Pope is overwhelming, interrogative and typically invites Nicky to tell him all about the cops. There is also, despite the immorality of what is going on, a sense that, for Pope, Nicky is more than just an I–It. He attempts to attend to her. He gets her a drink. He 'is tender with her'. The description 'holds his hand over her nose and mouth' almost disguises the true intent of the gesture. If one suspends full knowledge of what is happening in the scene, some of the description reads as a scene played between lovers. Furthermore, in the scene as written Darren works to establish Nicky's humanity. He attempts to warn Nicky off with the line 'I don't know where J is. I dunno if he's coming back soon'. And 'She just wants to go home'. In the written version of the script a series of visual cues further establishes Nicky's status as a You that is smiled at, or watched and watches.

There is a sense that, despite the horrific content, the scene could be described as 'ethical' within a particular set of parameters. This is because the violence is consistent with the representation of the Papal order of relations in the film, and secondly because the written scene makes some attempt to provide Nicky with humanity, to treat her more than an It. This brings us to an under-discussed aspect of narrative ethics, namely the question of whether characters themselves can be described as having ethical relationships and rights. This is unorthodox given a reluctance to theorize character in fiction in recent years (Price 2011, 202), and the difficulties facing an analysis of character in the scene text of the screenplay (Price 2010, 125). As Steven Price suggests, 'in the screenplay we see only the actions through which the character responds to, and carves out an identity for itself within the social world' (2011, 205). But we also see that the 'character's series of actions is orchestrated by the text' (2011, 205). However, our 'encounter' with characters is often unique, and highly relational in Buber's sense, to the point we often know actors through the characters they play. I suggest that the concept of relation provides a useful lens through which to frame character construction in the screenplay, one that emphasizes connections between characters in particular situations rather than realistic portrayals; and especially those points in the script where an I–You and I–It conception of humanity comes into contact. It forms a new frame in which to examine the idea that characters fit within logical structures, but at the same time can be imagined as autonomous, goal-oriented figures (Price 2010, 131).

As noted, this scene is not performed exactly in accordance with the script. Viewing this scene, a different weighting and emphasis in relations is evident. Firstly, as indicated by the action that is struck through, some actions are deleted. This diminishes some of the action tending to Nicky, which could be argued is more about Nicky being a You rather than an It. Secondly, the interaction in the written script (Pope smiles–Nicky looks up–Pope watches), part of a visual reciprocity, is in the edit replaced by a series of gazes that do not meet one another in any kind of reciprocal recognition. Nicky can barely respond to Pope's calls to 'look at me'. Thirdly, the scene as performed is difficult to describe as tender. For example, the holding of the nose and mouth is more accurately a smothering, whereby Pope's entire body overwhelms Nicky, not just his personality. Furthermore, the sexual tension of the scene is more explicit, and after lifting himself of Nicky's dead body Pope visibly adjusts his crotch for an erection. Nicky's life has been snuffed out. She has been used for sexual gratification and discarded.

Scenes such as this are complicated in ethical terms. They can leave viewers with a sense of ethical discomfort and even a sense of 'immorality'. 'Immorality' need not operate as some universal or absolute judgement. Here it can describe behaviours that transgress the set of rules and values underpinning a standard of wrong and right. This standard might be situational. The actions of a character might be criminal or unethical in terms of its consequences, but still moral if defined in terms of the norms and relations that define their conduct, or what Nicholas Wolterstorff calls the properties of a character (1980, 139, 146). As I have suggested, the script can be judged as ethical on the grounds that Nicky's You-ness is negotiated by the script, and the actions accord with the Papal order of relations and the kinds of actions one expects from Pope. Upon viewing, the same scene is open to a different interpretation and judgement. It is striking for the way Nicky is devalued and degraded as an object for Pope. Pope, for instance, slaps Nicky in action not detailed in the script. It can also be argued that the rendering of Pope through direction, performance and editing goes too far, possibly beyond what is required by 'the story', and that killing Nicky in this way takes him out of the Papal order. Overwhelming becomes not just suffocating, but smothering. From this perspective, when Darren cries 'What are you doing this for?', it points to an actual transgression in the script. Not only in the sense that if Pope's aim in the scene is to really find out who Nicky was talking too, it is unclear why he would inject her with a drug that sends her into a stupor. But also because Pope's abuse of Nicky is physical, bordering on rape in the sense of a sexual interaction without consent. The script demonstrates some self-consciousness around these issues. When Darren refers to Pope as 'Andrew' at the climax of this scene, it suggests we are no longer in the Papal order of things, but in a realm of shameless individual gratification.

Interestingly, given these transgressions, there is a sense that the killing of Nicky represents the beginning of a fall for Pope, or the symbolic properties that embody 'Pope'. In the rest of the script he never reclaims full power and seems cartoonish in his actions compared to his appearance in earlier parts of the film. The film actually provides a clearer sense of the transition here than the script. Pope has crossed into the Natural Order. A dolly shot positioned in front of Pope carrying Nicky's dead body into the backyard of the Cody house cuts to the camera zooming into the hotel room where J has been taken for his safety. The overall effect, taking into account the speed of Pope's walk and that of the zoom, reinforced by the soundtrack, is of Pope carrying Nicky towards the motel room where J is being held by Leckie.

CONCLUSION

This analysis of *Animal Kingdom* constitutes a kind of dialogue with the script. While methodologically speaking it would have been possible to track different scenes through different versions of the script, or interview script editors and actors on how they view and attend to different scenes, the scope of this chapter has been narrower, focusing on the way *Animal Kingdom* places ethical relations at the heart of the narrative. Through the depiction of a struggle between three distinct orders of social relations (the Maternal, the Papal, and the Natural order) the film forms an interesting case study in representation, using characters and situation to perform and explore different ethical or moral positionings in a world in which categories of Good and Evil are open to a range of powers and forces. On being awarded a star on the Hollywood walk of fame, film critic Roger Ebert said, 'Movies are the most powerful empathy machine in all the arts' (Ebert 2005). A central cog in this 'machine', screenwriters possess a unique power to cast objects, events and entities via an I–It relation or an I–You relation. This power raises significant ethical questions around whether characters and relations are used productively to explore a particular moral order, or abused. Furthermore, given the collaborative nature of moving image production, the screenwriter is not the only mediating agent when it comes to these relations. Directors, cinematographers, actors and editors can all be influential. This chapter has explored the hypothesis that central to screenwriting, however conceived, is the problem of relations, and how to mediate and represent them. The question of how relations interact with issues of identity, recognition and justice is an important one in contemporary cultural theory (see Fraser 2000; Taylor 1994). How the question of relations figures into the ethical analysis of screen writing represents, as the case of Animal Kingdom indicates, a potentially important and fascinating extension of this discussion.

NOTE

1. My analysis is based on the version of the script described as the 'Green Revisions' available in the public domain at http://www.sonyclassics.com/awards-information/animalkingdom_screenplay.pdf

REFERENCES

Booth, Wayne C. 1988. *The Company We Keep: An Ethics of Fiction*. Berkeley: University of California Press.

Buber, Martin. 1970. *I and Thou*. Translated by Walter Kaufmann. New York: Simon and Schuster.

Ebert, Roger. 2005 'Ebert's Walk of Fame Remarks' *Roger Ebert's Journal*, June 24. http://www.rogerebert.com/rogers-journal/eberts-walk-of-fame-remarks

Fraser, Nancy. 2000. 'Rethinking Recognition'. *New Left Review* 3: 107–120.

Maras, Steven. 2009. *Screenwriting: History, Theory and Practice*. London: Wallflower Press.

Michôd, David. 2010. Animal Kingdom [Script]. http://www.sonyclassics.com/awards-information/animalkingdom_screenplay.pdf

Price, Steven. 2010. *The Screenplay: Authorship, Theory and Criticism*. Basingstoke: Palgrave Macmillan.

Price, Steven. 2011. 'Character in the Screenplay Text.' In *Analysing the Screenplay*, edited by Jill Nelmes, 201–216. London: Routledge.

Taylor, Charles. 1994. 'The Politics of Recognition.' In *Multiculturalism: Examining the Politics of Recognition*, edited by Amy Gutmann, 25–73. Princeton: Princeton University Press.

Wolterstorff, Nicholas. 1980. *Works and Worlds of Art*. Oxford: Clarendon Press.

FILM REFERENCES

Animal Kingdom. 2010. Wr: David Michôd, Dir: David Michôd, Australia, 113 mins.

CHAPTER 11

Ethics, Representations and Judgement

Steven Maras

In the introduction to this collection I argued that discussion of ethics in screenwriting has been restricted by the grounding of questions of screen morality in a particular representational space that is focused on ethics as a moral code, and only partly interested in screenwriting as a practice due to a focus on compliance under the code. This representational arena allows for a very limited construction of the relationship between ethics and/in screenwriting. It constructs ethics primarily through concern over moral offence and indecency, and suspicion over entertainment, instead of grappling with the complexities or ambiguities of social ethics. It monitors representations in terms of whether they are manifestly transgressive of moral norms, rather than engage with representations as performances that seek to rework and even question norms. Screenwriting researchers interested in moving beyond this paradigm find themselves having to put ethics, representations and judgements together in new ways. This concluding chapter contributes to this task, examining different theories that account for the relationship between narrative and ethics, and putting forward a concept of 'ethical work' as a tool to help explore the ethical dimensions of screenwriting.

S. Maras (✉)
Media and Communication, The University of Western Australia,
Perth, WA, Australia
e-mail: steven.maras@uwa.edu.au

© The Editor(s) (if applicable) and The Author(s) 2016
S. Maras (ed.), *Ethics in Screenwriting*, Palgrave Studies
in Screenwriting, DOI 10.1057/978-1-137-54493-3_11

231

Through a focus on 'new perspectives' this collection has sought to transform and expand our understanding of the representational arena that is ethics in screenwriting by focusing on the impact of production environments on writers, and vice versa; issues to do with the relationship between actuality and history; and finally through a more creative treatment of issues of narrative and especially the way that character can form a basis for ethical reflection.

A central but still emerging concept in this rethinking of representational space is that of 'relation'. It is through this concept that many of the conceptual difficulties created by normative approaches to screenwriting and the historically low autonomy of screenwriters in the creative process can, I argue, be navigated. In this context I want to put forward a working hypothesis that central to screenwriting, however conceived, is the problem of relations, and how to navigate, mediate and represent them. The problem of relations can manifest itself in different ways. There are relations of practice (between non-professionals, professionals and between craft workers). There are also narrative relations (between characters, narrators and events). Relations can take what I call 'intrascriptural form', pertaining to the way relations are depicted in a script, and those that take an 'extrascriptural form', pertaining to the way relations are negotiated around a script, or the process of scripting. In distinguishing between intra- and extrascriptural modes my intention is not to set up some rigid dichotomy between what is inside the script and what happens around it. Indeed, like a Möbius band both can merge into one another, depending on the nature of the project at hand. A strongly collaborative project being developed through rehearsal may result in a script in which the extrascriptural relations are inseparable from intrascriptural relations. Or, a project working with non-professional actors may need to modify scenes to accommodate the strengths and weaknesses of the performer.

It is of course not a coincidence that issues of representation turn so quickly to questions of relation. Representations arise out of relations, and relations arise out of representations. Some key ethical terms, such as 'recognition' and 'identity', work at the intersection of these terms and the understandings that arise within them. As Charles Taylor puts it, 'our identity is partly shaped by recognition or its absence, often by the misrecognition of others, and so a person or group of people can suffer real damage, real distortion, if the people or society around them mirror back to them a confining or demeaning or contemptible picture of themselves' (Taylor 1994, 25). If identity is relational, a self-sufficient and self-created idea of the individual and their place in the world falls short. In its place, Taylor advocates a dialogic idea of ethics.

> In order to understand the close connection between identity and recognition, we have to take into account a crucial feature of the human condition that has been rendered almost invisible by the overwhelmingly monological bent of mainstream modern philosophy. ... This crucial feature of human life is its fundamentally dialogical character. We become full human agents, capable of understanding ourselves, and hence of defining our identity, through our acquisition of rich human languages of expression. (Taylor 1994, 32)

This focus on the 'rich human languages of expression' puts an important emphasis on the work of artists, and writers including screenwriters. While traditional debates might worry about the *influence* cinema or television might have on the prescriptive ensemble of moral code handed down through society, the focus on relation puts the work of artists and image-workers in a more positive light. Rather than cast suspicion over representation it gives the crafting of representations a generative role in our thinking about morality and ethics.

This revitalized idea of representation and its role in ethical formations brings with it a range of questions for any researcher seeking to do ethical analysis. One important question to pose here is, What is the role of the critic in ethical analysis? Is it merely to decide whether 'the work is in fact well-made' (Booth 1988, 137), or whether the work expresses a correct moral view? It is clear that the responsibilities of critics and analysts can extend further, to look not just at how well a work is made, but to be open to questions surrounding how the work sits within a broader ethical landscape or milieu. The role of the critic is more than dispensing absolute moral judgements about what is right and wrong, or about deciding what is good or bad in a script. Ethical analysis—which in its most broadest sense can be performed by academic critics and non-academic readers, practitioners in a critical or editorial relationship with their script, and viewers of moving image works—brings with it an additional responsibility to be cognizant of what we mean by 'good' and 'bad', and what we are doing when we make ethical judgements. As we reflect on the link between ethics and judgement, one particular question gains a special urgency; namely, how should we imagine the interconnection between representation and ethics? Or, put in a different way, how should we envisage the link between screenwriting practice and ethical practice?

STORYTELLING AND ETHICS

Thinking about ethics in screenwriting there can be a tendency to focus solely on case studies or particular texts. The benefits are that ethical issues (which are prone to becoming grey or murky) can be considered in a concrete form. A possible negative is that one can lose sight of the broader role or function of stories, narratives and writing in society. A wider exploration is needed. Needless to say, this is an enormous project. Thinking about the function of stories and narratives in culture represents one of the central projects in the humanities and social sciences. Stories help structure our world, but the world also 'comes to us' in the shape of stories (Turner 2002, 78–82). Focusing just on media studies, researchers are actively exploring the links between story, biology and neurology (Lambert 2013, 7–8). A long-standing approach looks at rituals via which we participate in stories and the links or 'condensations' that help organize the material world (Leach 1976, 37–41). In their study of television John Fiske and John Hartley link this to the 'bardic function', whereby the structure of messages is 'organized according to the needs of the *culture* for whose ears and eyes they are intended, and not according to the internal demands of the text, nor the individual communicator' (Fiske and Hartley 2003, 65). George Gerbner underlines the fact that the symbolic world is not primarily designed to be 'true to life' but to serve and perform cultural and social values. 'Fiction can act out purposes by presenting a world in which things seem to work out as they "ought to", regrettable or even terrible as that might be made to appear' (1973, 268–69). This perspective on the symbolic world and the 'ritual' dimensions of storytelling informs Horace Newcomb and Paul M. Hirsch's view of television as a 'cultural forum', in which the screenwriter could be said to work as a 'cultural *bricoleur*' (Newcomb and Hirsch 1994, 563).

Story forms an indelible link to one of the oldest forms of human interaction. Adam Ganz, thinking about the oral ballad tradition, encourages us to 'rethink the relationship between storytelling and screenwriting' (2012, 71–72). Nevertheless critics worry over the place of story in the modern world. The German critical theorist Walter Benjamin, in his 1936 essay 'The Storyteller', sounded a pessimistic note on the cultural place of storytelling when he declared the art of storytelling as coming to an end, with an age of information taking the foreground (1992, 83).

Several approaches to story present potentially useful ways of thinking about the relationship between screenwriting and ethical practice. One obvious path is to draw an ancient link between storytelling and morality through the existence of fables and tales that explain moral obligations and prohibitions (see Stadler 2008, 19–20). We could approach this from a different perspective through thinking of the role of story in Indigenous culture, and in an extension of this approach to the ongoing challenges of talking back to dominant, colonial culture (Gauthier 2012; Joyce 2013).

There are other perspectives through which we can directly construct the relationship between screenwriting practice and ethical practice. 'Communication rights' offers one avenue for exploring this link. The right to communication is a concept that has drawn a range of advocates and critics. Nevertheless, it usefully crystallizes a range of concerns around human rights-based approach to communication processes (Hamelink and Hoffmann 2008), and for listening to diverse voices from a wide political, economic and cultural spectrum (see International Commission for the Study of Communication Problems 1980, 20; Hamelink 2014, 22). A right to communication is based on the recognition of the importance of communication to human life and the centrality of relationships, interaction and solidarity to our existence. But it also seeks to redress historical injustices around these interactions, particularly technological and resource imbalances accumulated through colonial power, often following a division between countries and continents in the Northern hemisphere and the under-represented, and informationally dominated, global South. Accordingly, discussions of the right to communicate focus around issues of technological dependence between countries, Inequalities in information flows, ethical choice (Rennie et al. 2010), and also the status of Indigenous culture and communities (Lee 2004, 5). Without suggesting that all screenwriters become advocates for the right to communicate, a historical and theoretical understanding of the right to communicate can inform a progressive approach to ethics in screenwriting.

In the remainder of this section I want to briefly consider two other perspectives: narrative studies of morals and moral development, and theories of imaginative acquaintance.

Narrativity and Moral Life

Over the last few decades the question of the relationship between narrative and moral life has come to the foreground in philosophy and political theory (see Meyers 2004, 159–179). This work explores what seems an intrinsic link between morality and narrative, in the sense that we learn ethics *as* and *through* narrative. This link is further strengthened if one accepts the argument that human identity is not fixed and constant, but is in a sense crafted within stories and narratives. Indeed, such stories encompass our relationship not only with 'our' selves—or even what some theorists see as our different ethical selves—but also with others. Through narrative, we articulate and disarticulate moral problems and ambiguities central to our existence and being with others. Diana Tietjens Meyers suggests that narrative plays a key role in working out moral subjectivity, knowledge and agency. It helps form a bridge between moral codes and situations, allowing for moral knowledge that is both individualized and well justified (2004, 168). Judith Butler suggests that particular frames foster our apprehension and recognition of the lives of others (2009).

One area of intense interest in the relationship between narrative and moral life has to do with moral education and development. 'Moral development' is a vexed topic for feminist ethicists such as Carole Gilligan (1982) and Nell Noddings (1984). They identify, in the work of some ethicists, a masculinist privileging of concepts of individuality over intimacy, and individuals as separate entities over reciprocity. From this perspective, Gilligan criticizes Sigmund Freud's view that women possess a different idea of ethical normalcy, one with a lesser sense of justice and more influenced by emotions. Gilligan extends this into a wider critique of the way male views of maturity dominate the study of moral norms and development. Although we will not focus deeply on this feminist critique (often associated with the term 'ethics of care') it forms an influential touchstone in a number of different discussions about ethics, including moral education.[1]

In terms of moral education, researchers explore the role of narrative and dialogue in deepening our understanding of others, and expanding our understanding of our place in the world. As Carol S. Witherill notes: 'stories can serve as springboards for ethical action. Narrative invites us to come to know the world and our place in it' (1991, 240). For Janet Stadler, 'storytelling furthers ethical understanding of the process of articulating the relationships between characters and events' (2008, 19). She links it closely to processes of 'relating': 'of accounting for the complexity of ethical situations and the patterns of responsiveness and responsibility within them' (2008, 19).

Not all narrative theorists will go so far as Martha Nussbaum to declare 'the poet as the only judge' (1995, 79), but one important strand of thinking has to do with ethical judgement, and demonstrating the importance of imagination and empathy in our exercise of moral and legal judgement. From this point of view, Nussbaum suggests that literary understanding 'promotes habits of mind that lead toward social equality in that they contribute to the dismantling of the stereotypes that support group hatred' (1995, 92). Narratives provide insight into the nature of dignity and humanity. Of special interest here is Nussbaum's discussion of facts and neutrality. She questions whether lofty distance is the only model for neutrality and wonders whether empathy can work alongside neutrality (1995, 88). For Nussbaum, poetic imagination has a role in understanding the human and individual dimension of facts, and grasping the different dimensions of equality and inequality (1995, 105).

Imaginative Acquaintance

This view of the importance of imagination to ethics aligns with what Stephen Cohen regards to be one of the most important tools in making moral judgements, namely 'imaginative acquaintance': by which he refers to the process of imagining 'that we are in a situation that, in fact, we are not in; and then we ask how we should judge something about that situation' (2004, 93). Imaginative acquaintance can play an important role when a particular situation is beyond our own experience, or in introducing us to different viewpoints upon a situation we may already have some familiarity with. Most important from the perspective of screenwriting is that imaginative acquaintance is a process of storytelling. 'When you are imagining a different situation, you are, in effect, telling a story' (Cohen 2004, 96). For Cohen, storytelling actually goes beyond imaginative acquaintance and has a function in the reflective process, of rationalizing our decisions, and achieving that point at which our commitment to principles and understanding of a situation fit within a 'reflective equilibrium' (2004, 97). Ethical judgements involve more than simply tallying facts and details, in Cohen's view, but working through descriptions, perspective, as well as roles and loyalties.

This focus on the role of narrative as part of imaginative acquaintance and the weaving of moral tales is brought together in a sophisticated manner in Nussbaum's later work, where she develops a concept of ethical citizenship that incorporates an understanding of history and social facts into what she calls 'narrative imagination' (Nussbaum 1997). In doing so she furthers her work on poetic justice and social sympathy. For Nussbaum,

> narrative imagination is an essential preparation for moral interaction. Habits of empathy and conjecture conduce to a certain type of citizenship and a certain form of community: one that cultivates a sympathetic responsiveness to another's needs, and understands the way circumstances shape those needs, while respecting separateness and privacy. (1997, 90)

Nussbaum's concept of narrative imagination is focused around how characters foster compassion for the inner life of individuals and further to develop traits such as 'courage, self-restraint, dignity, perseverance, and fairness' (1997, 90). Furthermore, Nussbaum calls for 'an exercise of the compassionate imagination that crosses social boundaries, or tries to' (1997, 92). Here, Nussbaum takes the relationship between storytelling and ethics beyond moral edification. For Nussbaum, narrative imagination sits at the centre of our moral interaction and citizenship.

ETHICAL WORK

Research around moral development and narrative imagination allows us to posit a strong relationship between storytelling and ethics, and by extension screenwriting practice and ethical practice. The concept of narrative imagination pushes us further to consider the ethical or moral import of works of art. More than lessons in traditional moral codes, narrative works of art can explore issues and acquaint us with different possibilities. Intrinsic to thinking about the relationship between screenwriting practice and ethical practice is how should we conceive of the ethical work that screenwriters can do in or through their scripts? The remainder of this chapter explores the challenges posed by tackling this idea of 'ethical work'.

In his landmark 1988 work, *The Company We Keep: An Ethics of Fiction*, Wayne C. Booth makes the observation that most approaches to ethics focus on the interaction between the viewer or reader and the work, after the last page is turned (1988, 169). It is less common to focus on the ethical experience *during* the time of viewing or listening. He writes, 'Instead of asking whether this book, poem, play, movie, or TV drama will turn me toward virtue or vice tomorrow, we now will ask what kind of company it offers me today' (1988, 169). This is especially relevant in the context of discussion of screenwriting, and a long debate over whether scripts and screenplays offer the same reading experience to readers than novels and films. This discussion revolves around issues such as the 'completeness' of the script, the gratification or pleasure of the reading experience (or lack thereof), and whether or not the script 'ontologically' exists as a separate entity to the moving image work it anticipates (see Maras 2009, 49–50; Nannicelli 2011). There is an assumption in much work on moral development and imaginative acquaintance that the work of art is a kind of 'companion' in Booth's terms, like a friend that we can have a conversation with. However, the textual and industrial conditions of scripting are more complicated and—despite the special camaraderie of team-based creative projects—make such a friendship or companionship more instrumental and task focused. A common and contentious metaphor used to describe the script—the 'blueprint'—serves as a useful reminder of the broader production context that permeates our ideas of the script.

This is not to say that a literary work is not constructed, produced or realized. While Booth regards poetry as both an actualized and potential form (1988, 89), scripts structure the work of actualization differently. The focus on visualizing action that underpins writing for the screen—the way description and dialogue is laid out in a screenplay, for instance—can work against a kind of narrator-focused storytelling. Our experience of characters and narrators is mediated by actors, but also editors, directors, producers and cinematographers and so on. Scripts offer utility, a bridge to a world still-to-come, a guide to a range of technical and imaginative activities.

Scripting adds a complicated layer to the metaphors of people meeting and sharing stories that Booth tends to favour. For example, Booth bases the work of the reader or viewer on what he calls 'coductions' of various narratives, by which he refers to a specific approach to the act of judging which places the focus on comparison and *weighing up*. The neologism is drawn 'from *co* ("together") and *ducere* (to lead, draw out, bring, bring out)' (1988, 72). Scripts are possibly unique in that coduction is implicit in their architecture. Not just solely a work of interpretation then, coduction here functions as a principle of a material practice.

On this basis, screenwriting offers a unique case, and requires a more detailed account of the relationship between scripting and what I term ethical work. 'Ethical work' refers to the way that, through its depiction of actions and situations, scripts 'think through' ethical problems of loyalty, judgement, justice and human relations. It is my contention that understanding how this ethical work operates between the script, and the image-work arising from it, forms an important aspect of ethical judgement of screenwriting. Understanding ethical work can provide a useful lens on the way the screenwriter presents ethical ideas, and thus forms part of a potentially broader understanding of the responsibilities of the screenwriter.

The concept of ethical work raises important questions of how and where this work takes place. A careful navigation of author-text and reader-text relations is required. In terms of author-text relations, it is tempting to suggest that fiction operates as a kind of moral philosophy, making moral claims about objectivity and goodness (see Nussbaum 1983). D. D. Raphael suggests that the issue partly hinges on what one deems moral philosophy to be. If moral philosophy is the art of creating sharpened moral insight, then this may indeed be extended to fiction (1983, 5). Although Raphael hastens to suggest that classing works of fiction as moral philosophy should not be taken as a way to reduce them to philosophy: 'I do not think that a contribution to moral philosophy is in any way a central function of these works; it is tangential' (1983, 9).

Approaching fiction as a kind of moral philosophy often draws on ideas of 'teaching'. While asserting that 'all works *do* teach or at least try to' (1988, 152), Booth takes care to dismantle any sense of a communication situation that privileges the author as a singular voice: 'Whenever we read or listen to any story, whether it claims to be historical or fictional, we do not respond to a single, simple voice that is often implied by current theories of "communication": a "sender" or "source" who transfers bits of information to a receiver' (1988, 125). Instead, Booth highlights the dramatic and performative dimensions of fiction. Rather than relying solely on an author-centric intentionalist approach, Booth advocates an interactionist approach based on companionship and exchange. 'But our best narrative friends introduce us to the practice of subtle, sensitive moral inference, the kind that most moral choices in daily life require of us' (1988, 287). From this perspective, works and scripts appear not just as repositories for moral insights and dogmas, but schemes which suggest certain ethical actions and reactions, and which are then actualized by readers. Ethical work is, then, a largely representational activity, that encompasses the symbolic exploration of particular ethical representations and positionings.

Booth uses the concept of 'world' to capture this interaction:

> ...[C]riticism cannot be simply propositional, offering clear, firm "positions" that judge entire worlds as right or wrong, good or evil. We do not take in these worlds as isolated propositions, nor even as developed fragments of the kind I gave quoted. It is true that when we quote them wrenched out of their original narratives, we take those fragments in *as* propositions, and we can then discuss them in ordinary discourse. ... But when we meet them as part of a story of any scope (whether or not it offers explicit arguments along with narrative), what we re-constitute for ourselves is a vast articulated network of interrelated images, emotions, propositions, anecdotes, and possibilities, all embedded in more or less fixed norms. (Booth 1988, 336)

Booth emphasizes the fact that narrative form is determining, embedding the reader in norms. The medium, the narrative, matters to any message performed or gleaned from the work.

BUILDING ETHICAL WORLDS

Admittedly, Booth points to some difficulties faced in discussing entire worlds: 'If I am led to appraise whole commonwealths, religions, ontologies, am I not surely doomed to talk airy nonsense' (1988, 335). Despite the challenges, Booth encourages critics to engage with worlds. The issue remains, however, of finding an appropriate framework with which to explore world building and screenwriting as a form that offers a unique and even strange kind of companionship. To assist with this task, I want to draw on the work of Nicholas Wolterstorff and his theory of projected worlds, as filtered into film theory by Carl Plantinga (see Plantinga 1987; 1997, 16). Following this introduction to Wolterstorff's approach, I want to demonstrate how it can be put to work in the context of an analysis of the ethical work performed in Jimmy McGovern's 2014 television feature *Common*.

For Wolterstorff, the concept of world is analogous to that of 'story': 'consisting of the content, the chain of events (characters and settings), the objects and persons performing, undergoing, or acting as a background for them' (1976, 121). 'Projecting' is the term he uses to describe the work of expressing this story in a discourse. Distinguishing between 'a world projected' and the 'action of projecting a world', Wolterstorff argues that his approach is broader than the structuralist/narratological distinction of story and discourse (1980, 108).

For Wolterstorff a work of art lays down 'states of affairs' for our consideration. States of affairs are such when 'occurrences' have 'a certain property, or some things standing in a certain relation' (1976, 121). Each state of affairs implies a 'stance' taken on the world (Plantinga 1987, 49). Plantinga uses the idea to distinguish between works that foster a 'fictive' stance, and documentary in which 'an assertive rather than fictional stance is taken toward the world projected through the text' (Plantinga 1987, 50; see Wolterstorff 1980, 109).

For Wolterstorff each occurrence of a state of affairs is a kind of event (1980, 192). States of affairs imply certain claims, which we can take as true or false as long as the stance adopted is assertive. If the stance is fictive, then truth or falsehood is no longer the correct frame of evaluation. Fictive stances require a different kind of evaluation because the 'fictioneer' *fictionally*, rather than assertively, projects a world' (1998, 191).

> The fictive stance consists of *presenting*, of *offering for consideration*, certain states of affairs—for us to reflect on, to ponder over, to explore the implications of, to conduct strandwise extrapolation on. And he [sic] [the fictioneer] does this for our edification, for our delight, for our illumination, for our cathartic cleansing, and more besides. (1980, 233)

Wolterstorff's theory distinguishes between two kinds of states of affairs: existing and occurring. Historical events exist but may not be occurring now. He also refers to possible and impossible states of affairs: possible states could occur, impossible states cannot. Furthermore, there are different ways of indicating a state of affairs. They can be explicitly mentioned, or suggested. 'Narrations are never wholly explicit' (Wolterstorff 1976, 125; 1980, 115).

States of affairs, it should be said, are rarely singular. Wolterstorff notes that '…[T]he world projected by way of an artefact of art not only includes certain states of affairs but is itself a state of affairs' (1980, 127). As an artefact, the script lays down a world but might also assert or indicate certain states of affairs in terms of how the screen work would be made. 'The artist's activity consists in projecting an already existent but normally non-occurrent state of affairs by way of indicating certain states of affairs'

(1980, 130). Although Wolterstorff does not discuss the script, an analogy could be made with the way a scene can add and indicate a new state of affairs over an older one. Flashbacks, flashforwards and even camera angles could technically add new indications of states of affairs. The fluidity of states of affairs is an important dimension of Wolterstorff's work. 'We as human beings are created with the marvellous capacity to envisage states of affairs which never occur, even states of affairs which could not occur' (1980, 130).

Alongside projection, Wolterstorff also looks at the activity of interpretation on the reader or viewer's part. The activity of discovering what has been indicated is termed 'elucidation' (Wolterstorff 1976, 125).

> Elucidation is often a difficult and complicated procedure. We have to discern the presence and force of irony, the meaning of metaphors, the suggestions borne by emphasis, the presence of ambiguity (*double entendre*). And sometimes elucidation is stymied. Try as we might we cannot discern what an author mentioned in a certain passage or what he suggested. (Wolterstorff 1976, 125)

Wolterstorff rounds out his view of interpretation by exploring another aspect, namely extrapolation. This is the process of determining what is included in the projected world beyond what the author indicated. When we extrapolate what the author has, or may have indicated, we draw out the text according to certain 'strands' (1976, 126).

Mining Wolterstorff's work, a vocabulary or framework for the analysis of world building opens up consisting of: **states of affairs** which consist of a **world** that is **projected** according to certain **stances**. States of affairs can be **existing** or **occurring**; **possible** or **impossible**. States of affair can be **explicitly mentioned** or **suggested**, but are rarely singular. **Elucidation** is an activity of discovering what has been indicated. **Extrapolation** is the process of determining what is included in the projected world beyond what the author indicated, according to particular **strands**.

ETHICAL WORK IN JIMMY MCGOVERN'S *COMMON*

Having presented some of the key aspects of Wolterstorff's approach to world projection, I will now apply it to an example, specifically a 90-minute television feature *Common*, written by Jimmy McGovern, directed by David Blair and produced by McGovern and Steven McKeon, first broadcast in July 2014 on the BBC, the British public service broadcaster. My primary aim here is not to show how a screenwriter 'directs' from the page so that it is produced as written (Mehring 1990, 6). Rather it is to offer a concrete case study of a script engaged in 'ethical work'. My analysis hopes to show how, through its projection of different states of affairs and elucidation, ethical work can become a focus for the script and the screenwriter. *Common* provides a unique case to examine because it is highly dependent on the audience's understanding of a particular state of affairs. Indeed, this understanding is central to the way McGovern manipulates expectations of judgement, in the context of a complex narrative about working class morality, justice and the judicial system. Furthermore, as I show in the discussion of the script, McGovern offers important elucidations to the reader that guides the projection of this world.

One of the bonuses of focusing on *Common* is that the script (McGovern 2014) is available online, providing us with a unique opportunity to explore ethical analysis. The script available from the BBC website is a very late version. McGovern has explained that 'The director …would have seen earlier versions of this. Indeed he would probably have chipped in with his own ideas. But it's not the shooting script. That would have come immediately after this one' (McGovern, personal communication, 2015).

The 'common' of the title alludes to Common Purpose or Joint Enterprise laws in the United Kingdom. Under joint enterprise law, criminal liability for an action can be extended to any member of a group involved in that enterprise. Under the law, it is not necessary to determine exactly who in the group committed the crime. Critics have argued that this law has been applied unjustly, with a disproportionate number of convictions being faced by urban black and working-class youth. One of the profound aspects of the law is the way it changes our understanding of a state of affairs. Regardless of who wields a knife or throws a punch, regardless of their location or state of mind, criminal liability extends to all those implicated.

In a fictive challenge to this expansion, McGovern begins his script by indicating a particular state of affairs very narrowly, only gradually revealing more details. The script begins with a 'slice' of a situation and gradually indicates more and more about the state of affairs. As our understanding of the state of affairs grows, our interpretations and our extrapolations build into a more complex picture of what has gone on. I would further argue, in an elaboration of Wolterstorff's theory, that complicating the state of affairs are the activities of characters who in effect create projections of state of affairs from their own viewpoint.

Scene 1 begins with the simple description: 'Three young men (Tony Wallace, Colin McCabe and Kieran Gillespie) hurrying from a pizza parlour to a parked car. ... Johnjo O'Shea (17 years old, vulnerable) is at the wheel, a rap song blasting away'. Note here the specific indication of Johnjo's (Nico Mirallegro) vulnerability. The script makes other indications of character attributes (e.g. 'horrified') which are important mood-drivers in the script.

With the opening order to 'Drive!' the narrative pushes off even though we don't understand what has happened. Johnjo's dialogue, 'What's happened?', indicates his own lack of knowledge of the situation, but also highlights limitations in our (the viewer/reader's) understanding of the world. Is it too much to say that under joint enterprise we may be virtual accomplices?

Scene 2 starts by indicating the seating arrangements in the car, but there is more to it than this. This is an elliptical screen direction since what we will see in the played scene is a high energy and 'poly-phonic' situation in which different voices overlap with one another and compete for sense and dominance. It's something of a motif in McGovern's work, linked to moments of ethical and moral confusion and bewilderment. The placing of the characters also establishes a hierarchy of sorts, a zig-zagging pattern of communication and reasoning, with Tony Wallace, the older cousin, primarily responding to Johnjo.

Scene 2 reinforces the idea that an event has happened but we don't know the exact state of affairs. Furthermore, the structure of the scene means that what we know about the exact event or state of affairs is intertwined with or constrained by the projections of the event made by the characters. Colin McCabe voices this by stating 'You Stupid Prick, you've dropped us all in it now'.

Scene 2 also gives us a first insight into an explanation of what has happened, of the event. But here the state of affairs is contested and open to different perspectives.

```
                    COLIN MCCABE
          You've dropped us all in the
          shit, you prick. You crazy twat,
          you mad crazy...

                    KIERAN GILLESPIE
          He was asking for it.
     [...]
                    COLIN MCCABE
          How? How was he asking for it,
          you dick? He said nothing. He
          never opened...

                    KIERAN GILLESPIE
          He was looking at me.

                    JOHNJO O'SHEA
                 (really scared)
          What's happened?

                    COLIN MCCABE
          His mouth... He wasn't looking
          at you. He was...

                    TONY WALLACE
          Nothing's happened.

                    COLIN MCCABE
          ...watching the fight...
          "Nothing's happened?" He's only
          gone and stabbed someone, hasn't
          he...
```

Someone has been stabbed. They may or may not have asked for it, depending on whose projection of this world we accept. Faced with incomplete information, Johnjo tries to extrapolate 'Did he kill him?' It's a question that hangs in the air until the middle of Scene 3 when Kieran Gillespie acknowledges 'I don't know'.

In a script, actions can indicate new things about the state of affairs, and can foster new interpretations, or provoke new extrapolations and projections. McGovern is expert at using action to drive story forward in order to indicate or present a new aspect of the state of affairs. He is also skilled in delaying the presentation of action, and it is only in Scene 73 that we actually see the knife go into Thomas Ward. Another tool or indicator he uses is mood. Indications of 'Sheer Panic', 'Fear', 'More Fear', create momentum in the script, and (drawing on Booth's idea) embeds the ethical work of the script in narrative.

In the context of joint enterprise laws the structure of this opening to *Common* is provocative. It flags that the state of affairs in relation to any crime is complicated. It can stem from an act of madness, or a misplaced sense of righteousness. It also powerfully opens up issues of perspective, that what happened may look different according to the point of view of different participants. And finally we come to understand very strongly one state of affairs: that there is a powerful gap and asymmetry in what the different participants know. Johnjo, by serving as our proxy in the text, an interpreter with incomplete knowledge, is structured as a kind of innocent in the state of affairs, especially since he was not present in the pizza shop at the time of the stabbing. This illustrates Wolterstorff's point that states of affairs are never singular. Indeed different characters are already presenting different renderings of this world in the script, however incomplete our understanding of the state of affairs may be.

Scene 7 introduces the mother of the victim Margaret Ward (played by Susan Lynch) and the police. It inaugurates what is a dual-familial response (from Johnjo's family, and the family of the victim) and an institutional response (police and legal) to this state of affairs. But it also initiates a transformation of the state of affairs, and a projection of it, as the reality of the manslaughter, and the impact of joint enterprise, becomes apparent.

The script again adopts a technique of indicating an extremely narrow or constrained version of the state of affairs, this time within the context of policing.

```
                 POLICE OFFICER
      We've been told to bring you
      down to casualty, Mrs Ward.
      Thomas has had a bit of an
      accident.

                 MARGARET WARD
      What sort of accident?

                 POLICE OFFICER
      I don't know, love. we've just
      been told to get you.
```

The reality of Thomas Ward's situation, that we are dealing with more than just a bit of an accident, is revealed only gradually. In Scene 9 Margaret approaches the nurse's station; she is oblivious to the events that have transpired, but intuits something wrong from the weird machinations of the police and hospital procedure.

```
                 MARGARET WARD
      I'm Margaret Ward. My son Thomas
      is here. He's had an accident
      apparently.
```

The issue of who knows what, and how much is established through the script and the filmed scene, is described through glances.

```
Still nothing from the receptionist. Margaret is
getting frightened. She glances away...

She sees the nice friendly police officers who brought
her in. They're obviously getting some terrible news
from a colleague... They glance at Margaret. Look back
to the colleague. Glance at Margaret again...

She now sees other people staring at her....
```

At this point the social worker Jennifer Fieding makes her entrance, and she will eventually break the news in the 'Bad News Room'. The comment 'Make what?', and the way it is delivered, flags the fact that Margaret knows almost nothing about this state of affairs. In the face of her lack of knowledge Fieding gives us a cold, factual institutional account that falls on Margaret like a blow.

```
                    JENNIFER FIELDING (CONT'D)
        Thomas didn't make it, I'm
        afraid.

                    MARGARET WARD
        Make what?

                    JENNIFER FIELDING
        He was stabbed earlier this
        evening and died an hour or so
        ago. I'm really sorry.

                    MARGARET WARD
        I think you've got the wrong
        boy. I'm Thomas Ward's mother
        and he had a bit of an accident,
        that's all.

                    JENNIFER FIELDING
        He was stabbed in the pizza
        place on Holt Road, Mrs. Ward,
        and died here a short time
        later.
And mention of the pizza place makes it suddenly real.
```

I want to focus on this line, 'And mention of the pizza place makes it suddenly real'. Typically, scene description (that portion beneath the scene heading specifying place and time) relates to the action or business. 'The text gives general descriptive information, such as the physical appearance of the characters and the details of essential décor and ambience' (Miller 1986, 17). In the conventional understanding, description should only pertain to action that is seen and heard. There is no point dwelling on what is in the minds of characters.

Theoretically, this leaves little room for comments that are not about visible or audible action on the screen in the now. The screenwriter is strictly a presenter of audio-visual descriptions. In the context of this orthodoxy it is interesting to note the presence of what we can term, after Wolterstorff, authorial 'elucidations' in McGovern's script. These include descriptions such as:

Scene 8: 'They all giggle at that—all blissfully unaware'
Scene 9: 'There are other officers here but Margaret doesn't see them'
Scene 9: 'It's the Bad News Room'
Scene 14: 'She shakes her head: such a task is beyond her'
Scene 14: 'She's clutching at straws: it breaks his heart'
Scene 35:' Another little wound to lick. Another pause'
Scene 37: 'DI Hastings's reaction: Oh, how he despises the yobs who have caused all this pain...'
Scene 44: 'Hastings's reaction. He can't believe his luck'
Scene 60: 'Way below the belt. And the banker can't respond'
Scene 68: 'The gloves are well and truly off now'
Scene 70: 'Cards on the table time...'
Scene 75: 'She puts the phone down. She feels soiled, humiliated...'

McGovern explains he gives very few stage directions, rarely describing places and people. In these comments, there's an element of 'directing from the page' but they serve other purposes as well. These include: timing, usually slowing things down; writing for the actor to suggest background; protecting against sentiment; and foreshadowing things of importance, moments of realization (McGovern, personal communication, 2015).

A significant issue in thinking about the script as a companion in Booth's terms is that there are scenes that are in the script but deleted, and also a scene that appears in the film but not in the script. Scenes 79–80 were dropped in the edit due to length (McGovern, personal communication, 2015). The scene that appears in the film but not in the script is inserted between the end of Scene 30 and the start of 31. It is a powerful encounter of a mother with her deceased son. In terms of the mortuary scene, McGovern explains that he 'wanted to avoid the "first visit to the mortuary" stuff because, he'd seen it lots of times. I wrote about a *subsequent* visit in Scene 34. But David Blair [the Director] wanted the first visit so, unbeknown to me, he scheduled it and shot it. He gave Susan Lynch hardly any direction and, crucially, did not tell her that her son would be visible behind the glass—hence the powerful reaction'.

What is remarkable about this additional scene is how it extends some of the key fictive strategies of *Common*, the idea that point of view matters, reinforced by use of the hand-held camera. That actually grasping the full state of affairs can be terrifying and even soul-destroying. Using the beating of the glass to guide the editing is a powerful device, underlined by the muted audio. But also that a state of affairs can sit beyond one's response and reaction: visible but inaccessible and out of reach, and subject to shifting focus. Point of view is a device used elsewhere in the film and script, in Scene 61 where Kieran Gillespie is taken away in handcuffs, written from Johnjo's parents' point of view. It's apposite here to acknowledge David Blair's ongoing creative collaboration with McGovern, as he has directed numerous episodes of *Accused*, *The Street* and *The Lakes*.

Having noted some salient aspects of the script for *Common*, there is a sense that I am still in the realm of what Larry Gross terms the Watergate theory of screenwriting, which he formulates in terms of the question who knows what and when, or more expansively, 'what do the characters know—about narrative context, about themselves, and about each other, and when do they know it?' (2014, 313). For Gross, screenwriting is a kind of information game: 'screenwriting is basically a set of decisions about information, a confidence game played with and for the audience … trying to convince them that you know where you're leading them and that you're taking them somewhere they ought to want to go' (2014: 314). However, in response I would highlight that McGovern's manipulation of states of affairs and our access to it provides the basis for a radical critique of joint enterprise law. This is more than an information problem or confidence game for McGovern, but a matter of justice.

In the context of joint enterprise law, it is also an ethical issue. As with any crime, admitting guilt can have serious effects. But, under joint enterprise, any disclosure by any party risks expanding criminal liability. This makes any attempt to tell the truth fraught. In addition to the strategy of contesting joint enterprise through its construction of states of affairs, the script does additional ethical work, explored through numerous strands, to do with exploring different ethical commitments that flow into this state of affairs. I want to summarize these under three headings:

- Grassing and loyalty
- Dignity and decency
- Truth-telling and justice

Grassing and Loyalty

Taking 'grassing' first. This is brought home in an exchange between Johnjo and Kieran O'Shea in Scene 17, where Johnjo is burdened by what is the right thing to do, especially since he believes the police will eventually track down the car (which belongs to his brother), but is confronted by threats to his family if he grasses. The focus on family becomes poignant when in Scene 25 Johnjo's brother is arrested.

The script explores a number of moral injunctions against breaching loyalty. But there are exceptions to the rule, if only in the confines of the family home where a kind of community justice is in play (see Scene 38). The exceptions to the rule often involve mothers, and an ethical imperative that they deserve to know the truth. The mother as a key figure for working-class young men appears again in Scene 87, when Kieran Gillespie admits he is not willing to tell the truth because he told his Ma he didn't do it.

Dignity and Decency

Another strand of ethical work surrounds dignity or respect and decency. Margaret Ward and Tommy Ward, the victim's parents, are a focal point here, particularly in terms of Tommy's past treatment of Margaret. Respect can be a powerful motivator, but also destructive. Need we be reminded that Kieran Gillespie stabs the young Ward because he was 'asking' for it? In terms of it being a motivator, there is a powerful speech by Tommy Ward in Scene 36 when he confesses to imagining a reconciliation with his son.

```
         COMMON by JIMMY MCGOVERN        As at: 5 June 2013      P32
36       CONTINUED:                                              36
                              TOMMY WARD (CONT'D)
                     I'd meet him one day when he was
                     older, knew more about men and
                     women, and we'd go for a pint
                     and I'd talk to him man to man,
                     brutal honesty, "one life, one
                     shot at happiness", all that
                     stuff, and after that he'd have
                     some sort of grudging... Well,
                     not respect, no. Grudging
                     acceptance maybe. And I'd build
                     on that and build on it... But
                     he's gone. and so has the
                     prospect of reconciliation. And
                     that makes me so.... That makes
                     me so...
```

And of course we could unpack this subplot, this ethical strand, into a state of affairs that extends back before the pizza parlour, to do with Tommy Ward leaving the family, which makes the speech about the prospect of reconciliation, now destroyed, so poignant.

Truth-Telling and Justice

As well as grassing and loyalty, dignity and decency, truth-telling represents a third important strand. Truth-telling is essential to *Common* because on one level, joint enterprise laws by-pass one understanding of it. There is no need to establish certain legal facts over what really happened, and who held the knife for instance. It also, as becomes evident in McGovern's script, forces distortions to the truth as parties plead to lesser charges because of their fear of the consequences of joint enterprise. In Johnjo's case the debate is over whether he will tell the truth and plead not guilty and risk joint enterprise, or whether he will plead guilty to the lesser charge of grievous bodily harm.

This strand is set up across numerous scenes (38; 44; 46; 53; 58) in which the idea that one has nothing to fear by telling the truth is explored, and that because Johnjo has done nothing he will be safe. The strand is intertwined with a question of innocence and justice (see Scene 20 when Tony Wallace talks to Johnjo by the seaside).

The belief that the innocent should go free is put in the address of Johnjo's barrister in Scene 84:

```
            Nobody entered that shop intent
            on harming Thomas Ward. His
            murder was a moment of madness.
            With no forethought. No plan.
            So, again, your honour, only he
            who was responsible for that
            moment of madness, he who
            wielded the knife, should face
            trial. The innocent should go
            free.

    Johnjo. His parents. Ever rising optimism...
```

It is a case of natural justice, he explains, not to proceed with a charge against Johnjo with such flimsy evidence. 'Joint enterprise might allow it, your honour; natural justice should not'.

McGovern's script reminds us that just as there can be multiple or dual states of affairs in existence there can be multiple forms of justice. Institutional justice. Community justice. Rough justice. Community justice is invoked by a shot from Scene 84 that doesn't appear in the film:

```
    Johnjo's parents give him the thumbs up and whatnot.
    They think he's coming home with them.

    But Coleen's smile fades when she realises that, from
    across the courtroom, Margaret Ward is staring at her...
```

This begins a strand to do with a need to accept Johnjo's version of the story, perhaps not of his innocence, but of his honesty, that is taken into Scene 85 and ends in Scene 102 with Margaret Ward's acceptance of a letter from Johnjo written from prison. The struggle for community justice is in stark contrast to the battle for institutional justice where in Scene 86 the judge pronounces that 'Justice for four is surely better than justice for none'.

The judge's decision that the joint enterprise case against Johnjo should proceed marks a turning point, prompting a last ditch attempt to find justice for those who knew nothing about the stabbing, but it relies, in Scene 87, on Kieran Gillespie pleading guilty to the stabbing. At this point, the strand regarding truth-telling intersects with the strand to do with grassing and loyalty to mates.

Here, it is the threat of joint enterprise that is powerful as much as the legal nuances. A special case is not argued for Johnjo. But the ethical strand linked to 'We've done nothing' is furthered and the most likely outcome becomes a charge of grievous bodily harm, with between six and ten years in jail. This choice between two evils—joint enterprise or pleading to grievous bodily harm — crystallizes the injustice. It is Johnjo's mother, Coleen (Jodhi May), who voices the issue in Scene 90.

```
                         PETER O'SHEA
                      (eventually)
             Take the six years.

                        COLEEN O'SHEA
             Take the six years?

                         PETER O'SHEA
                      (to Johnjo)
             Could you do six years?

                        COLEEN O'SHEA
             He couldn't do a week in Butlins.

                        JOHNJO O'SHEA
             I could do six years.

                        COLEEN O'SHEA
             It's not just the six years, is
             it? you'll be saying you played a
             part in that boy's death.
That really gets to Johnjo.

                        JOHNJO O'SHEA
             I didn't.

                        COLEEN O'SHEA
             I know.

A buzzer goes. Visiting is coming to an end. Johnjo
arrives at a massive decision...

                        JOHNJO O'SHEA
             I'm pleading guilty to nothing,
             Mum. They can do what they want.
```

Johnjo is sticking by his innocence and the vision of justice behind it. It's a vision not shared by his barrister in Scene 97, who threatens to resign because he sees it as a question of choosing the lesser of two evils. But it is a bigger issue for Johnjo and his mother.

Scene 95 takes this discussion and explores it through Johnjo's eyes, in a scene of ethical agony in the back of a police wagon, with each of the boys/men in a separate cell crying out to Johnjo to try to convince him to plead to grievous bodily harm and not opt for an innocent plea. Loyalty, grassing, decency, respect are all played out. It's the inverse of the getaway car in Scene 2, this time Johnjo is not extrapolating a state of affairs, he now confronts a quite new state of affairs around sentencing, pleading, truth-telling, innocence and guilt, intertwined with his immanent incarceration. This analysis of *Common* teases out how the script and the programme does ethical work, by reexamining and repositioning the state of affairs at the heart of the narrative. Earlier in this chapter I asked, How should we envisage the link between screenwriting practice and ethical practice? In my discussion, as well as exploring the many interconnections between narrative and ethics, I have explored one way of figuring the relationship between screenwriting practice and ethical practices, through the idea of ethical work and world building. This is to say that rather than simply work through moral teaching, scripts can engage us in forms of ethical work that encourage the viewer to reconsider states of affairs and the judgements associated with them. In terms of a broader argument around ethics, representations and judgement, my contention is that ethical analysis needs to be open to some conception of ethical work performed by the script and screen work. The ethical work performed within or around the narrative forms an important point of understanding against which to form our ethical judgements and viewpoints. Against the idea that critical ethical analysis represents casting judgements of right or wrong over a clear state of affairs, the example of *Common* demonstrates the need for careful engagement with the ethical work of the text, and a reflective approach to ethics in screenwriting, in which one discerns nuances in the state of affairs and the situation as written and as portrayed on the screen.

NOTE

1. Jeff Rush's chapter, in this collection, explores the interplay of an ethics of care and an ethics of justice in the context of HBO serial, *The Wire*.

REFERENCES

Benjamin, Walter. 1992. *Illuminations.* Translated by Harry Zohn. London: Fontana Press.

Booth, Wayne C. 1988. *The Company We Keep: An Ethics of Fiction.* Berkeley: University of California Press.

Butler, Judith. 2009. *Frames of War: When is Life Grievable.* London: Verso.

Cohen, Stephen. 2004. *The Nature of Moral Reasoning: The Framework and Activities of Ethical Deliberation, Argument and Decision-Making.* South Melbourne: Oxford University Press.

Fiske, John, and John Hartley. 2003. *Reading Television*. 2nd ed. London: Routledge.

Ganz, Adam. 2012. '"Leaping Broken Narration": Ballads, Oral Storytelling and the Cinema.' In *Storytelling in World Cinemas, Volume One: Forms*, edited by Lina Khatib, 71–88. New York: Wallflower Press/Columbia University Press.

Gauthier, Jennifer L. 2012. 'Ghosts in the National Machine: The Haunting (and Taunting) Films of Tracey Moffatt.' In *Storytelling in World Cinemas, Volume One: Forms*, edited by Lina Khatib, 177–91. New York: Wallflower Press/Columbia University Press.

Gerbner, George. 1973. 'Teacher Image in Mass Culture: Symbolic Functions of the "Hidden Curriculum".' In *Communication Technology and Social Policy*, edited by George Gerbner, Larry P. Gross and William H. Melody, 265–68. New York: Wiley-Interscience.

Gilligan, Carol. 1982. *In a Different Voice: Psychological Theory and Women's Development*. Cambridge: Harvard University Press.

Gross, Larry. 2014. '"The Watergate Theory of Screenwriting": a keynote presentation at SRN, Wisconsin, 2013.' *Journal of Screenwriting* 5 (3): 313–22.

Hamelink, Cees J. 2014. 'Communication Rights and the History of Ideas.' In *Communication Rights and Social Justice Historical Accounts of Transnational Mobilizations*, edited by Claudia Padovani and Andrew Calabrese, 17–28. Basingstoke: Palgrave Macmillan.

Hamelink, Cees J., and Julia Hoffmann. 2008. 'The State of the Right to Communicate.' *Global Media Journal (American Edition)* 7 (13). http://www.globalmediajournal.com/open-access/the-state-of-the-right-to-communicate.pdf

International Commission for the Study of Communication Problems. 1980. *Many Voices, One World: Towards A New More Just and More Efficient World Information and Communication Order*. London, New York: UNESCO.

Joyce, Hester. 2013. '*Taonga* (Cultural Treasures): Reflections on Maori Storytelling in the Cinema of Aotearoa/New Zealand.' In *Storytelling in World Cinemas, Volume Two: Contexts*, edited by Lina Khatib, 21–34. New York: Columbia University Press.

Lambert, Joe. 2013. *Digital Storytelling: Capturing Lives, Creating Community*. Hoboken: Taylor and Francis.

Leach, Edmund. 1976. *Culture and Communication: The Logic by which Symbols are Connected*. Cambridge: Cambridge University Press.

Lee, Philip. 2004. 'The Right to Communicate Affirms and Restores Human Dignity.' http://www.direitoacomunicacao.org.br/index2.php?option=com_docman&task=doc_view&gid=130&Itemid=99999999

Maras, Steven. 2009. *Screenwriting: History, Theory and Practice*. London: Wallflower Press.

McGovern. Jimmy. 2014. *Common* [Script]. http://www.bbc.co.uk/writersroom/scripts/common

Mehring, Margaret. 1990. *The Screenplay: A Blend of Film Form and Content*. Boston: Focal Press.

Meyers, Diana Tietjens. 2004. *Being Yourself: Essays on Identity, Action and Social Life*. Lanham: Rowman & Littlefield.

Miller, Pat P. 1986. *Script Supervising and Film Continuity*. Boston: Focal Press.

Nannicelli, Ted. 2011. 'Why Can't Screenplays Be Artworks?' *The Journal of Aesthetics and Art Criticism* 69 (4): 405–14.

Newcomb, Horace and Paul M. Hirsch. 1994. 'Television as a Cultural Forum.' In *Television: The Critical View*, edited by Horace Newcomb, 561–573. 5th ed. New York: Oxford University Press.

Noddings, Nel. 1984. *Caring, a Feminine Approach to Ethics and Moral Education*. Berkeley: University of California Press.

Nussbaum, Martha Craven. 1983. 'Flawed Crystals: James's The Golden Bowl and Literature as Moral Philosophy.' *New Literary History* 15 (1): 25–50.

Nussbaum, Martha Craven. 1995. *Poetic Justice: The Literary Imagination and Public Life*. Boston: Beacon Press.

Nussbaum, Martha Craven. 1997. *Cultivating humanity: A Classical Defense of Reform in Liberal Education*. Cambridge, Mass.: Harvard University Press.

Plantinga, Carl R. 1987. 'Defining Documentary: Fiction, Nonfiction, and Projected Worlds.' *Persistence of Vision* 5 (Spring): 44–54.

Plantinga, Carl R. 1997. *Rhetoric and Representation in Nonfiction Film*. Cambridge, UK: Cambridge University Press.

Raphael, D. D. 1983. 'Can Literature Be Moral Philosophy?' *New Literary History* 15 (1): 1–12.

Rennie, Ellie, Leo Berkeley, and Blaise Murphet. 2010. 'Community Media and Ethical Choice.' *3CMedia* 6: 11–25.

Stadler, Jane. 2008. *Pulling Focus: Intersubjective Experience, Narrative Film, and Ethics*. New York: Continuum.

Taylor, Charles. 1994. 'The Politics of Recognition.' In *Multiculturalism: Examining the Politics of Recognition*, edited by Amy Gutmann, 25–73. Princeton: Princeton University Press.

Turner, Graeme. 2002. *Film as Social Practice*. 2nd ed. London: Taylor and Francis.

Witherell, Carol S. 1991. 'Narrative and the Moral Realm: Tales of Caring and Justice.' *Journal of Moral Education* 20 (3): 237–242.

Wolterstorff, Nicholas. 1976. 'Worlds of Works of Art.' *Journal of Aesthetics and Art Criticism* 35 (2): 121–32.

Wolterstorff, Nicholas. 1980. *Works and Worlds of Art*. Oxford: Clarendon Press.

FILM AND TELEVISION REFERENCES

Common. 2014. Cr: Jimmy McGovern; Dir: David Blair, BBC1, UK, 90 mins.

INDEX[1]

A

Accused, 80, 86, 87, 93, 242
Alternate Reality Games (ARGs),
  xiii, 146, 147, 152–9, 161–7
Animal Kingdom, xiv, xvi, 215–28
Ankersmit, Frank, 102, 104, 105,
  116, 117
ANZAC Girls, xii, xvi, 99–117
Arbuckle, Roscoe 'Fatty,' 2
ARGs. *See* Alternate Reality Games
  (ARGs)
Aristotle, 15, 17
Association of Motion Picture
  Producers, 11
autonomy, viii, ix, 23–5, 25n10,
  26, 36, 203, 224

B

bardic function, 226
Bateson, Gregory (NOTE: His
  Christian name isn't given in the
  text - as is usual practice), 148,
  152, 154, 156, 157, 166, 167

Beker, Marilyn, 16, 19, 22, 23,
  23n9, 24, 25, 44, 104, 107,
  109, 113, 115
Benjamin, Walter, 227
Berkhofer, Robert, 104, 112
Bloody Sunday, xi, 82, 89–91,
  94n3, 94n6
blurred boundaries, blurred lines, 158
blurring boundaries, xii, 143–67.
  See also blurred boundaries,
  blurred lines
Booth, Wayne C., vii, 20n8, 178, 215,
  225, 230–3, 238, 241
Borgen, 34, 45–51
Born, Georgina, 37, 38
Braveheart, 99
Breen, Joseph I., 4, 4n2, 6, 10, 13
Bridge, The, 37
Broadcasting for Remote
  Aboriginal Communities
  Scheme (BRACS), 65
Brookside, 81
Buber, Martin, xiv, 18, 215–20,
  222, 225

[1] Note: Page numbers with "n" denote notes.

© The Editor(s) (if applicable) and The Author(s) 2016   259
S. Maras (ed.), *Ethics in Screenwriting*, Palgrave Studies
in Screenwriting, DOI 10.1057/978-1-137-54493-3

Buñuel, Luis, 196, 197, 199, 201, 203–8, 212n2
Butler, Judith, xv, 14, 18, 228

C
Caldwell, John T., xi, 25n10, 44, 151
care ethics, 187, 190. *See also* ethics of care
censor(s), 1–3, 12, 13, 131
censorship, 1–3, 7, 8, 13, 22, 62, 126, 129, 138. *See also* censor
Cohen, Stephen, 14, 16, 20, 229
common, xv, xvi, 12, 22, 23, 40, 73, 77, 83, 85, 88, 146, 207, 230, 231, 233, 235, 236, 238, 242, 244, 247
communication rights, 227. *See also* right to communication
conflict(s), 42, 115, 116, 181–6
consequentialist approaches, 16
Corner, The, 182, 183
Cracker, 77, 82, 83
cultural forum, xiii, 179, 188–90, 226

D
de los Reyes, Aurelio, 123, 125–7, 129–31, 133–5, 138n1, 139n8, 139n11, 139n14
Deontology or duty, 16, 17, 19, 20, 63, 87, 90–2, 100, 113, 215
dialogic ethics or dialogism, xiv, 18, 215–28
disclaimers, xii, xiii, 17n1, 144, 152, 154, 155, 157
Dockers, 82, 84, 93, 94n4
docudrama, 83, 84, 103, 129, 139n10. *See also* docudrama
documentary, vii, viii, ix xii, xv, 18, 36, 71, 72, 89, 104, 108, 110, 112, 115, 122–4, 127–9, 135–7, 139n11, 234. *See also* nonfiction film

Dogma '95 Manifesto, 43
doubled ethics, xiii, 175–91
double story (distinct from double storytelling), xii, 100, 101, 104–10, 117
double storytelling (distinct from double story), vi, x, xi, 33–51, 191n2
Dunne, Philip, 13

E
1864, 36, 50
entertainment, vii, x, 5, 8–12, 21–3, 33, 41, 43–5, 48, 50, 67, 123, 134, 136, 143, 155, 157, 160, 223
ethical decision-making or decision-making, 15, 18–20, 35, 38
ethical turn, 16
ethical work, xv, 77, 223, 230–3, 235–43, 247
ethics of blindness, 196, 200–4
ethics of care, xiii, xv, 18, 177, 187, 228, 247n1. *See also* care ethics
ethics of creativity, 209, 210
ethics of cultural work, 37, 38
ethics of justice, xiii, 177, 182, 187, 190, 247n1. *See also* justice ethics
existentialism, 16

F
fabrication, xii, 121–3, 126, 128, 131, 132, 135–7
fan labor, 151
Field, Syd, 209
Final Punishment, 114, 157, 161–6
Footnote, The, 105, 106
Foucault, Michel, 14–16
fractured intimacy, 205

G
Gilligan, Carol, 18, 186, 187, 228
Grafton, Anthony, 104–6, 109
Green Bush, 56, 65
Grierson, John, 122, 127, 137

H
harm(s), 8, 17, 19, 155, 156, 201,
    244, 246
Hays code, 5
Hays Office, x, 4, 5, 13, 13n7
Hays, Will H., 2, 3, 3n1, 4, 5, 6n3,
    13, 13n7
Hecht, Ben, 13
Held, Virginia, 186, 187
Hillsborough, xi, 77, 80–4, 89–91, 94n2
Hillsborough Family Support Group
    (HFSG), 80, 82
Hirsch, Paul M., 179, 189, 226
Home Box Office (HBO), 177, 247n1
Huston, John, 12

I
imaginative acquaintance, 227, 229–31
improvisation, 23, 199–200
indexing, 127, 129, 137

J
Jenkins, Henry, 143, 147, 151
Jenkins, Keith, 101, 102, 114, 117
Johnston, Eric, 13, 13n7
joint enterprise, xi, 83, 85, 94n5,
    236–9, 242, 244–6
Joy, Colonel Jason, 3, 6
justice ethics, 187, 190

K
Kant, Immanuel, 15–17
Kes, 92
Killing, The, xi, 34, 45–50, 90, 227

L
Levinas, Emmanuel, vi, 196,
    201–4, 209
Liverpool Docks dispute, xi, 82
Lord, Father Daniel, 3, 4, 6, 9–11,
    15, 90

M
Maibaum, Richard, 12
Mankiewicz, Herman, 14
McGovern, Jimmy, vi, xi, xii, xiii, xv,
    xvi, 77–94, 233, 235–45
McKee, Robert, 209
Miller, Jacqui, 6, 10, 13, 36, 241
Mill, John Stuart, 15–17
Mimi, 56, 57
moral development, 227,
    228, 230, 231. *See also* moral
    education
moral education, 228
morals, morality, vii, x, xi, xiii,
    xiv, 1–3, 5–12, 14–20,
    22, 26, 58–60, 64, 66,
    77–94, 147, 148, 215,
    223–8, 236
Motion Picture Producers and
    Distributors of America
    (MPPDA), 2–4, 6. *See also* Hays
    Office

N
narrative alignment, 177–81, 189
narrative imagination, 230
neutrality, 229
Newcomb, Horace, viii, 179,
    189, 226
Nichols, Bill, 122
Noddings, Nel, 18, 228
non-consequentialist approaches, 16
normative theory/ies, 23–6
Nussbaum, Martha, xv, 229,
    230, 232

O
objectivity, xii, 101, 105, 121, 123, 126, 127, 129, 132, 137, 187, 232

P
Payback, 56, 57, 66, 67
Peirce, Charles Sanders, vi, xii, xiii, 143–67
Pervasive Fiction, 154
Phelan, James, xiii, 177, 178
Phillips, Andrea, 151, 154, 155
Plantinga, Carl, 127–9, 137, 233, 234
poetic imagination, 229
'Potter box,' 19
Potter, Ralph, 19. *See also* 'Potter box'
prescriptive agencies, 14
prescriptive ethics, 16, 35
Priest, 62, 78, 79, 82, 217
production code, x, 1, 4, 5, 6n3, 8, 12, 13, 15, 21, 25. *See also* Hays code
Production Code Administration (PCA), 4, 6, 12
public interest/s, 3, 25, 33, 39, 126
public service broadcaster/s, 33, 37, 39, 50, 51, 145, 236. *See also* public service broadcasting (PSB)
public service broadcasting (PSB), xi, 33, 34, 38–41, 45–9, 159, 191n2

Q
Quigley, Martin, 3, 4, 15, 29

R
Rawls, John, 17, 181, 183
Redfern Now, 93
reflective equilibrium, 229
relational ethics, xiv, 18
right to communication, 227. *See also* communication rights

Robinson, Casey, 12
Rosenstone, Robert, 103, 104, 115
Ross, William David, 17, 19
Rushmore, 176, 177, 186, 190

S
Samson and Delilah, xi, 55–8, 61–5, 67–9, 71, 74, 75
screen ideas, 38–40, 45, 48, 50
Secret Language of Film, The, 195, 196, 212n1
showrunner, 178, 179, 182
Shurlock, Geoffrey, 13, 13n7
situational ethics, 18
Stewart, Donald O., 13
Street, The, 77, 79, 83, 86, 88, 93, 158, 182, 242
Studio Relations Committee (SRC), 3, 4, 6, 13
summum bonum, 144, 148, 149, 155, 158, 162, 163, 166, 167
suspension of disbelief, 164
Sveistrup, Søren, 34, 47, 48

T
Taxa, 34, 42
Taylor, Charles, 225, 228
Thalberg, Irving, 3, 9, 9n4, 10, 11, 11n6
That Obscure Object of Desire, 196, 197, 200–4
Those Who Kill, 37
three-act structure, 59
three-plot structure, 47, 48
Truth About Marika, The, 144, 157–61, 165, 166
truth, or truth-telling, xi, xv, 61, 83, 89–91, 101, 104–6, 108–10, 113, 115–17, 123, 126, 128, 134, 137, 144, 153, 155, 157–61, 164–6, 234, 242–7

U

Unit One, 43, 44, 47

V

vanishing screenplay,
  The, 195, 198, 210, 212
violence, xv, 13, 37, 49,
  134, 138, 162, 165,
  166, 189, 201,
  208, 225
virtue ethics, 16
virtuous screenwriter, 20–6

W

Welles, Orson, 155
Wire, The, xiii, 175–91, 247n1
Wolterstorff, Nicholas,
  xv, 226, 233–6, 239, 241

Y

Yousef, Nancy, xiv, 206, 207

Z

zone of responsibility, viii, 25